THE PATAGONIAN SUBLIME

THE PATAGONIAN SUBLIME

The Green Economy and Post-Neoliberal Politics

MARCOS MENDOZA

RUTGERS UNIVERSITY PRESS

New Brunswick, Camden, and Newark, New Jersey, and London

Library of Congress Cataloging-in-Publication Data
Names: Mendoza, Marcos, author.
Title: The Patagonian sublime : the green economy and post-neoliberal politics /
Marcos Mendoza.
Description: New Brunswick, New Jersey : Rutgers University Press, 2018. |
    Includes bibliographical references and index.
Identifiers: LCCN 2017059111| ISBN 9780813596754 (hardback : alk. paper) |
    ISBN 9780813596747 (paperback : alk. paper)
Subjects: LCSH: Ecotourism—Patagonia (Argentina and Chile) |
    Ecotourism—Economic aspects—Argentina. | Capitalism—Environmental
    aspects—Argentina. | Nature conservation—Economic aspects—Argentina. |
    Argentina—Politics and government—2002– | BISAC: SOCIAL SCIENCE /
    Anthropology / Cultural. | TRAVEL / Special Interest / Ecotourism. |
    POLITICAL SCIENCE / Public Policy / Environmental Policy. | NATURE /
    Ecosystems & Habitats / Mountains. | TRAVEL / South America / Argentina. |
    TRAVEL / South America / Chile & Easter Island.
Classification: LCC G155.A7 M46 2018 | DDC 338.4/791827—dc23
LC record available at https://lccn.loc.gov/2017059111

A British Cataloging-in-Publication record for this book is available
from the British Library.

♾ The paper used in this publication meets the requirements of the American
National Standard for Information Sciences—Permanence of Paper for Printed
Library Materials, ANSI Z39.48-1992.

www.rutgersuniversitypress.org

Manufactured in the United States of America

CONTENTS

List of Acronyms   vii

List of Spanish Terms   ix

Preface   xi

Introduction   1

PART I: THE SPHERE OF TOURISM CONSUMPTION

1   Alpine-Style Mountaineering: Resolve and Death
in the Andes   25

2   Adventure Trekking: Pursuing the Alpine Sublime   43

PART II: THE SPHERE OF SERVICE PRODUCTION

3   *Comerciante* Entrepreneurship: Investment Hazard
and Ethical Laboring   67

4   *Golondrina* Laboring: Informality and Play   87

PART III: THE SPHERE OF THE CONSERVATION STATE

5   Community-Based Conservation: Land Managers
and State–Civil Society Collaborations   109

6   Conservation Policing: Education and Environmental
Impacts   128

PART IV: THE POLITICS OF THE GREEN ECONOMY

7   Defending Popular Sustainability in *la Comuna*   149

8   Kirchnerismo and the Politics of the Green Economy   168

Conclusion   183

Acknowledgments   189

Notes   193

References   201

Index   213

ACRONYMS

APN	Administración de Parques Nacionales (National Parks Administration of Argentina)
CAP	Consejo Agrario Provincial (Provincial Agrarian Council of Santa Cruz)
CBC	Community-based conservation
DTP	Delegación Técnica Regional de Patagonia (Patagonian Regional Technical Delegation)
GNI	Gross national income
IANIGLA	Instituto Argentino de Nivología, Glaciología y Ciencias Ambientales (Argentine Institute for Snow, Glacier and Environmental Sciences)
IMF	International Monetary Fund
INDEC	Instituto Nacional de Estadística y Censos (National Census and Statistics Institution of Argentina)
OAS	Organization of American States
PMLG	*Plan Preliminar de Manejo, Parque Nacional Los Glaciares* (Preliminary Management Plan for Glaciers National Park)
PNLG	Parque Nacional Los Glaciares (Glaciers National Park)
SLV	Seccional Lago Viedma (Lake Viedma Ranger Station)
STP	Sustainable Trails Project NGO

SPANISH TERMS

A pulmón	By lung, by sheer will, by the bootstraps
Asociación de Vecinos	Association of Neighbors
Blanco	White, formal, visible
Blanquear	Whiten, launder, make legitimate
Brigada de senderos	Trail crew
Brigadista	Seasonal ranger
Buena onda	Good vibes
Cámara de Comercio	Chamber of Commerce
Charla	Informal talk
Comerciante	Small-business owner
Comisión de Fomento	Development Commission (state-appointed administrative council)
Compañeros de rubro	Market-sector partners
Comuna	Collective, community
Empresario	Big-business owner
Escalador	Climber
Estanciero	Ranch or farm owner
Fantasma social	Social ghost
Gente humilde	Humble or common folk
Golondrina	Patagonian swallow, seasonal service worker
Hostería	Bed-and-breakfast
Kirchnerismo	Political ideology of the Kirchner-Fernández governments
Los Kirchners	The Kirchners as individuals
Mirador	Scenic viewpoint
Negro	Black, informal, obscured
No deje rastro	Leave no trace (rules of outdoor conduct)
Paisano	Gaucho, horseman, agrarian laborer
Porteño	Person from Buenos Aires
Prestador	Guiding company owner
Recorrida	Patrol
Refugio	Chalet, hut
Retenciones	Export taxes
Seccional	Park ranger station

Tierra fiscal	Public land (administered by the Consejo Agrario Provincial)
Tirolesa	Tyrolean traverse (a cable spanning a river or chasm)
Villa	Settlement

PREFACE

This book examines post-neoliberal politics and the green economy in Argentina at a time of weakening faith in global neoliberalism. Since the election of Hugo Chávez as president of Venezuela in 1998, Latin America has witnessed the proliferation of New Left governments that have adopted a wide range of responses to the crises, conflicts, and contradictions associated with neoliberal policies and principles. Over the course of two decades, the New Left has sought to promote "growth with equity" and challenge the ideology of the self-regulating market (Grugel and Riggirozzi 2009, 19). Though facing a number of recent setbacks, the New Left—whether its adherents hold office or are in the opposition—remains a key front of resistance within the Americas. The Néstor Kirchner (2003–2007) and Cristina Fernández de Kirchner (2007–2015) presidential administrations are associated with post-neoliberal politics in Argentina. The Kirchners have worked to promote stronger state control over the economy, expand welfare programs, protect real wages, and accelerate the exploitation of natural resources, whether through extraction or conservation. With respect to the green economy, the Kirchner-Fernández governments have implemented a green productivist agenda. I explore how strategies of capitalist development, political rule, and national representation operating within green productivism affect the Patagonian region. A binational zone that includes parts of Chile, Patagonia encompasses the Argentine provinces of Neuquén, Río Negro, Chubut, Santa Cruz, and Tierra del Fuego (see Map P.1). In particular, I focus on the mountain village of El Chaltén and the adjacent Parque Nacional Los Glaciares (Glaciers National Park). I document the sociocultural responses of actors to a green productivist project based on ecotourism and community-based conservation within alpine landscapes. I attend to subjectivity formation and risk consciousness within the green economy, charting the enactment of concrete visions for sustainable development.

I arrived in Buenos Aires for the main period of my field research in October 2008, just after the collapse of Lehman Brothers on Wall Street, in New York City. In addition to spending time at the National Parks Administration library on Avenida Santa Fe, I attempted to follow the breaking new stories coming out of the United States as some journalists and public intellectuals began to openly question whether the financial crisis signaled the impending disintegration of global capitalism. This seems laughable in hindsight, but such predictions arose from experiences of uncertainty, horror, and loss whose repercussions we are still dealing with today. Traveling to El Chaltén, I arrived in a village where internet access was difficult, though it had improved since my previous trips. It typically

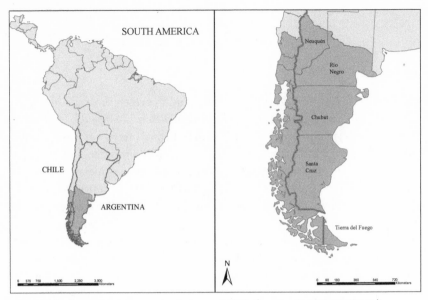

MAP P.1. The Patagonia region in Argentina and Chile (map by Stephen G. Harris)

took fifteen minutes to load the content of one news article at an internet café. I quickly lost touch with the latest twists and turns in the international arena. The global financial crisis, however, came to permeate everyday life in this remote ecotourism destination, since residents worried about how ongoing events would affect the season, and tourists wondered whether they would have a job when they returned home to Buenos Aires, Berlin, or Boston. Focusing on the years 2008–2011, this ethnography recounts the stories of park rangers, land managers, mountaineers, trekkers, service workers, tourism entrepreneurs, and others involved in building a green economy during and immediately following the Great Recession. This period was marked by growing acrimony between the park administration, tourism company owners, and residents over the shifting contours of development under the Kirchners.

This ethnography is based on eighteen months of fieldwork carried out in 2006–2011, with the research periods occurring in August–September 2006, November–December 2007, October 2008–November 2009, and December 2011. I spent the vast majority of this time living in El Chaltén, where I used participant observation, interviews, and photography to collect ethnographic data. El Chaltén is adjacent to the national park, which means that one can move efficiently between the village, trail system, campsites, and backcountry. Such a concentrated space enabled me to research the wide variety of social groups involved in the green economy. To supplement my primary research in El Chaltén, I conducted interviews with rangers, land managers, climatologists, glaciologists, and representatives of environmental organizations at various locations throughout Argentina and Chile. I consulted historical documents at libraries and archives in Buenos Aires, Bariloche, El Calafate, and Río Gallegos. All translations of interview data and documents from Spanish into English are my own unless otherwise noted.

Through ethnographic research, I sought to acquire a multiperspectival understanding of the politics of the green economy. My initial concern regarding ethnographic research in El Chaltén centered on gaining access to park rangers. During an initial conversation, the ranger station director suggested that I join the volunteer program for the national park service, which accepted citizens and foreigners. Following his advice, I worked as a volunteer ranger from late 2008 through early 2009, giving environmental education talks to tourists, patrolling the trails and campgrounds, doing manual labor such as trail restoration and building bridges, participating in rescues, and working on revegetation projects. Though I had experience as a wildland firefighter in the U.S. Pacific Northwest, I was never called upon to help suppress fires in Parque Nacional Los Glaciares. Luckily, these were extremely infrequent in El Chaltén, though the scars of massive burns from the early twentieth century were still visible in the landscape. Working for the park service opened up lines of communication with land managers and scientists who periodically traveled to the zone to check on the ranger corps and assess sustainability plans. After this, I moved my tent—which had been pitched in the forest behind the ranger station—to a private campground in town to begin research with service workers and entrepreneurs. This involved interviews and frequent visits to retail shops, cafés, restaurants, hostels, and other establishments. With the approach of the austral winter, I moved inside into a series of budget hostels where I continued to learn about the labor market, investment patterns, and capital accumulation. Beyond seeking to understand the politics of the park and pueblo, I also spent time conducting research with tourists. The trekking population proved relatively easy to access while I was working as a volunteer ranger (and thus talking to tourists every day) and living in the village, where trekkers cycled in and out. I participated in trekking excursions with tourists and spent scores of hours at each of the main destinations in the park, conversing with visitors and gathering perspectives on landscape aesthetics, adventure, and Patagonia's position in the global consumer economy. The most difficult group to research was the mountaineering population. I pursued an ethnographic strategy of immersive training to acquire the embodied techniques and competencies needed to gain entry into this social group (Wacquant 2006). This involved practicing at the local climbing gym and on rock-climbing routes surrounding the village. With minimal prior climbing experience, I decided to mountaineer on the peaks requiring the least amount of technical difficulty, given the high degree of risk assumed by practitioners and my desire to survive to raise a family. As one climber candidly told me, "I can do what I do [extremely technical alpinism] because I don't have any children." I took that message to heart.

This book engages scholarly debates in anthropology, political ecology, Latin American studies, risk studies, and related fields. First, I contribute to anthropological theories of capitalism by developing the model of the semiotic estate to underscore the centrality of ground rent capture and rentier dynamics to the green economy. Second, I provide the first book-length study of how ecotourism and community-based conservation are being appropriated by post-neoliberal governments, building on prior work in political ecology on neoliberal conservation. Third, I contribute to contemporary studies of Latin American resource politics by theorizing and documenting the green productivist agenda implemented by the Kirchner-Fernández regimes, while drawing attention to the representational pluralism of post-neoliberal politics. Fourth, I advance a distinctive approach to the ethnographic research and analysis of capitalist spaces. Drawing on work in the interdisciplinary field of risk studies, I develop an ecology of risk approach to understanding the conjunctural terrains of capitalist production, consumption, and state formation. Beyond its contributions to academic debates, though, this ethnography—I hope—illuminates the sociocultural life of Patagonia in a compelling fashion that does justice to the time, friendship, and interest poured into the project by the people of El Chaltén.

THE PATAGONIAN SUBLIME

INTRODUCTION

In March 2015, President Cristina Fernández de Kirchner of Argentina addressed a crowd of supporters that had gathered outside the administrative center for Parque Nacional Los Glaciares (PNLG). As her second term in office was drawing to a close, Fernández had traveled to her family home in El Calafate, a bustling tourism destination on the shore of Lake Argentino—which was turquoise on sunny days and occasionally dotted by icebergs. These icebergs alerted visitors and residents alike to the proximity of the Andean glaciers and massive ice field that the adjacent park sought to protect. In office from 2007 to 2015, Fernández was the surviving member of Latin America's most powerful political couple during the early twenty-first century. Her late husband, Néstor Kirchner, had been president from 2003 to 2007, dying unexpectedly of a heart attack in 2010 at the age of sixty. Her visit officially celebrated the opening of a new tourism information center at the largest (726,927 hectares) and second-most-visited national park in Argentina, but her message—at turns leavened by nostalgia and humor—was sharply political. Fernández took stock of the Kirchnerist presidential legacy ahead of the upcoming national elections.

Holding power from 2003 to 2015, Kirchner and Fernández forged a national political movement known throughout Argentina as Kirchnerismo that responded to the perceived failures of the neoliberal development approach pursued by President Carlos Menem, in office from 1989 to 1999. Menem was a devoted pupil of the so-called Washington Consensus that was brokered between the U.S. government, the World Bank, and the International Monetary Fund (IMF) to promote free-market policies during the 1980s and 1990s (Stiglitz 2003). This trio of powerful actors helped usher into being a global economy based on the neoliberal principles of privatization, liberalization, fiscal conservatism, and deregulation (Stiglitz 2003; Harvey 2007). Though Menem enjoyed some early success, the Argentine economy entered a deep depression lasting from 1998 until 2002. Enacting policies prescribed by the IMF, the Argentine government—first under Menem and then, from 1999 to 2001, under his successor, Fernando de la Rúa—greatly exacerbated the downturn. The country soon faced growing poverty, ballooning unemployment, and social dislocation (Weisbrot et al. 2011).

Recognizing an impending collapse, the IMF cut the Argentine government loose by ending its access to emergency loans. The ensuing crisis culminated in massive nationwide protests, riots, a bank run, and a debt default in December 2001 (D'Avella 2014). Four presidents came and went over the course of two weeks before Eduardo Duhalde took office in January 2002 (P. Lewis 2009). Kirchnerismo offered a new vision of state power, market capitalism, social rights, national sovereignty, and the use of natural resources that rejected the neoliberal approach.

Fernández's speech to the sympathetic Patagonian audience in El Calafate used the growth of national park tourism as a metaphor to understand Kirchnerismo: "The truth is that today we have achieved many things, but most importantly as a woman from this place, more than as president, I feel profound emotion. When this park was created by the National Parks Administration, Calafate barely had a population of 100 people and 15 people per year came in 1937 to visit the glacier [Perito Moreno Glacier]. . . . Look, from 1937 until 1991, we went from 100 to 2,000 beds, and, from 1991 until today, we now have almost 8,000 beds, more than 20,000 residents, and more than half a million tourists who every year visit El Calafate" (Fernández de Kirchner 2015). The Kirchners began their political careers in Santa Cruz, the province in which the PNLG is located. Kirchner was provincial governor before becoming president, while Fernández was a provincial deputy, national senator, and national deputy for Santa Cruz. Fernández's speech alluded to the slow growth experienced by El Calafate from 1937—the year the PNLG was founded—until the end of the 1980s. Following the election of Kirchner as governor in 1991, El Calafate experienced robust development as measured by the numbers of tourism jobs, new businesses, permanent residents, and total visitors, as well as by growing public investment in conservation. Fernández framed the rise of El Calafate and the PNLG as a symbol for Kirchnerismo writ large. From the beginning of 2003 until the end of 2015, Argentina's gross domestic product enjoyed a robust but volatile annual growth rate of 4.58 percent (World Bank 2018a). During this time, the country's per capita gross national income (GNI) grew from $3,550 to $12,430, reflecting a massive economic expansion with respect to the collapse that occurred from 1998 to 2003, when per capita GNI declined by some $4,440 (World Bank 2018b). Beyond this, the speech noted the integral role that the green economy played within the politics of Kirchnerismo. In Argentina, the dominant understanding of the green economy was related to ecotourism and the conservation of protected areas. Fernández communicated the commitment that the Kirchners had displayed for more than two decades to promote parks and the tourism industry across the nation and within the Patagonian region. It was certainly not lost on the crowd that the Kirchners had invested their own capital in the green economy as owners of hotels and real estate in El Calafate and El Chaltén, the ecotourism destinations situated at the southern and northern entrances to the

PNLG, respectively. In many ways, then, the Kirchners were fundamentally entangled in the green economy, with personal, family, and financial concerns coexisting—uneasily for many—with presidential power and national politics.

POST-NEOLIBERAL POLITICS AND GREEN PRODUCTIVISM

Over the past two decades, global neoliberalism has begun to face growing opposition. The triumphal march of market fundamentalism associated with the Washington Consensus has given way to anti-neoliberal social movements, civic groups, nongovernmental organizations (NGOs), political parties, and governments, which have taken many forms and drawn very different conclusions. In Latin America, some New Left governments have called for the restoration of socially responsible, progressive capitalism to replace neoliberal policies associated with social upheaval and slow growth. Others have embraced what they call twenty-first century socialism. Scholarship on the New Left, however, has often focused on the crisis of neoliberalism, constitutional reform, political parties, moderate versus radical ideologies, economic programs, intraregional cooperation, social movements, and resource extraction (Castañeda 2006; Santiso 2007; Brand and Sekler 2009; Robinson 2010; Flores-Macias 2012; Webber and Carr 2013; Ellner 2014; Arsel, Hogenboom, and Pellegrini 2016). The green economy has received little sustained attention despite the fact that protected areas are often the largest territorial assets controlled by states and crucial to how nations are represented to citizens and to other countries. Ecotourism continues to increase across the region, providing valuable sources of investment, income, and employment for communities. Moreover, the green economy offers governments a highly visible platform on which to establish the meaning of post-neoliberal political rule. Indeed, some governments have enshrined constitutional protections for nature and sought to link New Left political ideologies to indigenous ethical principles and alternative development approaches such as buen vivir (Radcliffe 2012; Villalba 2013).

This book examines the intersection of post-neoliberal politics and the green economy in Argentina. Focusing on the Kirchner-Fernández administrations and the Patagonian region, this ethnography asks a series of interrelated questions: What is the post-neoliberal development approach pursued by the Kirchners? How does the green economy fit into this development model? What strategies of capital accumulation, political rule, and national representation are advanced to promote the green economy? How do local actors and communities formulate different modes of risk consciousness and practice to understand and respond to post-neoliberal politics and the shifting currents of global capitalism? To answer these questions, I draw upon my field research in the Patagonian village of El Chaltén and the PNLG. I focus on the key actors present in the El Chaltén zone: mountaineers, trekkers, park rangers, land managers, tourism entrepreneurs, and service workers. Rather than providing an abstract, despatialized state-level view of the politics of the green economy, this book instead offers a grounded ethnographic account of subjectivity, risk, power, and place within the El Chaltén zone that illuminates key features of Kirchnerist post-neoliberal green politics.

Much confusion has arisen regarding the "post" in post-neoliberal. I take the "post" to refer to an immanent, multisite struggle to forge a counterhegemonic front from within global neoliberalism. Rather than "an era after neoliberalism," post-neoliberalism—as Laura MacDonald and Arne Ruckert assert (2009, 6)—involves the search for "policy alternatives arising out of the many contradictions of neoliberalism" (quoted in Wylde 2012, 23). As Jean and John Comaroff note, however, "there is little reason to expect a retreat of the precepts and practices of neoliberalism, even though its triumphal assertion as ideological paradigm may be more muted at the moment" (2012, 25). Neoliberalism remains the dominant political-economic paradigm for global capitalism, but the Latin American New Left has created a diverse set of alternatives ranging from the pragmatically modest to the more radically committed (Escobar 2010; Goodale and Postero 2013). Though linked to left-of-center politics in Latin America, scholars should understand "post-neoliberalism" as a polysemic term that can be associated with any number of ideologies, including right-wing authoritarianism and fascism.[1] While some scholars have emphasized the continuities between New Left governments and global neoliberalism (Webber and Carr 2013), various others have focused on the creation of new forms of governance, development, social consensus, and logics of capital accumulation that are distinct from previous neoliberal regimes (Grugel and Riggirozzi 2009; Féliz 2012; Wylde 2012; Ebenau and Liberatore 2013; Weisbrot 2015).

Neo-developmentalism is one development strategy embraced by New Left governments. Neo-developmentalism seeks to synthesize elements from both the neoliberal policies advocated by international financial institutions like the IMF and import substitution industrialization policies pursued by many Latin American developmentalist states following World War II (Ban 2013; Bresser-Pereira 2016).[2] Neo-developmentalism advances the ideal of a mixed economy and emphasizes not only market capitalism and global integration, but also stronger state control over national development and taxation schemes that rebuild social welfare programs. In Argentina, the Kirchner-Fernández administrations have advanced a neo-developmentalist approach to national growth and criticized the neoliberal legacies of privatization, deregulation, and liberalization (Féliz 2012; Wylde 2012). The Kirchnerist governments have halted and begun to reverse the privatization of state companies and utilities, implemented tighter regulations, imposed tariffs and export taxes, and advocated for stronger labor protections.

Kirchnerist neo-developmentalism has formulated a unique macroeconomic logic that depends upon the government maintaining fiscal and trade surpluses (though this has not always been accomplished) and intervening in foreign exchange markets (Féliz 2012; Wylde 2012). State intervention to create a depreciated peso allows "domestic industry to compete more effectively against imports and also in world markets" (Weisbrot 2015, 68). The government has faced a delicate balancing act between fiscal pragmatism and investing heavily in social programs, redistributing wealth, and protecting real wages through public subsidies for transportation, food, and energy (Calvo and Murillo 2012, 152). Export taxes on agricultural commodities like soy have provided a pool of discretionary revenue the Kirchners could use to finance the social state.

This book develops the argument that green productivism is the agenda the Kirchners advanced to promote the green economy. This strategy seeks to develop the green economic potential of the nation in ways that do not conflict with key tenets of Kirchnerist neo-developmentalism, such as its emphasis on commodity exports and natural resource exploitation (Ebenau and Liberatore 2013). At the macroeconomic level, green productivism depends upon the interventionist approach taken by the Argentine central bank to devalue the peso on the foreign exchange market to boost the competitiveness of the tourism industry and commodity exports (Organisation for Economic Co-operation and Development 2014, 336). The green economy is thus part of the natural resource sector that is oriented toward global competition and foreign consumer markets. Much has been made of the New Left's embrace of agro-extraction (Arsel, Hogenboom, and Pellegrini 2016). This body of scholarship, however, typically treats extraction and conservation as opposing forces, rather than including the green economy within a broader pattern of natural resource exploitation that includes both conservation and agro-extraction.

THE TREKKING CAPITAL OF ARGENTINA

On a sunny day in late 2008, Rolando Garibotti and I hiked out of the PNLG from the mountaineering base camp at Río Blanco, passing scores of trekkers who were headed up to see Monte Fitz Roy.[3] Referred to by residents as "Chaltén," this zone of Argentina includes the bohemian village of El Chaltén and the northern section of the national park (see Map I.1). As indicated by a large sign erected at the entrance to town, El Chaltén is the "trekking capital of the nation." The village attracts over 65,000 tourists each year, visiting the zone to hike its famous trekking circuit and take commercial tours of backcountry glaciers. Rolando and I hopped into his old Datsun pickup and drove back to town along the unpaved Route 23. He stopped to pick up a hitchhiker along the way, as is customary throughout much of Patagonia.

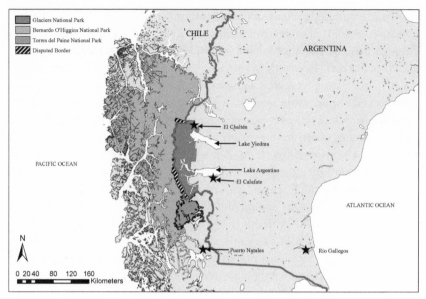

MAP I.1. The El Chaltén zone and Glaciers National Park (map by Stephen G. Harris)

El Chaltén is an aesthetically stunning and remote corner of the Southern Patagonian Andes located on the Argentina-Chile border that takes its name from Cerro Chaltén, a mountain more commonly referred to as Monte Fitz Roy (3,405 meters), the most prominent peak in the Chaltén Massif (see Figure I.1). The ice-covered spires of the massif dominate the skyline and are subject to the almost constant westerly winds that race across the continent. Situated in a canyon, El Chaltén is surrounded on three sides (north, south, and west) by the national park, while privately owned farms occupy the foothills to the east of town. Fed by tributaries coming from the high mountains, the De las Vueltas River defines the eastern boundary of the village. The river then winds its way south into Lake Viedma. One of the largest freshwater lakes in Argentina, Lake Viedma is the major drainage basin for the El Chaltén zone. The arid steppe begins to the east of Lake Viedma and continues across the province of Santa Cruz, ending at the Atlantic Ocean. On the steppe are farms devoted primarily to raising herds of sheep, goats, and cattle, where the famous Patagonian gauchos— or *paisanos*, as they are called locally—serve as the main source of agrarian labor. West of the Chaltén Massif is the daunting Southern Patagonian Ice Field, referred to as the Hielos Continentales.[4] Adjacent national parks—Glaciers in Argentina and Bernardo O'Higgins and Torres del Paine in Chile—comprise one megapark that covers almost all of the Southern Patagonian Ice Field, the principal source of fresh water in the region. The ice field is uninhabited, with arctic conditions prevailing year-round.

FIGURE I.1. El Chaltén and Monte Fitz Roy (© Dörte Pietron)

Rolando drove the truck down the gravel road that ran parallel to the De las Vueltas River. After initially discussing mountaineering, Rolando abruptly switched topics as the village appeared in the distance. He talked about the difficulties facing El Chaltén as the U.S.-precipitated financial crisis affected the global economy: "If there is an economic crisis (in Argentina), and it looks like there will be one, then we might see three or four years of no growth or even a decrease in tourism, which should be good for the village. It will give everyone a chance to establish better infrastructure, to get the waste treatment and water systems in place, to have the better businesses stay and the worst ones leave. The quick growth that the town has experienced over the last few years is like a moraine after its supporting glacier has retreated. It's completely unstable." Rolando reflected a popular concern among residents reacting to what economists call contagion, as the Great Recession spread beyond the United States. Indeed, the Argentine economy had already gone into recession by late 2008 (Weisbrot et al. 2011, 4). The domestic economy rebounded in 2009, but the PNLG tourism industry entered a period of stagnation that lasted for the next few years.[5] The heady years of the ecotourism boom from 2003 to 2007 coincided with the presidential term of Néstor Kirchner and yielded accelerating growth and an employment bonanza. By contrast, the presidential terms of Cristina Fernández de Kirchner (from 2007 to 2015) witnessed a slowing rate of economic growth and inaugurated a period of ecotourism consolidation. For Rolando, growth threatened to undermine the sustainable development plans authored by land managers working for the National Parks Administration of

Argentina (Administración de Parques Nacionales, or APN). He likened El Chaltén to a moraine: the soil and rock formations that consolidate at the edges of glaciers. With the growing impacts of climate change on the Andean environment, Patagonian glaciers had begun an accelerating process of thinning and retreating. A moraine becomes destabilized after its "supporting glacier" vanishes. Boulders unexpectedly shifted on this terrain, resulting in injuries for trekkers and climbers. However, Rolando expressed the hope that hitting the pause button on accelerated growth would buy time for the park service, community residents, and the tourism industry to make the changes needed to increase sustainability.

This book takes the El Chaltén zone as its ethnographic theater of inquiry to understand post-neoliberal politics and the green economy. At the general level, the term "green economy" refers to any mode of economic activity that facilitates environmental protection, health, and well-being.[6] In the global public sphere, however, the term refers to sustainable development and the international debates that began over the limits to growth in the 1970s. As the United Nations Environmental Programme defines it, the green economy is a mechanism to achieve sustainable development: "In its simplest expression, a green economy is low-carbon, resource efficient, and socially inclusive. In a green economy, growth in income and employment are driven by public and private investments that reduce carbon emissions and pollution, enhance energy and resource efficiency, and prevent the loss of biodiversity and ecosystem services. These investments need to be catalysed and supported by targeted public expenditure, policy reforms and regulation changes. The development path should maintain, enhance and, where necessary, rebuild natural capital as a critical economic asset and as a source of public benefits. This is especially important for poor people whose livelihoods and security depend on nature" (2011, 16). What is interesting about this statement is that the United Nations Environmental Programme implicitly limits the green economy to a development approach that only makes sense in a world defined by the nation-state system, public and private investment, and market capitalism. A more appropriate phrase, then, is the green capitalist economy. In Argentina, "sustainable development" is a ubiquitous term of reference in national politics, appearing in policy positions and planning documents as well as being enshrined in the state bureaucracy with its own dedicated federal agency—the Ministry of the Environment and Sustainable Development. Amid the omnipresence (and thus thinness) of sustainability as a national discourse, people concretely understand this term by locating the green economy. Though relevant to farming, energy, forestry, resorts, and fund-raising for environmental causes, among other things, the green economy is most closely associated in Argentina with protected area conservation and ecotourism. The El Chaltén zone provides a key vantage from which to understand the green capitalist economy and the local forms of sustainable development that worried Rolando and many other residents.

El Chaltén's green economy includes the spheres of tourism, the service industry, and the conservation state. Tourism involves hundreds of mountaineers who contend with a gauntlet of environmental dangers as they seek fame in the Andes, as well as the tens of thousands of trekkers who pursue alpine adventure on "frontcountry" trails and backcountry glaciers. The service industry includes the hundreds of seasonal workers who struggle against socioeconomic barriers that prevent their upward mobility and the scores of tourism entrepreneurs who develop investment strategies to facilitate capital accumulation. The conservation state refers to the dozens of park rangers and handful of land managers who work for the APN to foster sustainable development and diminish the environmental impacts of the tourism industry. These different actors offer concrete points of entry into understanding subjectivity formation within the capitalist economy.

Tania Li has developed an "analytic of the conjuncture" to make sense of how social formations are constituted within the dynamic, unfolding, and uncertain interactions between different historically situated "elements" (2014, 16). Focusing on rural Indonesia, Li shows how capitalist processes and relations are embedded within a conjuncture of economic, ecological, emplaced, spiritual, and institutional elements, which in turn shape subjectivity formation. Li conceptualizes the subject as an agent that is "capable of action and reflection" but whose practices, desires, and habits are situated within fields of power deriving from the conjuncture. Subjects are both "formed within" and "formative in turn" of the conjuncture (2014, 18–19). I apply this conjunctural approach to the Patagonian green economy by focusing on the interactional terrain of tourism, the service industry, and the conservation state. Though situated in Patagonia, this conjuncture involves translocal movements, articulations, and imaginations that bring visitors, rangers, entrepreneurs, workers, scientists, and others from afar to engage in particular types of activities. In El Chaltén, subjects forge an interactional sense of their positionality through sensorial, discursive, and imaginative practices. Subjects gain this positional understanding by exercising agency to access aesthetic experiences, political power, social status, economic capital, and natural resources. At the same time, the existing capitalist relations of production, consumption, and state power place limitations on agency, stabilizing subject positions that contribute to the reproduction of the green economy. My analysis of subjectivity draws attention to how actors "thematize" (Heidegger 1962, 414) their position in the world through the exercise of agency that occurs in ways that tend to subjugate them to the wider operations of power (Foucault 1979; Agrawal 2005). To anticipate a subsequent point, the experience of risk provides a central thread of perception, understanding, communication, and imagination for actors to thematize their position in the world. The green capitalist economy is constituted by risk subjectivity. Though uncertainty is central to Li's conjunctural approach, I specifically foreground risk as a creative force within the subject's understanding of and engagement with the world.

The Patagonian Sublime focuses narratively on the tourism seasons following the Great Recession. Ecotourism development slowed, and El Chaltén entered a more turbulent period during the Fernández administration, as anticipated by Rolando in his commentary. The trekking masses and mountaineering expeditions continued to arrive, but the rate of growth of their numbers slowed. The dreams of opportunity that had attracted entrepreneurs and seasonal workers faded in the face of surging inflation, a heightened cost of living, and increasing concern about state corruption. Rangers and land managers struggled to mitigate the ecological harms linked to the rapid expansion of tourism. Tensions flared between representatives of the tourism industry and the park service and seasonal workers over access to park resources. Despite these rifts, coalitions formed across class, racial, and gender boundaries to confront communal threats.

THEORIZING GREEN PRODUCTIVISM

The Logic of Capitalist Development

Kirchnerist green productivism is based on state control of protected areas and the aggressive drive to promote ecotourism. The broader category of nature-based tourism refers to conventional "travel to unspoiled places to experience and enjoy nature" (Honey 2008, 7). By contrast, ecotourism is a form of alternative travel that fetishizes the ideal of people and landscapes as "pristine, unspoiled and untouched by westernization, industrialization, and even mass tourism" (Brockington, Duffy, and Igoe 2010, 135). This ideal, however, contradicts the social, cultural, and economic realities of ecotourism destinations as sites saturated by processes of marketing, branding, and service provision (Duffy 2002; Fletcher 2014).[7] I view ecotourism as a flexible market discourse of alternative travel to and within pristine nature—ideally but not always associated with an indigenous, non-Western other—that evolves in relation to consumer notions of mass tourism. Ecotourism also involves a commitment to forms of environmental conservation that improve the livelihoods and welfare of surrounding local communities (Honey 2008, 28–33). In Argentina, foreign and domestic tourists seek out remote parks—such as the PNLG—as alternative sites of travel beyond the mass tourist and vacation destinations of cosmopolitan Buenos Aires and the Atlantic beaches (Pastoriza 2011). There is a dialectic of mass and alternative tourism that spatializes Argentina for travelers in specific ways. Moreover, the Argentine park service has sought to promote environmental protection in a democratic manner that improves the welfare of communities (Administración de Parques Nacionales 2012). Ecotourism is the central development strategy taken by the APN to achieve the goal of community-based and community-legitimized conservation.

Ecotourism reflects a specific mode of capitalist development. Anthropological scholarship on capitalism has increasingly sought to create a balanced portrait of how production, consumption, exchange, and circulation dynamics affect diverse human and nonhuman worlds.[8] With respect to capitalist production, anthropologists have focused on the dialectics of capital and labor, but they have largely neglected to scrutinize land and ground rent as crucial elements within the productive process. I follow Fernando Coronil's (1997) lead in seeking to redirect scholarly attention to Karl Marx's "trinity form" of capital or profit, labor or wages, and land or rent—as well as the central role of the state in mediating the productive interactions between capital, labor, and land (1991, 953). In his classic theorization of industrial capitalism, Marx (1990) attended to capital and labor, but land largely dropped out of the analysis. This emphasis on the capital-labor nexus influenced subsequent anthropological scholarship to the detriment of assessing ground rent and the impacts of rentier processes. Moreover, scholarship in political ecology on ecotourism has adeptly explored issues of marketing, branding, spectacle, labor exploitation, consumer hype, and community impacts (see Duffy 2002; Walley 2004; Vivanco 2007; and Fletcher 2014). What is missing is an appreciation of how ecotourism—and tourism more generally—can operate as a form of rentier capitalism. My analysis of the Patagonian green economy focuses on capital (tourism entrepreneurs), labor (service workers), consumers (mountaineers and trekkers), and state actors (park rangers and land managers), but it ties production, consumption, and the state to a rentier logic based on place branding and land ownership.

Ground rent refers to the monetary value that results from landownership and monopolistic control over private or public resources, such as forests, farms, mines, and wilderness. This monopoly position allows landowners—states, corporations, and individuals—to charge users for physical access to these assets, concessions and use rights, and the privilege of extracting resources.[9] Coronil has argued that rents are central to how contemporary Latin American nations generate surplus value and obtain foreign exchange, given their position in the international division of production as "nature intensive" or "resource-based economies" (2011, 242).[10] Building on Coronil's work, I conceptualize protected areas as landed property over which the park service exercises direct monopoly control and the tourism industry exercises subsidiary control. The park service directly controls territory and accrues rental income by charging user fees to tourists and tour companies. By paying a user fee to the park service, tourism companies obtain subsidiary rights to commercialize destinations inside a park. As a rentier state agency, the park service concerns itself with maximizing ground rent. In a parallel process, the tourism industry develops a rentier operation through its subsidiary ability to monopolize access to consumer spaces in parks. Under Kirchnerist green productivism, the drive to promote ecotourism involves a form of rentier capitalism that generates expanding sources of revenue for the conservation state and the tourism industry.[11]

Beyond territorial control, ecotourism involves place branding and commodification strategies to increase the consumer value of monopolized spaces. David Harvey has conceptualized the global tourism industry as invested in the commodification of "place" and the attempt to control access to the "collective symbolic capital" tied to distinct localities (2001, 405). By branding destinations with exclusive place identities, tourism industries—working together with the state—contribute to the formation of symbolic monopolies. Indeed, the Patagonian green economy relies on the formation of place-based brand images and the commodification of park landscapes in which tourists accumulate signs of distinction (Bourdieu 2002). In southern Patagonia, the primary ecotourism circuit involves four destinations with different brand images: Ushuaia and Tierra del Fuego National Park as the "End of the World"; Puerto Natales and Torres del Paine National Park as the "Trekking Capital of Chile"; El Calafate and the PNLG (southern sector) as the "Glacier Capital of Argentina"; and El Chaltén and the PNLG (northern sector) as the "Trekking Capital of Argentina" (Mendoza et al. 2017, 101). I have coined the term "semiotic estate" to refer to the creation and ongoing development of coupled territorial and symbolic monopolies that facilitate rent capture.[12] In Patagonia, the conservation state and the tourism industry have forged a public-private alliance to control a semiotic estate based on park territory and place branding.

A Strategy of Political Rule

Kirchnerist green productivism depends upon ecotourism as the primary engine of capital development and upon community-based conservation (CBC) as a form of political rule. At the general level, the strategies of political rule that neoliberal and post-neoliberal governments have implemented are diverse since they respond to the shifting conditions of local, regional, and national terrains constituted by class, racial, ethnic, and gender differences. Neoliberal regimes have employed terrorism, military force, and paramilitary violence to pacify populations, promote capital accumulation, and secure resources (Paley 2001; Watt and Zepeda 2012; Hristov 2014). Neoliberal governments have also used democratic elections, technocratic managerialism, and the dream of foreign investment to build consent among citizens (Babb 2001; Dezalay and Garth 2002). Post-neoliberal governments are no different insofar as they have the powers of repression and tools to build popular consent at their disposal. In Argentina, Kirchnerismo is a center-left ideology that has created a populist political front (Laclau 2007) through antipathy to neoliberalism, the international financial system, Euro-American power, and domestic political foes who have stood in the way of Kirchnerist programs. Though organized around center-left populism, Kirchnerist politics have involved an array of practices ranging from the use of emergency measures to expedite the passing of laws (Alvarez 2007) to the promotion of zones of environmental sacrifice tied to expanding soy production (Gordillo 2014) to the celebration of human rights and curbing of the impunity of military personnel who committed crimes during the Dirty War (Faulk 2013). Green productivism provides a window onto a different type of Kirchnerist politics based on promoting civil society participation, the decentralization of power, and community involvement. This suggests that the green economy is a platform from which to signal democratic involvement in state governance of natural resources, presenting a counternarrative to critics suggesting that the Kirchners are anti-environmental—given their close ties to mining companies, megadam boosters, and foreign agribusiness.

Under the Kirchners, ecotourism-led development has involved a form of political rule that promotes CBC. The APN began promoting CBC in the 1990s and consolidated this approach during the 2000s. The field of political ecology has examined CBC as a form of environmental governance associated with the global turn toward ecotourism and participatory development during the 1980s and 1990s (see Igoe 2004; Walley 2004; Haenn 2005; and Agrawal 2010). CBC emerged as a corrective to the "fortress conservation" approach that employed centralized state power to frame protected areas as environments preserved for tourism, which often involved the eviction or marginalization of local communities (Neumann 1998; Brockington 2002). There is a rich field in political ecology that focuses on how ecotourism and CBC facilitate the implementation of "neoliberal conservation" based on: the decentralization of state power; the shifting of responsibility for environmental governance to local communities, NGOs, and market actors; and the promotion of tourism-based entrepreneurialism and the commodification of parks as reservoirs of natural capital (Brondo 2013, 10–11).[13] Scholars have drawn attention to how multilateral lending and aid organizations such as the World Bank and the U.S. Agency for International Development have promoted participatory development and ecotourism as part of a wider neoliberal agenda (Duffy 2002; Brockington, Duffy, and Igoe 2010). Of course, it is important not to move from the claim that ecotourism and CBC facilitate neoliberalism to the much stronger assertion that they are inherently neoliberal. This book pushes scholars to consider how post-neoliberal governments have enlisted ecotourism and CBC to construct popular environmental fronts of support for sustainable development. The Kirchners have taken up ecotourism and CBC as useful vehicles to promote their social, economic, and political goals. Argentine post-neoliberal conservation utilizes the master tools associated with neoliberal conservation within a national political movement working to restructure the country along different capitalist principles and modes of building social consensus.

As a strategy of political rule, CBC intersects with the rentier logic at work within ecotourism. The creation of a semiotic estate based on a symbolic branding and landownership monopoly privileges the conservation state and the tourism industry, which have direct and indirect control, respectively, over the national park as a commoditized space. Not only do they monopolize ground rent capture, but the conservation state and entrepreneurial capital also work together to determine what place brand will be employed in a particular destination, as well as what investment work needs to be undertaken to improve the landscape for consumption. This form of rentier capitalism thus depends upon a state-capital alliance that marginalizes other actors, such as agrarian laborers, ranchers, and tourism workers. By capturing rent and growing their institutional capacities, the conservation state and the tourism industry have become more powerful and equipped to establish hegemonic rule over ecotourism destinations. As a strategy of political rule, CBC works to incorporate ecotourism community members into a form of resource management that reproduces state-capital domination, though of course not without dissent and conflict. I document how CBC aspires to create localized domains of sustainable development that expand popular consent for procapitalist practices, which result in a stronger state apparatus and a more powerful tourism industry.

Representing National Nature

Green productivism is also a cultural project of national representation that intertwines the ecotourism industry and protected area conservation with the global consumer economy. To promote capitalist development and political rule within the green economy, the Kirchner-Fernández administrations have sought to encourage increased tourism from both domestic locations and abroad. Landscape aesthetics figures centrally in recruiting visitors and directing them toward high-priority destinations. Within the federal park system, Iguazú National Park in the far north of Argentina is the most visited destination, protecting Iguazú Falls—the largest waterfalls system in the world—and the surrounding subtropical zone of the Paranese rainforest. By contrast, Andean Patagonia is a very different landscape that contains a series of national parks abutting the Chilean border. This belt of parks protects the Andean Patagonian forest and the high-mountain ecoregion and sells an alpine aesthetic of forests, lakes, glaciers, and snow-capped peaks. Patagonian parks account for over 50 percent of the number of tourist visits within the entire federal protected area system and generate the most domestic and foreign consumer interest when compared to other types and images of national nature, such as rainforest, marine, steppe, grassland, or desert environments (Ministerio de Turismo de Argentina 2014, 153–155).

Through the promotion of specific destinations, the Kirchner-Fernández administrations have fostered an uneven spatial representation of national nature in which the alpine environment constitutes the core feature.

In addition to ecotourism and CBC, the alpine landscape sublime is a constitutive pillar of green productivism. Ecotourism-led development depends on the semiotic estate and the enlisting of CBC to generate community consent. Ultimately, though, this political-economic logic doesn't make a whit of difference without an aesthetically compelling landscape to attract tourists, thereby generating the consumer demand to power the capitalist economy. Andean Patagonia gains much of its meaning within the global consumer economy by belonging to the category of alpine destinations that includes the Canadian Rockies, the Peruvian Andes, the Southern Alps in New Zealand, the Himalayas in Nepal, and the European Alps. Moreover, there are long-standing forms of outdoor recreation associated with alpine environments, such as mountaineering, skiing, trekking, kayaking, rafting, cycling, and fishing. As Robert Fletcher (2014) notes, Patagonian ecotourism is productively blended together with adventure sport. The Patagonian region has exploited growing global interest in alpine landscape linked to adventure travel and media consumption, extreme sports, and the outdoor recreation industry (Beedie 2003; Wheaton 2004; Vivanco and Gordon 2009). Though concerned with ecological integrity, Patagonian tourists discursively privilege adventure within sublime wilderness as the primary rationale for visiting the region. The "sublime" refers to the incredible awe and reverence experienced by people beholding the immense power and magnitude of nature (Bell and Lyall 2002, 4). Patagonian tourists experience the sublime as a sense of wonderment, intense connection, and even rapture before the majesty of the Andean wilderness, a sentiment that they take back home with them, where it works to recruit the next wave of travelers. The semiotic estate thus involves the alpine sublime as a site of commodification for the tourism industry and the bases of aesthetic value for tourist consumers traveling to Patagonia.

The alpine sublime is a political project as much as a strategy of national representation. The formation of Patagonian national parks is related to the history of genocidal violence visited upon indigenous societies by the Argentine armed forces in the nineteenth century to open up the region for settler colonization, European immigration, and agrarian capitalism based on livestock farming for the world market (Bandieri 2005). The Argentine state's push to colonize Patagonia emerged out of geopolitical concerns regarding Chilean expansion, but livestock farming failed to establish territorial sovereignty over the disputed region. In the 1930s, political elites created a series of national parks in geopolitically sensitive border zones like Andean Patagonia (Administración de Parques Nacionales 2012). The first president of the park service, Exequiel Bustillo, viewed Patagonia as Argentina's version of the Swiss Alps and established the alpine landscape as vital to the conjoined tourism, colonization, and sovereignty mission of the federal agency (Bustillo 1999). The Kirchnerist embrace of the alpine sublime thus relies upon a long history of geopolitical disputes, border conflicts, and state efforts to promote development in Patagonia (Mendoza et al. 2017).

The Risk Society

Economists have long recognized the centrality of risk taking to the competitive ethos driving capitalism. Separated by over a century, Adam Smith (1976) and John Maynard Keynes (1997) sought to distinguish between rational enterprise and unsound speculation, examining the role of risk taking in securing higher returns but also in generating the conditions for ruin, bankruptcy, and economic disaster. Radicalizing Smith's insight (and anticipating Keynes), Marx developed a theory of capitalism that emphasized creative destruction and the constant revolutionizing of the social relations and productive conditions arising from market competition. The corollary to this is that capitalism generates and spreads uncertainty across the world in ways that affect the states, industries, regions, and communities within its orbit. A central feature of social life under global capitalism is that people generate different notions of risk exposure as they attempt to understand and respond to uncertainty (LiPuma and Lee 2004). The ongoing expansion of the global economy generates various types of risk exposure—often at multiple scales—that become the object of action or inaction for individuals, groups, corporations, and states. As anthropologists and sociologists have discussed, actors gain social membership through collective exposure to different types of risk, such as planetary megahazards like climate change (Beck 2012), toxic spills and environmental disasters (Petryna 2002; Auyero and Swistun 2009), or the specter of nuclear annihilation and terrorism (Masco 2006 and 2014). Despite collective notions of exposure, risk consciousness often remains highly variable within communities and populations. This book develops an ecology of risk approach to the ethnographic research and analysis of capitalist spaces. Such an approach examines the conjunctural (Li 2014) terrain of subject positions, each of which is informed by a concrete mode of risk experience. These risk subject positions emerge within and are stabilized by a capitalist network of production, consumption, and statecraft. A key issue for research is how—if at all—this plurality of risk experience is integrated into the collective imagination of security, and how this social imaginary is tied into broader constellations of state power.

Patagonian society has developed in response to green productivism based on ecotourism, CBC, and the alpine landscape sublime. Risk enters the ethnographic analysis when we locate actors as living beings who face uncertainty about how to achieve specific outcomes (Keane 1997). The green capitalist economy represents a concrete form of risk society. As I use the term, "risk society" refers to the network of social relations and interactional space in which actors deal with uncertainties—the possibilities of gain or loss, safety or danger, and advancement or decline—under specific conditions of production, consumption, and state power. Inhabiting distinct subject positions, social actors cultivate modes of risk consciousness and practice to perceive, understand, imagine, and thematize their world. The Patagonian risk society involves actors contending with different scales of risk, of which three are most significant to this study. First, actors are exposed to the interactional risks deriving from their local position in the green economy, particularly as groups jockey for power, status, or resources. Second, they are exposed to the risks deriving from the national politics of Kirchnerismo. Third, they are exposed to the challenges of the global economy. Actors respond to these different perceived scales of risk—local, national, and global—as they formulate a collective response. The Patagonian risk society is both the outcome of and the basis for an expanding green capitalist economy.[14]

In Patagonia, an ecology of risk approach highlights how subject positions within the green capitalist economy reflect diverse modes of thematizing the world through attention to risk exposure, but in ways that converge around the social imagination of security.[15] There are different clusters of risk experience that define the fields of tourist consumption, service production, and the conservation state. Mountaineering and trekking tourists thematize risk around the body in nature, fashioning a discourse of adventure in vertical and horizontal spaces. Workers and owners construct risk around the economy of nature, creating specific understandings of productive labor and opportunities for advancement in the ecotourism industry. Rangers and land mangers develop risk through the politics of nature, seeking to protect biodiversity and limit tourism's impacts. As I show, these diverse forms of risk subjectivity coalesce around the issue of how to achieve sustainable development. Sustainable development is the security charter produced by the Patagonian risk society to ensure the longevity of the community and the park. This logic of sustainability takes account of: the local conditions of capital, power, and resources; the national dynamics of the Kirchner-Fernández administrations; and the global situation of the consumer economy affected by the Great Recession.

The Political Culture of Kirchnerismo

The Kirchner-Fernández administrations have developed the political ideology of Kirchnerismo to legitimize their policies and programs, and their values and visions for Argentina. Drawing upon the political legacy after World War II of President Juan Perón and his celebrated wife, Eva Perón, the Kirchners have represented themselves as the standard bearers for twenty-first century Peronism. Classic Peronism focused on issues of economic nationalism, territorial sovereignty, and social rights that built an electoral coalition through antagonism to political opponents, foreign capital, and imperialism. The Kirchner-Fernández regimes have blended classic Peronist positions with a commitment to global market competition and export-led development through the exploitation of natural resources. As a political ideology circulated throughout Argentina, Kirchnerismo is the lens through which Patagonian communities have interpreted and responded to green productivism. As they grapple with the outcomes of this agenda, the communities formulate cultural representations of Kirchnerismo that embrace or reject the legitimacy sought by Kirchner and Fernández.

Political economists and political scientists have often painted Kirchnerismo with an overly homogenizing brush that fails to account for concrete variations in cultural representations of the state, governance, and citizenship. This book draws attention to the representational pluralism of post-neoliberal politics. The political culture of Kirchnerismo is unevenly circulated, received, and reinterpreted within regional and local contexts. Much of the existing scholarship on Kirchnerismo focuses on the presidencies of Kirchner and Fernández, neglecting the Patagonian historical context in which this political ideology was initially forged, as well as the impacts this regional connection has had on communities. As noted above, Kirchner and Fernández entered politics in the province of Santa Cruz. During this period, Kirchner and Fernández helped forge a center-left faction within the Partido Justicialista, commonly known as the Peronist party, that opposed the party's center-right wing, then led by President Menem. The couple built a patronage machine within Santa Cruz through oil royalties, public works projects, and business networks (P. Lewis 2009, 153–154). As governor, Kirchner invested public funds in the nascent tourism industry, helping commercialize the PNLG and build transportation and urban infrastructure in the towns of El Calafate and El Chaltén. During the 2000s, the Kirchners established their family home in El Calafate—the southern site of entry into the PNLG—and made personal investments in the green economy. Residents of El Chaltén have long-standing personal connections with the Kirchners as political leaders and investors.

Cultural representations of the Kirchnerist state, governance, and citizenship vary from region to region in Argentina. I attend to how actors within the Patagonian green economy recognize the existence of a personalized state—associated with the Kirchners as individuals—alongside the center-left political agenda of Kirchnerismo within the federal state; the effect this "double state" has on creating ambiguous governance, which is seen as both highly successful and often corrupt; and a tiered system of citizenship that provides full legal recognition only to the privileged middle class. The political culture of the double state, ambiguous governance, and tiered citizenship provides the basis of meaning in which social groups and communities understand the green productivist agenda.

BOOK OVERVIEW

I thus argue that the Kirchner-Fernández green productivist agenda mobilizes ecotourism-led development, CBC, and the alpine sublime to accelerate the exploitation of protected nature. Public-private alliances have crystallized to control the semiotic estates and place branding activities in distinct parks. The expanding green capitalist economy has facilitated the emergence of a risk society grounded in tourism consumption, service production, and the conservation state. Risk subjectivity has plural lives that cluster around the body, economy, and politics of nature. Sustainable development is the charter of collective security around which risk subjectivities converge. Though ultimately successful in generating socioeconomic development, the green agenda has also facilitated cultural responses to Kirchnerismo—centered on representations of the state, governance, and citizenship—that question the rectitude and authority of post-neoliberal politics. Green productivism has exacerbated social tensions and fostered cultural responses that threaten to undermine the legitimacy of the post-neoliberal turn.

The Patagonian Sublime consists of four parts and a brief conclusion. Part 1 examines the sphere of tourism consumption pertaining to the alpinist and trekking populations, focusing on how risk subjectivity is thematized around the body-nature relationship in ways that intersect with the political project of the alpine sublime. Chapter 1 focuses on the hundreds of mountaineers who climb in the Chaltén Massif every year, scrutinizing performances of resolve in the face of existential threat as well as the linkages between this adventure sport and the Euro-American outdoor industry. Chapter 2 attends to the tens of thousands of trekkers who visit the PNLG and the global consumer economy of adventure travel. I look at how trekking subjectivity depends on the tourist genre of adventure and the imaginative exposure of the trekking body to the sublime landscape. These two chapters demonstrate how mountaineering and trekking practices configure the consumer aesthetic and symbolic bases of El Chaltén's place identity as the trekking capital of Argentina. These chapters also show how Kirchnerist neo-developmentalism advances its political ends by framing and representing national identity in ways that tap into global consumer markets.

Part 2 addresses the sphere of tourism service production that encompasses entrepreneurs and service workers, scrutinizing how risk subjectivity is thematized around the economy of nature involving productive laboring, social standing, and local citizenship. The rise of tourist consumption has enabled an industry to develop around the exploitation of place identity and rent capture, which in turn has fostered a growing service industry for investment and employment. The rentier logic of ecotourism anchors the struggle between entrepreneurial capital and tourism service labor over access to resources and the establishment of local citizenship in the pueblo. Chapter 3 focuses on the formation of entrepreneurial subjectivity in relation to the difficulties of capital investment, differentiating the ethical accumulation of small business owners from the illicit wealth of big business owners. Chapter 4 discusses the hundreds of seasonal laborers who come to El Chaltén every season from elsewhere in Argentina and from surrounding countries. I examine how worker subjectivity emerges through aspirations for upward mobility that are increasingly stymied by socioeconomic barriers both local and national in scope. These two chapters foreground the capital-state alliance that shapes the semiotic estate and the selling of the alpine sublime, the growing exclusion of seasonal workers, and the limits of the progressive political ideology of Kirchnerismo related to citizenship. The tiered system of citizenship highlights a key contradiction with the expansionary agenda of green productivism that has resulted in jobs and economic growth.

Part 3 investigates the sphere of the conservation state that includes park rangers and land managers, attending to how risk subjectivity is thematized around the politics of nature and environmental protection. To do so, the conservation state has embraced CBC and participatory development approaches that seek to get communities to buy into the sustainability plans authored by land managers and enforced by park rangers. Chapter 5 examines the discourse of scientific sustainability and the public conservation subject position created by land managers and others during their efforts to author and update park management plans. Chapter 6 analyzes the policing practices of the park rangers tasked with conserving the northern sector of the PNLG. Rangers formulate an educational policing approach that responds to the variety of threats they face from residents, the tourism industry, and tourists. These two chapters demonstrate the strategy of political rule employed by the park service to foment rentier capitalism. The conservation state works with entrepreneurial capital to maintain control over the semiotic estate and the shifting conditions of sustainability. Nevertheless, the conservation state becomes the local representation of the post-neoliberal state, which is increasingly viewed as corrupt, authoritarian, illegitimate, and a source of ambiguous governance.

Part 4 addresses the politics of the green economy. Chapter 7 focuses on the popular understanding of sustainable development, not as a scientific plan authored by land managers but rather in terms of the politics of security necessary to ensure the long-term viability of El Chaltén as an ecotourism destination. This chapter scrutinizes sustainability as a collective social charter formed against internal and external threats. Chapter 8 examines the Kirchners' entanglements with the green economy across their time as provincial politicians and national leaders. The green productivist agenda communicates key values of Kirchnerismo, such as the defense of territorial sovereignty, economic development through resource exploitation, and the building of a stronger state through rent capture. The conclusion provides a brief review of the argument with attention to the key contradictions fostered by the green productivist agenda and Patagonian engagements with Kirchnerismo.

PART 1 THE SPHERE OF TOURISM CONSUMPTION

1 · ALPINE-STYLE MOUNTAINEERING

Resolve and Death in the Andes

Hundreds of mountaineers travel annually to El Chaltén and Parque Nacional Los Glaciares (PNLG) to contend with the mixed-condition (snow, ice, and rock) routes of the Chaltén Massif. Located in the Southern Patagonian Andes, the Chaltén Massif contains two iconic peaks—Monte Fitz Roy (3,405 meters) and Cerro Torre (3,102 meters)—that have long served as proving grounds where climbers can establish their global expertise (Kearney 1993). Mountaineering, or alpinism, is a sport based on the imagined global reach and mobility of its practitioners—including every continent, even Antarctica. Key ranges such as the Patagonian Andes, Canadian Rockies, Himalayas, and European Alps have supreme status. Climbing in Patagonia positions alpinists at the cutting edge of exploration, but it also exposes teams to existential peril. From 2007 until 2017, there has been an average of one fatality per season out of a climbing population of 200–400 people. An elevated risk of death is an enabling condition for many so-called risk, alternative, extreme, or lifestyle sports such as whitewater kayaking, BASE jumping (buildings, antennas, spans, and earth), and big-wave surfing (see Lyng 1990; Wheaton 2004; Fletcher 2008; Laviolette 2016). Though dangerous, Patagonian alpinism has attracted participants from two sources. First, foreign mountaineers, mostly from Europe and North America, travel to the zone on expeditions. Second, Argentine alpinists head to El Chaltén to work in the commercial guiding sector; rather than climbing full time, these locals are leisure-time practitioners. Mostly unmarried young men, both foreign and local alpinists come from middle- or working-class families and are typically employed—in El Chaltén or elsewhere—as guides, porters, or carpenters, or in related occupations requiring skilled labor. Alpinism is thus productively connected to the types of employment that sustain the bodily skills necessary to the sport.

Mountaineering provides the first point of entry into the Patagonian green economy and risk society. Oriented toward ascending the Andes, mountaineering subjects engage in performances of resolve in the face of death.[1] Through rigorous training over years or decades, alpinists acquire bodily techniques that enable them to ascend and descend nearly vertical routes without succumbing to the paralyzing fear that a nonclimber feels when clinging by his or her fingertips to a razor-sharp ledge thousands of meters above the ground. Resolve is a type of practical mastery that climbers cultivate to confront, adapt, and improvise within the uncertain conditions of the mountain environment.[2] Resolve is also a key symbol of what it means to be a mountaineer. An alpinist demonstrates resolve by confronting possible death. This engagement with death is ennobling to the sport's practitioners and produces a social distance from the crowds of tourists who fail to take such risks when hiking the trail system and being led on commercial tours of glaciers. Climbers thus thematize risk through the existential dangers of placing the body in vertical nature.

Mountaineering intersects with a green productivist agenda based on ecotourism in the alpine landscape. The sport has historically played a central role in establishing the value of El Chaltén as an alpine landscape for wilderness adventure. Mountaineering has worked within the geopolitical vision pursued by the Argentine state during the twentieth century to shift the Patagonian borderlands away from livestock farming and toward protected area tourism. Alpinists have also helped create a theater of alpine adventure defined by vertical and horizontal terrains into which trekking is incorporated. Tourism consumption depends upon linking the horizontal spaces of trekking with the vertical spaces of mountaineering. Below, following a brief history of Patagonia, I examine alpinist risk subjectivity through debates about the ethics of climbing style, status games played to gain fame, and engagements with death in the mountains. I then look at how alpinism provides high-risk images used by entrepreneurs to commodify the park.

A POLITICAL HISTORY OF THE PATAGONIAN LANDSCAPE

Ecotourism depends upon exploiting the alpine landscape protected by Patagonian national parks. The understanding of Patagonia as an alpine wilderness entails a long history of geopolitical conflict and changing landscape ideologies related to how the region should be exploited.[3] For centuries, the notion that Patagonia was *terra nullius* (empty land) dominated the European imagination of the region (Briones and Lantana 2002, 7–8). As terra nullius, Patagonia invited colonization by European powers and marginalized the presence of indigenous peoples. In the sixteenth century, the expedition of Ferdinand Magellan gave rise to the image of Patagonia as a monstrous landscape populated by giants

(Duviols 1997, 129). While the *Beagle* expedition in the early nineteenth century put to rest the myth of giants, Charles Darwin (1989) popularized the conception of Patagonia as a forbidding desert. The Darwinian notion of this desert—a variation on the image of terra nullius—positioned its indigenous peoples along a continuum from savagery to barbarism that dissociated them from any claims to the environment that they had inhabited for millennia. The Darwinian perspective influenced the conceptions of the region held by the Argentine elite, whose members long regarded it as useless for potential colonization (Nouzeilles 1999).[4]

Following independence from Spain, Argentina and Chile struggled to determine how to divide up Patagonia. In the mid-nineteenth century, Chile established a settlement at Punta Arenas on the southern tip of the mainland, which became a commercial port of entry for settlers. This growing Chilean threat to Argentina's claim over Patagonia spurred national elites to revisit the region's potential. Francisco Moreno, a scientist and explorer, traveled extensively throughout Patagonia. His scientific explorations provided a catalogue of the resources that could be acquired by settler-colonists working to advance the progress of the nation-state. He sought to overturn the Darwinian landscape ideology of the Patagonian desert, replacing it with a vision of abundant resources (Moreno 2002 and 2006). The cavalry followed. Seeking to subjugate indigenous peoples and open up new lands for settlers, the Argentine military began a campaign known as the "conquest of the desert" (Gordillo 2004, 48). The military's genocidal liquidation of indigenous peoples in Patagonia prepared the way for "white settler" colonialism (Gott 2007). The nomadic Aonikenk Tehuelche inhabited the El Chaltén zone. The Aonikenk had created a diversified economy that drew upon foraging practices using the domesticated horses introduced by the Spanish, as well as manufactured goods acquired through trade. Following the conquest of the desert, the surviving Aonikenk were confined to reservations and intermarried with the rural proletariat.[5]

The Argentine government pursued the counsel of Juan Bautista Alberdi, a political theorist who advocated for having European immigrants settle the frontier deserts. Political elites sought to populate Patagonia with yeoman farmers cultivating livestock for the world market. Instead, land policies consolidated the power of foreign capitalists who developed oligarchic control over vast estates, commercial operations in the territories, and import-export firms (Bandieri 2005). By the end of the nineteenth century, Patagonia was marked by a *latifundista* regime (large landed estates) of estancias controlled by a few wealthy families (Bayer 2008, 21–22). Waves of European settler-colonists moved into the El Chaltén zone, where they built estancias around Lake Viedma, growing sheep on the steppe and cattle in the forested foothills. Settlers exploited local resources for subsistence living, while cultivating livestock to be sold in Atlantic ports for the world market.

The Chilean territorial threat persisted into the twentieth century, prompting Argentine elites to develop new understandings of the Patagonian desert. In the 1930s, a group of upper-class conservationists promulgated the creation of a system of national parks located in geopolitically sensitive zones, such as Patagonia and the triple frontier area with Brazil and Paraguay. In 1934, the federal government passed legislation creating the National Parks Directorship (later renamed the National Parks Administration [Administración de Parques Nacionales]), which received jurisdiction over parklands totaling more than 22,000 square kilometers: Iguazú along the Brazilian border; Nahuel Huapi, Los Alerces, Perito Moreno, Lanin, and Glaciers along the Chilean frontier (Administración de Parques Nacionales 2012). Regarding livestock farming as having led to low population densities, national elites viewed parks as mechanisms for tourism-led development based on urban centers. Conservation elites helped cultivate a new landscape ideology that aestheticized the Andean desert as alpine wilderness, viewing Patagonia as Argentina's version of the Swiss Alps.[6] The first president of the park service, Exequiel Bustillo, imagined the newly created town of Bariloche in northern Patagonia as a future St. Moritz, the famous Swiss alpine resort (Bustillo 1999, 133). From the beginning, the landscape ideology of alpine wilderness was tied to elite aesthetic tastes and the pursuit of class status through leisure practices. In the El Chaltén zone, the government expropriated land from the owners of estancias to create the PNLG in 1937. Without an urban node around which to develop tourism infrastructure, the zone remained committed to livestock farming. However, federal parkland had been established on paper, providing the legal conditions of possibility for the future turn toward ecotourism.

Following the creation of the national park system, Patagonia remained a landscape of perceived emptiness and extensive nature, but that nature was increasingly of two kinds. In the Andean zone, there was an aesthetically valuable alpine wilderness that park officials set about creating through land expropriations and population resettlement.[7] There was also what remained: a vast steppe and *monte* desert marginalized from early conservation efforts. Not aesthetically valuable for parks and tourism, the steppe and monte were an extensive natural area earmarked for livestock farming and extractive industries such as mining and oil production.

Mountaineering expeditions to the El Chaltén zone opened up the area to international climbing in the early twentieth century and configured the initial meaning of alpine landscape as a site for high-risk adventure sport. This worked in concert with the political goal of fashioning the Andes into a wilderness with touristic appeal. In the 1950s, the first high-profile expeditions descended on the Chaltén Massif, seeking to tackle Monte Fitz Roy and Cerro Torre. Aided by President Juan Perón, a French team led by Lionel Terray became the first

FIGURE 1.1. Cerro Torre, Southeast Ridge (Compressor Route) (photo by author)

ascenders of Fitz Roy in 1952. This expedition proved crucial to establishing the reputation of Patagonia as an elite destination within global mountaineering. In 1958, an Italian team led by Bruno Detassis arrived in the Torre Valley. Judging Cerro Torre impossible, Detassis forbade his team to try climbing the peak (Kearney 1993, 60). The aura of impenetrability surrounding Cerro Torre further heightened the standing of the Chaltén Massif (see Figure 1.1).

As provincial and national politicians, Néstor Kirchner and Cristina Fernández de Kirchner contributed to the expansion of tourism and conservation through public investment, which provided the context for the growth of alpinism. In the 1970s, it took some climbers one month to travel from Buenos Aires down the Atlantic coast to the city of Río Gallegos and then west to the cordillera on a mail truck. Climbers then had to ford large rivers to pack in provisions to last weeks. Amid continuing border struggles with Chile, the Argentine government founded the village of El Chaltén in 1985 to promote tourism, grow the permanent population, and secure territorial sovereignty. As governor, Kirchner provided the foundational public investments—in road and bridge construction, bus route development, and the first wave of local infrastructure—for a nascent tourism industry that initially revolved around mountaineering but soon attracted young European and Argentine backpackers. With improvements in connectivity and travel infrastructure, alpinism in the zone grew from a handful of annual expeditions prior to the 1990s to hundreds by the end of the 2000s.

Contemporary mountaineering has configured a set of cultural meanings and social relations associated with the exploration of vertical space. Alpinists have engaged in ethical debates, status games, and confrontations with death that relate the local sporting terrain to the wider fields of global mountaineering and the Euro-American outdoor industry. Granting sponsorships to top alpinists, the outdoor industry includes companies like The North Face, Patagonia, Inc., Mammut, and Black Diamond. Patagonian mountaineers compete for status and recognition in the Andes that has the potential—in some cases—to translate into professional opportunities, while companies use sponsored athletes to sell retail goods and the outdoor adventure lifestyle (Chouinard 2006).

THE ETHICS OF STYLE

In global mountaineering, the Compressor Route that follows the southeast ridge of Cerro Torre is an iconic line. Once considered by elites to be impossible, Cerro Torre became a topic of ongoing controversy when Cesare Maestri claimed to have reached the summit in 1959 (Kearney 1993). After allegedly making an ascent heralded as one of the greatest of all time, Maestri found his account to be the subject of intense scrutiny and faced accusations that he lied about reaching the top (Garibotti 2004). Maestri returned to Cerro Torre in 1970 with a pneumatic air compressor, a drill, and hundreds of bolts. Working his way up the southeast ridge, he and his team drove in nearly 400 bolts, reaching the head wall but never setting foot on the true summit. Bolts are metal anchors that have been drilled into rock to protect climbers in the event of falling. Condemned by alpinists around the world, Maestri's Compressor Route became synonymous with unethical mountaineering. Since Maestri engineered the Compressor Route, alpinists have sought to "free" it in the sense of climbing the southeast ridge without using his bolts. The aim to "free the Compressor" is wrapped up in ongoing debates about the ethics of climbing style and how mountaineering resolve ought to be performed. Implicit in these debates is the issue of how much risk alpinists should be willing to take as they confront death.

During the 1990s, Patagonian mountaineers employed so-called siege tactics to deal with environmental hazards. As the term suggests, these tactics depended on a warlike, conquest-of-nature ethos in which teams probed for weaknesses or flaws in the defenses of routes (see, for example, Ortner 1999, 46–48). The siege style provided the dominant model for how teams should ascend and equip routes in the Andes. Over much of the twentieth century, Patagonian climbers strung lines of fixed ropes up routes. When the weather turned bad, they rappelled down the mountain. When conditions improved, they climbed the fixed ropes back to the highest point they had reached, where they continued their ascent. Often numbering 4–10 members, siege teams took weeks, months, or even years to complete routes by virtue of climbing in piecemeal fashion, rather than ascending in one continuous push from the bottom to the summit that is the hallmark of alpine style. Weighed down by big teams and large amounts of equipment, siege teams made slow, methodical progress and were lucky to ascend one or two routes during a season. Though siege tactics predominated, alpine-style proponents gradually gained influence, ushering in a different way to climb. Over the course of the twentieth century, foreign climbers from the United States and Europe dominated Patagonian alpinism.

During the 2000s, alpine-style proponents gained greater influence and promoted the values of light, fast, and self-contained ascents. The alpine-style logic emphasized the use of small teams (two or three people), carrying minimal gear, ascending in one continuous push from the bottom to the summit, and a greater dependence on team members. This strategy increased each team member's exposure to the technical difficulty of routes by decreasing the number of people who could be called upon in emergency situations. Alpine-style climbers rejected the use of fixed ropes as life lines, safety lines, or umbilical cords that aided retreat in the event of accidents or approaching storms. The alpine-style logic stressed greater technical confidence and training, thereby creating a seemingly more radical engagement with death in the mountains as compared to the more conservative siege logic.

In recent years, Patagonian mountaineers have increasingly wedded alpine style to free climbing, thereby creating a new free alpine standard. "Free climbing" refers to the use of only hands and feet to make upward progress.[8] The use of ropes is permitted for catching falling climbers, but not for aiding an ascent. Indeed, free alpine climbers have rejected using bolts as aids. In the past, climbers have used special stirrups (called *étriers*) as aid on a key section of Maestri's bolts on the Compressor Route. The free alpine ethic takes the view that the drilling and use of bolts makes a team complicit in environmental degradation, as well as lowering the technical skills of climbers.

In January 2012, Hayden Kennedy and Jason Kruk accomplished the first "fair means" free alpine ascent of the Compressor Route, using only five bolts (none of which were placed by Maestri). On the summit, the pair of North American climbers moved toward a more radical ethical stance, debating whether or not to cut the bolts off the Compressor Route:

> We talked about what was going to happen on the internet. We talked about what was going to happen with our sponsors. We talked about the reasons it should be done. We traced it back for us to the definition of alpine climbing: the sense of the unknown; that the summit isn't the end-all; it's about this experience; it's about having this partnership with your buddy, going on this wild adventure, not knowing what's going to happen. Maybe coming down, maybe summiting. And also not bringing the mountain down to your level.... [One,] mainly it was to restore Cerro Torre back to its natural state. Two, to make a statement that alpine

climbing should be done without the use of heavy machinery, without the use of fixed ropes, and that Cerro Torre is the most amazing, fantastic, unreal mountain in the world. . . . That mountain deserves more respect, and we felt that the bolts really disrespected that mountain. (Kalous 2012)

Kennedy and Kruk decided to "free" the Compressor Route in the more permanent sense of destroying the bolted route. As the pair rappelled down from the summit, they chopped close to 120 bolts off of the upper half of the route, provoking a major controversy as news quickly spread through El Chaltén and internet climbing forums.

The actions of Kennedy and Kruk had unintended local consequences. Upon returning to El Chaltén, they encountered a group of livid residents who declared them *personae non gratae*. While many residents viewed the route as an abomination, they also regarded it as part of the local patrimony. Protestors gathered outside the climbers' apartment, and the translator for the group remarked: "We feel like you have stolen the bolts from us. This route is part of our cultural heritage and you have taken them, and you have no right. We want the bolts" (quoted in Cordes 2014, 299–300). The police confiscated the bolts and took them briefly into custody. Days later Kennedy and Kruk left town, traveling back to the United States and Canada, respectively. In an interesting twist to the story, an Austrian climbing team, led by David Lama, climbed the Compressor Route shortly thereafter using no bolts at all, taking the laurels for the first completely free, alpine-style ascent from the North American team. As a sponsored athlete, Lama had climbed while being filmed by a production crew hired by the Austrian beverage company, Red Bull, which anticipated that the film would document a landmark mountaineering accomplishment.[9]

The Compressor Route controversy underscores the politics of style.[10] Beyond local concerns about destroying a part of their cultural heritage, Kennedy and Kruk faced vocal critiques from alpinists around the world. What made the Compressor Route's debasement so infuriating to many is that the pair's unilateral action made the route inaccessible to everyone except a tiny cohort of top climbers. Moreover, the implication seemed to be that the scores of alpinists who had previously climbed the Compressor Route had not actually climbed the real route, but rather an illegitimate one tainted by Maestri's bolts. The debates that followed in the print media and online climbing forums divided largely elite Patagonian alpinists—both foreign and local—who heralded the freeing of the Compressor Route as ethical progress from a sizable group of non-elite Patagonian climbers who condemned the pair. While Kennedy and Kruk viewed their actions as restoring ethical purity to Cerro Torre, other climbers (and local residents) regarded their decision as an elitist exercise in cultural imperialism (Manica 2012). No one argued that free alpine was not the ideal style in which to climb. However, many stood ready to reject the imposition by elites of this stylistic standard on others.

The 2012 Cerro Torre debate draws attention to the contested grounds of risk taking within mountaineering. From the 1990s to the present, alpinists have increasingly sought to raise ethical standards by embodying the values of being fast, light, self-contained, and (increasingly) "free." Embedded within this project is the attempt to refashion alpinist subjectivity and collective notions of what constitutes the proper degree of risk exposure to assume during a climb. Moreover, these debates are not easily divided across national lines that pit locals against foreigners. Though local climbers played a large role in condemning Kennedy and Kruk, a cadre of elite Argentine mountaineers joined with foreign elites to denounce Maestri's Compressor Route and celebrate its destruction. As indicated by the Cerro Torre debate, mountaineers establish the meaning of the alpine landscape through ethical debates about the relationship of sport to the environment.

STATUS GAMES

During their breakout season in 2008–2009, Jorge Ackermann and Tomy Aguiló ascended a number of classic routes, which included the famed West Face of Cerro Torre. As accomplished local climbers, Ackermann and Aguiló attempted to follow in the footsteps of their Italian-Argentine mentor and resident of El Chaltén, Rolando Garibotti. Garibotti had achieved global fame as a climber during the early 2000s, in part by moving to the United States to work as a mountain guide and gain access to the outdoor industry. In doing so, he developed a friendship with Yvon Chouinard, the founder of Patagonia, Inc. To achieve global fame and become professional climbers, Ackermann and Aguiló set their sights on completing the Fitz Roy Traverse: covering the entire Fitz Roy Range in one continuous climb along its seven peaks.

The status hierarchy within Patagonian mountaineering depends upon establishing first ascents of new routes with high degrees of technical difficulty. Mountaineers celebrate those climbers who perform resolve to confront death under the most radical situations, emphasizing technical difficulty and exposure to environmental dangers. The social hierarchy of Patagonian climbing includes novices, veterans, and elites and reflects ascending competencies to make "significant" first ascents. "Novices" are those climbers who take lesser individual risks insofar as they ascend peaks at the lowest level of difficulty. "Veterans" take mid-range risks by repeating classic routes on smaller and larger peaks. The members of these categories account for more than 90 percent of the climbing community. At the upper end of the spectrum are the "elites" who take the greatest risks by "trying to do something new and interesting," as one Argentine climber noted. Among elites, there are a handful of alpinists who have achieved global fame, possessing a "name" that "circulates" among climbers and people in the outdoor industry, to adapt a phrase from Nancy Munn (1992, 108). On the streets of El Chaltén, climbers display an almost obsequious respect for these super-elites, who are known around town by sight. Garibotti is the only super-elite among the locals, and he thus provided a key source of mentorship to up-and-coming Argentine mountaineers like Ackermann and Aguiló.

Super-elite status is the condition of possibility for becoming a professional alpinist. Euro-American outdoor companies grant sponsorships to the super-elites within global alpinism (and other adventure sports), providing funding in exchange for the use of photos, videos, stories, and other content for marketing campaigns, advertisements, and corporate branding (Logan 2011; Dumont 2015). Companies capitalize on the sporting profile and global fame of mountaineers known for their extreme first ascents. The industry, however, awards the vast majority of sponsorships to European or American climbers who can appeal to national markets, drawing attention to the differential opportunities enjoyed by core Euro-American practitioners and the slim chances that peripheral Argentine athletes have to become professionals. This is the corporate nationalism that shapes global mountaineering. Garibotti's example is instructive since he had to leave Argentina and move to the United States to cultivate a super-elite status attractive to Patagonia, Inc. For alpinists, sponsorship creates an exchange logic rife with opportunity and threat. Framed positively, this exchange enables super-elites to climb full time rather than working at regular jobs to save money to go on occasional expeditions. Moreover, the sponsorship offers a point of entry into the outdoor industry, providing—for some—future job opportunities when they retire from climbing. Represented negatively, this exchange signifies a form of financial dependency and the commodification of reputation. This reduces alpinism to a mode of corporate laboring, a position that climbers reject by framing their actions as spiritual. Indeed, alpinists discussed the sense of camaraderie that develops between climbers who rope up together, the kinetic pleasures felt in dangerous environments, and the sublime experiences in the mountains that frame the sport as a spiritual endeavor (Ortner 1999; Le Breton 2000).

The outdoor industry has facilitated the alpine-style embracing of enhanced technical risk taking and team exposure. Garibotti remarked to me:

> One of the downsides, from my perspective, and the reason I have always tried to escape it [sponsorship] is because most people want to know ahead of time what you're going to do and they want freaking updates while you're on the trip and I think that's a recipe for disaster, on two counts. Number one, you might be risking too much because you feel the pressure of having to succeed. Or [number]

two, another thing that could happen is that if you don't succeed it feels like much more of a defeat. . . . I don't know, but the point is: if you're doing a dangerous activity, any extra pressures you have is probably a bad fucking idea, you know?

Garibotti speaks to the political economy of risk taking implicit in the sponsorship world (Johnston and Edwards 1994). The growth of the Euro-American outdoor industry has put a premium on sponsoring athletes at the cutting edge of their respective sports. This creates the expectation that super-elites will continue to ratchet up the risk taking to maintain their competitive position with respect to up-and-coming elites. This emphasis on risk taking filters down to veterans and novices who follow the lead of elites, intersecting with the alpine-style dictum emphasizing the need for more radical engagements with death. Mountaineering, then, entails a mode of risk subjectivity synchronized to a corporate world that promotes an aggressive cycle of one-upping and profits from a continuously replenished pool of climbers who risk death. Given the dangers of mountaineering, Garibotti likens the extra pressures applied to practitioners as a "recipe for disaster." As the industry has embraced alpine style, Patagonian mountaineers have had to follow this practice to maintain the global competitive position of the Patagonian Andes.

Patagonian climbers have adopted the stylistic tactics by which super-elites are made, even if the chance of becoming a professional is very small. During the 2009–2010 season, Ackermann and Aguiló returned to El Chaltén to expand upon their previous success. They had achieved national fame as part of the "new generation of Argentine climbers" in the climbing magazine, *Vertical Argentina* (Aguiló 2009, 46–49). Attempting to become super-elites and follow the trail blazed by their mentor, the pair had tremendous success but were never able to complete the Fitz Roy Traverse. Ultimately, an American super-elite duo, Alex Honnold and Tommy Caldwell, made its first ascent in 2014. While there are dozens of super-elites across the world, there is a much larger pool of elites—like Ackermann and Aguiló—who labor near the cutting edge of the discipline, seeking global fame though radical engagements with death. Ackermann and Aguiló struggled against the north-south inequalities defining the sponsorship market, placing Argentine climbers at a disadvantage compared to rising U.S., French, or German stars who can appeal to national markets. By engaging in status games, then, mountaineers have injected social hierarchies of adventure into the project of alpine exploration.

CONFRONTING DEATH ON THE MOUNTAIN

Anticipating the opening of a window of good weather, mountaineers prepare their gear, recheck the forecast, and hike into the national park. They cross the rivers that mark entry into the Andean zone, clipping their harnesses onto cables, hanging supine, and pulling themselves across the *tirolesas* (Tyrolean traverses, or specialized cables spanning rivers or chasms) to the other side. Teams then hike off trail to the base of their intended routes, establishing an advanced camp and preparing for the looming physical test of their competencies in an environment—once climbers enter vertical terrain—in which every move has the potential to preserve or kill the climber (Abramson and Fletcher 2007, 6). In the mountains, alpine-style climbers perform their radical resolve to confront death by embodying the values of being light, fast, and self-contained. However, teams face fear, injuries, and fatalities, underscoring the chance that performances of resolve may fail.

In addition to Ackermann and Aguiló, there was another alpine-style team that had a breakout season in 2008–2009. After an initial climb on Aguja Mermoz, Bjørn Årtun (of Norway) and Cullen Kirk (of the United States) turned their sights on Cerro Torre's West Face—a more than 600-meter-long route consisting of near-vertical to overhanging walls of ice. The pair left their advanced camp in the dead of night, wearing crampons, carrying ice axes, and packing minimal gear to facilitate their speed. They headed for the West Face where they ran a gauntlet of difficulties (see Figure 1.2). They "free soloed" the easiest sections of 70-degree ice ramps at the beginning, which means they climbed without being roped together or using any protective devices like ice screws. This tactic saved time, but a fall might have led to injury or death. Then they "simul-climbed" (simultaneously climbed) the moderate 80-degree sections roped together, with Årtun taking the lead and placing ice screws every few meters. Like free soloing, simul-climbing saves time—but at the expense of security. On the very difficult 90–95-degree stretches, one person climbed at a time while the other person "belayed," passing the rope through a friction-generating device to stop a fall. After fifteen hours of arduous climbing, they reached the summit of Cerro Torre. Unbeknown to them at the time, they had created a new speed record, climbing the West Face faster than anyone else ever had. In addition to establishing their reputations as rising stars, Kirk and Årtun embodied the values of being self-contained by rejecting the use of large teams and fixed ropes, minimizing the amount of gear brought on the trip, and ascending as fast as possible to the summit. Embodying the values of alpine style, they performed radical resolve to confront death by climbing not just "on belay," but also free soloing and simul-climbing, thereby ratcheting up team and individual risk.

Alpinists like Årtun and Kirk perform resolve by drawing upon embodied sporting competencies. Climbers make ongoing decisions about tactics—where to free solo, simul-climb, or climb on belay—and the bodily movements necessary to overcome specific spatial problems. These concrete movements reflect forms

FIGURE 1.2. Cerro Torre, West Face (© Rolando Garibotti)

of judgment integrated into the expert body's sense of how to deal with rock, snow, and ice conditions.[11] At the same time, alpinists attempt to assert control over the environment, organizing the route in terms of identifiable subjective and objective risks that materialize as a team makes progress. "Objective risks" refer to environmental hazards or difficulties such as razor-thin cracks, hanging glaciers, avalanche zones, and brittle rock. "Subjective risks" correspond to the potential dangers associated with the climber, such as becoming paralyzed with fear, misjudging the intensity of an incoming storm, or succumbing to fatigue. As they ascend, mountaineers chart the line of least resistance that enables them to minimize objective risks while evaluating any subjective risks beginning to manifest themselves. During an interview, Kirk described in minute detail the step-by-step pathway he and Årtun followed up the West Face and the concrete objective risks they encountered. Kirk recognized a domain of radical uncertainty that outstripped their mastery. The pair remained hypervigilant about the unanticipated rockfall, avalanche, or equipment failure, but they also understood that they could not eliminate the many incalculable chances they faced.[12]

Climbers confront the ambiguous threshold between living and dying to prove their resolve. There are, however, many ascents in which resolve is inadequately performed, resulting in injury or death. At the same time that Kennedy and Kruk were freeing the Compressor Route, a Canadian climber, Carlyle Norman, was struggling for survival on Aguja Saint-Exupéry. A freak rockfall had struck her, prompting her partner to climb down for help. She held out for a couple days, as park rangers in El Chaltén organized a high mountain rescue that enlisted the helicopter being used for Lama's ascent of Cerro Torre. The helicopter dropped a team at the base of the mountain. The team members climbed into a tempest but were forced to retreat as conditions grew increasingly dangerous (Lavigne and Wood 2012). During the storm, Norman fell off the mountain. Kennedy reflected on the impact of this death: "It [their reaching the summit] wasn't at all important anymore, because of her death. Didn't matter what we did. And that's the thing that comes back to me all the time. It's not worth dying in the mountains. It's not worth seeing friends die in the mountains. That's the risk we take. . . . We were thinking about why we do alpine climbing. Is it worth it? All the risks we take?" (Kalous 2012). While climbers risk death, ultimately, he decided, "it's not worth dying in the mountains." Yet like so many others, Kennedy continued to climb. His words echoed a maxim from Gregory Crouch's mountaineering classic, *Enduring Patagonia*: "Mountains aren't worth dying for, but they are worth risking dying for" (2002, 53). This maxim speaks to the double meaning of "death" in the sport. Death is not just the negative condition of biological demise. There is also the positive sense of risking death as a way to create a community of practitioners organized around a shared sense of value and fellowship. Though alpinists grieve at the passing of their companions, they remain committed to risking death as a way to ennoble life. Rather than measuring life in terms of its temporal duration, climbers judge existence in terms of its vitality. Risking death helps forge a social identity and represents a critique of nonclimbers' failing to live life with the same zeal. In Friedrich Nietzsche's words, there is "the feeling of fullness, of power that seeks to overflow, the happiness of high tension" (1966, 205). By risking death, climbers create an authenticating world of resolve that literally and figuratively elevates them above a quotidian existence. In short, mountaineering configures the alpine landscape as a space of authenticity and exception from the conditions of everyday life.

Kirk and Årtun's speed record highlights key features of mountaineering risk subjectivity at the interface with the outdoor industry: the emphasis on speed, lightness, and minimalist tactics; the intersection of their record-breaking effort and status games played to elevate social standing; and the proximity of risking death to biological demise. Their ascent also underscores the socioeconomic inequalities that operate across the local-foreign climbing divide. Global mountaineering is predicated on a north-south asymmetry in the circulatory flow of athletes. Euro-American climbers draw upon savings from jobs back home to finance trips abroad. By contrast, mountain guides like Ackermann and Aguiló who work in El Chaltén do not have the discretionary income to organize ascents abroad in North America, Asia, or Europe, reflecting differences in currency values, purchasing power, and standards of living. Local climbers have the economic means to explore Argentina and surrounding South American nations, but foreign mountaineers have the economic capital to establish partnerships to travel to remote ranges around the world. This divide fundamentally constrains the chances of aspiring Argentine elite climbers. As a result of their speedy ascent, Kirk won a scholarship from the American Alpine Club to return to Patagonia the following year to climb. Årtun established partnerships with super-elite climbers and quickly became one of Norway's alpine stars, traveling throughout Europe, Patagonia, and Alaska. However, his rise to fame within global alpinism came to a tragic conclusion in February 2012. Attempting a new ice route in Norway, he and his climbing partner died in an accident, the cause of which is unknown.

THE THEATER OF ALPINE ADVENTURE

During the twentieth century, global alpinism represented the Chaltén Massif as a landscape for alpine adventure, with its own pantheon of climbing heroes, tall tales, and iconic peaks. With the rise of trekking, mountaineering has receded as the primary leisure pursuit in the area, but the sport has left its cultural imprint on popular conceptions of nature. Alpinists represent only a small fraction of the tourist population and have a very modest impact on consumption receipts. Given the high degrees of technical difficulty associated with the Chaltén Massif, there has been little effort on the part of local business to create the type of mountaineering tourism that exists on Aconcagua and Everest (Ortner 1999; Logan 2011). Instead, mountaineering has primarily served as a cultural resource for entrepreneurs to promote tourist consumption among trekkers. Tourism entrepreneurs have used the high-risk performances of climbers as a key way to narrate and imagine wilderness adventure. Trekking and mountaineering coexist within a shared theater of alpine adventure, operating in horizontal and vertical environments, respectively.

Public officials and entrepreneurs have identified El Chaltén as the official trekking capital of Argentina. Though they foreground trekking as what El Chaltén is all about, entrepreneurs enlist mountaineering to help market their tours. Businesses have incorporated mountaineering imagery into the signs and placards that hang outside their stores, the photographs that adorn interior walls alongside pictures of mountains and glaciers, and the online advertising campaigns used to market tour options such as day hikes and ice-trekking excursions onto glaciers. There is a productive cultural equivocation at work, in which entrepreneurs invite trekkers to imagine themselves as mountaineers traipsing through the park and traversing glaciers with technical gear such as crampons and ice axes. The brand image of El Chaltén as a trekking capital becomes more symbolically resonant because of its association with high-risk alpinism. Although its practitioners never intended this, alpinism is crucial to tourism commodification and the branding logics of El Chaltén.

Patagonia, the company, has played a major role in identifying Patagonia, the Latin American region, with outdoor adventure. Indeed, the story of this corporation's origin relates to the local history of the El Chaltén zone. Doug Tompkins (cofounder of The North Face) and Chouinard (future founder of Patagonia, Inc.) traveled to the Chaltén Massif in 1968, where they (together with other climbers and a filmmaker) made the first ascent of the southwest buttress on Monte Fitz Roy, which they christened the "California Route" (Chouinard et al. 2013). After returning from Patagonia, Chouinard founded Patagonia, Inc., and appropriated the silhouette of the Fitz Roy Range—with Monte Fitz Roy in the middle—as its corporate logo. The image of the Fitz Roy Range appears on coats, jackets, T-shirts, and other material objects bearing the Patagonia, Inc., logo, above which is written "patagonia." As its brand-name commodities circulate through this Latin American region via the global tourism industry, the corporation achieves a kind of semiotic closure by creating a representational loop that feeds back upon itself, in which hardcore adventurers wear and use Patagonia commodities in the field. Moreover, the corporate sponsorships that Patagonia, Inc., grants a select group of super-elite alpinists, who climb in the Andes and other ranges, provide a steady stream of climbing content (photos, online videos, and narratives) that reinforce this representational loop.[13] Like local entrepreneurs, the Euro-American outdoor industry appropriates alpinist imagery as a cultural resource to give their commodities the patina of serious commitment to adventure. The outdoor industry works together with the global tourism industry to facilitate adventure travel to distant sites like Patagonia that have become archetypes of wilderness adventure in the global public sphere (Mendoza et al. 2017).

Beyond brand imaging, Chaltenenses (residents of El Chaltén) embrace mountaineering as a key part of their public culture. Alpinist imagery floods the signs that trekkers see as they walk down the streets of El Chaltén. Climbing photos and paraphernalia adorn cafés, restaurants, and hostels, and the visitors' center at the ranger station has an entire exhibit devoted to mountaineering history. Throughout the season, the park service and commercial venues frequently play documentary films about Patagonian alpinism to entertain crowds of tourists and educate them about El Chaltén's history. Moreover, first ascenders have the right to christen routes. The toponymy of mountains and routes reflect the history of Patagonian exploration during the nineteenth and twentieth centuries, including the names of explorers (Robert FitzRoy, Antoine de Saint-Exupéry, and Ernst Standhardt) and climbers who perished in the zone (Jacques Poincenot, Toni Egger, and Rafael Juárez). Mountaineers are dramatis personae: the actors who make the Chaltén Massif a world stage. Indeed, mountaineers make history every season in El Chaltén with new ascents. While it is certainly a very niche kind of world history making, mountaineering elevates this remote pueblo to the forefront of the status games being played around the planet in sites like the Himalayas, the Alps, and Alaska. El Chaltén may be the only place in Argentina where climbing is more popular than soccer as an everyday leisure activity. In short, alpinism is a key element in how Chaltenenses configure the global identity of El Chaltén.

RESOLVE AND DEATH IN THE ANDES

Mountaineering risk subjectivity arises through the attempts by climbers like Årtun, Kirk, Ackermann, and Aguiló to perform resolve in the face of death through ascents that are meaningful to the local sporting community, global mountaineering, and the Euro-American outdoor industry. The growth of mountaineering in tandem with that of the wider ecotourism industry has brought increasing numbers of foreign and local climbers to the zone. A few local climbers have gained elite status and challenged the Euro-American monopoly on symbolic honors deriving from first ascents. Nevertheless, the corporate nationalism of the Euro-American outdoor industry has continued to privilege the Euro-American risk-taking subject through the unequal granting of sponsorship funding. Mountaineering operates alongside trekking tourism within Chaltén's alpine landscape. Through ongoing performances of resolve to confront death, alpinists have helped transform the Andean backcountry and the PNLG into a theater of alpine adventure defined by high-risk activities.

Mountaineering thematizes risk around the adventuring body in nature. Historically, mountaineering has helped configure the sporting value of the Patagonian Andes in ways that reinforce the landscape ideology of alpine wilderness and the political vision of promoting protected area tourism. Mountaineers are the vanguard tourist group in El Chaltén and have established key registers of meaning that collectively constitute the alpine landscape: registers that include ethical debates over the environment, the search for symbolic value in nature that fosters social distinction, and the embrace of risk taking as a way to transcend everyday life and recover an authentic relationship to the world. These mountaineering meanings incorporate Patagonia into the global consumer economy of alpine adventure. Trekkers will modify this set of landscape meanings for their own ends, in concert with the staging practices of the tourism industry and conservation state.

Kirchnerist green productivism has built on the historical basis of alpine landscape meanings that exist within the Patagonian Andes, seeking to accelerate the growth of the ecotourism industry. In El Chaltén, green productivism has facilitated the rapid expansion of mountaineering and the high-risk imagery the sport produces. This has created two separate streams of commodity images. The local tourism industry has employed this imagery to commodify the PNLG as an iconic space for wilderness adventure. And the Euro-American outdoor industry has taken up the high-risk imagery produced by its super-elites in the Chaltén Massif and used it in fashioning a global consumer economy of alpine adventure in which Patagonia is considered an elite destination. These two streams of high-risk imagery help direct the tourist gaze toward Patagonia as a promising, exotic site for the fashioning of adventure subjectivities.

2 · ADVENTURE TREKKING
Pursuing the Alpine Sublime

Tourists crowded the microbrewery in late November 2007. The global financial crisis had not yet come to a head, and the Patagonian green economy was still booming under President Néstor Kirchner. Workers in the U.S. financial industry, Josh Fawkes and Evan Marchmain fit the Patagonian tourist profile as white, affluent professionals. Political conservatives, they reacted harshly to what they perceived as widespread "anti-American sentiment" linked to the Iraq War. They dismissed most travelers as liberal environmentalists. "It's a fucking joke," Josh remarked about the "crunchy Patagonia tree-hugger scene":

> Everyone, all these Europeans, are so anticapitalist, and yet it's precisely because of high earning potentials in their home countries—precisely because of capitalism—that they can afford to be here. I mean this [beer] is expensive. These parks charge American prices. Christ, $15 for a meal, $20 for a bottle of wine, $30 dollars to wash my clothes. . . . Don't get me wrong, these parks are stunningly beautiful. [But they] are perfectly designed to generate revenue. I mean driving right up to the Moreno Glacier in a bus! Now that's a national park I can stand by! That you gotta love! And all these Europeans pretending they're in the wilderness, pretending they're communing with nature.

Ordering more beer, Josh and Evan continued to fume about their experiences along the southern Patagonian ecotourism circuit that includes Ushuaia as the "End of the World," Puerto Natales as the "Trekking Capital of Chile," El Calafate as the "Glacier Capital of Argentina," and El Chaltén as the "Trekking Capital of Argentina" (Mendoza et al. 2017, 101). Defined by complementary place brands, this circuit organized and represented tourism as taking place within an alpine landscape focused on outdoor adventure activities like trekking, climbing, kayaking, and boating.

Their narrative raises a number of key points about Patagonian ecotourism. First, Evan and Josh recognize that many tourists are eco-friendly and affluent, able to visit the region because they have professional jobs at home. Indeed, adventure-seeking tourists are predominantly from the upper middle class, traveling to Patagonia primarily from countries in Latin America, Europe, and North America (Fletcher 2014). This globe-trotting bourgeoisie has the resources to fund travel to Patagonia to gain access to its symbolic capital: the one-of-a-kind experiences of forests, trails, lakes, glaciers, and mountains that have symbolic value and reinforce social divisions along class, gender, racial, and national lines. Upper-middle-class tourists gain the social distinction (Bourdieu 2002) that derives from experiencing these places, gathering images, videos, and stories that enable them to construct self-narratives tied to an adventure-seeking lifestyle. In the process, affluent travelers distinguish themselves from lower-middle-, working-, and lower-class populations in their home countries. Second, Josh and Evan identify the Patagonian green economy as capitalistic. Parks are "perfectly designed to generate revenue" for the national park service, which charges user fees, and for tour companies, which sell bus rides, boating trips, and glacier tours. By virtue of controlling access to parkland, the conservation state and entrepreneurial capital exercise a monopolistic hold over access to the symbolic capital of place. Third, the pair sees "communing with nature" as a touristic ideal, while disparaging the notion that visitors are actually "in the wilderness." Their critique reflects the idea that wilderness exists as a space of nature set apart from society and the economy (Cronon 1996; Neumann 1998; Nash 2001). What the two fail to grasp is that "wilderness" and "capitalism" have long coexisted in Argentina through park-centered tourism (Pastoriza 2011). Despite their critique, the two men did regard the parks as "stunningly beautiful." Implicit in this aesthetic judgment is the category of the alpine landscape, which positions the Patagonian Andes within a global category of alpine wilderness that includes the Rockies, the Alps, and the Himalayas. The symbolic capital of Andean Patagonia emerges in concert with this global class of aesthetically complementary landscapes and preparatory work by mountaineers during the twentieth century to produce an alpine landscape associated with the pursuit of social distinction and status, ethical debates about nature, and risk-taking practices that create authentic relations to the world beyond everyday life.

Evan and Josh eventually retired for the evening. The microbrewery hummed with conversations in a variety of languages, as tourists planned their forays into Parque Nacional Los Glaciares (PNLG). Was the weather forecast correct? Would there be sun or rain? Would Monte Fitz Roy be visible? By ten o'clock, most tourists had returned to their hostels, hotels, or bed-and-breakfasts, anticipating the adventures to come. And as the tourists left, the young seasonal workers began to arrive. The expensive microbrews became less common among the crowd, replaced by cheaper domestic beer varieties such as Quilmes and Schneider.

THE TREKKING CAPITAL OF ARGENTINA

El Chaltén is the trekking capital of Argentina. There are various sites throughout the nation—such as Bariloche, Salta, and Mendoza—with significant trail systems for day hiking or extended backpacking trips. However, El Chaltén has official claim to this title, announced in a large sign at the entrance to town (see Figure 2.1). Created by park rangers and residents, this sign is the materialization of the ongoing work by Chaltenenses to create a place brand that is globally renowned. Whereas mountaineering involves some 200–400 visitors annually the adventure trekking market draws over 65,000 tourists every year. This place image emerged within a landscape once primarily based on livestock farming. The creation of the PNLG in 1937 sought to reorder capitalist production in the Patagonian borderlands. The National Parks Administration of Argentina (Administración de Parques Nacionales, or APN) tried to convert the supposed Andean desert into a desirable wilderness for tourists. Rejected by the *estancieros* (ranch or farm owners) and the paisanos living in the El Chaltén zone, the alpine landscape ideal remained dormant—apart from mountaineering—until the 1990s, when it began to flourish with the growth of youth backpacking. Under Governor Kirchner, El Chaltén took definitive steps towards pushing livestock farming aside in favor of ecotourism. In the national park, this involved the phasing out of its social uses as pasture. Rangers attempted to reduce visible signs of human impact and create the image of a pristine wilderness.

Trekkers provide the second point of entry into the Patagonian risk society and the sphere of tourism consumption in the green economy. Trekking subjectivity is meaningfully organized around the alpine sublime. Unlike mountaineers, trekking subjects do not engage in high-risk activities based on existential peril. Instead, trekkers pursue more modest adventures deriving from day hiking and backpacking within the frontcountry trail system that includes forested valleys and hills but stops at the edge of the glaciated backcountry that the APN has defined as off-limits for everyone except mountaineers. Trekkers enter the frontcountry either autonomously (often in small groups of 2–5 people) or under the direction of hired guides. To access the backcountry, trekkers pay for commercial tours with registered trekking or mountain guides. Adventure trekkers pursue the alpine sublime inside the park. The "sublime" refers to aesthetic experiences of the overpowering force or scale of nature. A tempest gathering over the ocean and a towering ice-covered mountain are phenomena that can inspire experiences of imagined peril. Rather than physical danger, the sublime refers to a state of imagined vulnerability and pleasurable "terror" (Burke 1990, 36) in the face of

FIGURE 2.1. El Chaltén (photo by author)

nature. Trekkers pursue sublime experiences that derive from contemplating the might and magnitude of alpine environments defined by physical forms such as mountains, glaciers, and lakes, as well as dynamics such as avalanches, rockfalls, and the calving of glaciers to create icebergs.

Adventure trekking is one component of a regional ecotourism market fashioned around place brands. In the case of El Chaltén, the place brand of the national trekking capital remains an abstract signifier until the concrete practices of tourists create particular routes, destinations, and ways of perceiving, imagining, and narrating nature. The brand, then, depends upon the concrete tourism practices that flesh out the abstract image of trekking. Some travelers have pushed the tourism industry to expand its offerings to new destinations inside the PNLG, such as remote vistas off the primary trail system or guided excursions up nontechnical mountains that do not require ropes, harnesses, or other rock-climbing tools. With enough money and time, an enterprising tourist can hire a guide to visit any part of the PNLG, including the Southern Patagonian Ice Field. Nevertheless, the vast majority of trekkers stick to the routes and practices established by previous travelers and the tourism industry. The scope of trekker agency, then, typically involves selecting between a predetermined set of consumer options. To this end, El Chaltén is an alpine landscape staged and improved upon for the tourist gaze (Urry 2008) by the commercial guiding sector and the conservation state to enhance its commodity value.[1] Visitors typically travel throughout the Patagonian region for one or two weeks with the intention of visiting two or three of the main destinations, and they rarely stop in El Chaltén for longer than three days. Travelers circulate quickly and efficiently through the zone, seeking to reach as many destinations as possible in this short timeframe.[2] After I discuss the national politics of ecotourism, I examine the risk subjectivity of adventure trekkers as they experience a sense of being with nature on front-country trails, communicate feelings of the sublime at scenic viewpoints, take commercial tours onto glaciers, and situate El Chaltén within the global consumer economy of alpine nature.

THE NATIONAL POLITICS OF ECOTOURISM

Following the national crisis of 2001–2002, Presidents Néstor Kirchner and Cristina Fernández de Kirchner developed a neo-developmentalist approach to national recovery and growth premised on maintaining a depreciated peso that made natural resources attractive to foreign markets (Féliz 2012; Wylde 2012). Resource exploitation involved the agro-extractive sector and the ecotourism industry. The green productivist goal was to stimulate and accelerate the growth of the national green economy in comparison to the 1990s under the neoliberal-friendly President Carlos Menem. Menem had tackled the serious problem of hyperinflation by establishing a one-to-one currency peg that tied the Argentine peso to the U.S. dollar. Though effective in curbing hyperinflation, this policy radically diminished the competitive standing of Argentina's ecotourism industry. Beyond working to foster macroeconomic conditions that made ecotourism more globally competitive, the Kirchners moved the APN under the bureaucratic oversight of the Secretary of Tourism, which was part of the Ministry of Production, signaling the drive to foster greater capital accumulation, job growth, and state revenue capture.

From 2003 to 2014, the green productivist strategy increased national park tourism from approximately 1.8 to 3.5 million visitors annually (Ministerio de Turismo de Argentina 2014, 153). In 2014, Iguazú attracted 1,188,563 visitors (56 percent of whom were domestic and 44 percent foreign), with the PNLG coming in second at 666,340 (54 percent domestic and 46 percent foreign)—though when all of the Andean Patagonian parks are taken into account, this number jumped to 1,802,188 visitors (155). The protourism policies of the Kirchner and Fernández governments facilitated the near doubling of traffic to the parks. At the local level of the PNLG, this strategy proved effective as well. During the season from October 2002 to March 2003, El Chaltén hosted some 20,000 visitors, while El Calafate in the heavily commercialized southern zone of the park received 156,000. During the season from October 2013 to March 2014, El Chaltén received over 56,000 visitors, while El Calafate garnered more than 420,000—reflecting increases of 280 percent and 269 percent, respectively, over this eleven-year period (Administración de Parques Nacionales 2014). The agenda was tremendously successful in promoting ecotourism-led growth.

The Kirchner governments have created a tourism policy focused on national, regional, and place branding that frames resource exploitation around a rentier logic. The Kirchners have invested in building institutional capacity within the federal government and the domestic tourism industry to promote the market, as well as rolling out a "country brand" strategy to "revive the tourism sector and homogenize the national image in international markets" (Echeverri Cañas and Estay-Niculcar 2013, 191).[3] As scholars have noted, the Argentine resource economy depends primarily upon agricultural commodities with low and medium value-added inputs—such as soybeans and soy-based derivatives—that compete with commensurate products from other countries (Ebenau and Liberatore 2013). Pursuing a nation-branding strategy, the Kirchnerist governments have turned toward a rentier approach based on cultivating and commodifying the symbolic monopoly capital that exists within popular destinations, such as national parks. Green productivism has worked to develop the national patrimony of inalienable nature.

Green productivism depends on a politics of visibility. The agro-export sector churns out undifferentiated commodities sold in mass markets. The politics that drive the production of soy, gold, and other goods often remain invisible to consumers. By contrast, the green economy provides a highly visible platform on which to perform the meaning of post-neoliberal politics. Engaging upper-middle-class domestic and foreign tourists, the conservation state—through the actions of park administrators and rangers—enacts concrete forms of environmental governance that work to create ecotourists and sustainable development. Rather than the violence, land grabbing, environmental destruction, and market value associated with mining and soy production, the green economy highlights the classed politics of the post-neoliberal state premised on environmental education and an aesthetic appreciation of the alpine landscape. The success of green productivism has resulted in the uneven representation of national nature. Unlike mass tourism in Buenos Aires and Atlantic beach destinations, alternative ecotravel to Patagonia is far less accessible to members of the working and lower-middle classes. Indeed, ecotourism works to reinforce the separation between social elites, who have access to the aesthetic experiences through which the nation is imagined, and people who are marginalized.

TREKKING ON FRONTCOUNTRY TRAILS

Katrina Lange and Rick Davis head for the Loma del Pliegue Tumbado (see Figure 2.2). Katrina is a recent university graduate from Munich, Germany. Rick is a teacher from Minneapolis, in the United States. Both are on their first trip to Patagonia, and they are visiting El Chaltén as one stop on a wider tour of Argentina. An infrequently visited destination, the Loma is one of the few sites that provides an excellent panoramic view of both the Fitz Roy and the Torre Ranges.

FIGURE 2.2. Trekkers en route to the Loma del Pliegue Tumbado (photo by author)

With light daypacks, the three of us climb through an alpine meadow above Lake Viedma, which looks azure on this sunny day, talking at first and then settling into the rhythms of our mobile bodies. We begin a gradual ascent through the southern beech forest to a denuded highland. The winds bear down on us, kicking up dust and making our eyes water. After it reaches the base of the Loma, the trail climbs into a steep set of switchbacks that deliver us to the top of the hill, where we find a windbreak. The winds pummel us, while the temperature is pleasantly chilly. We take cover, sitting on the ground to eat our lunch, and then spend the next half-hour gazing upon the vast landscape that spreads out beneath us. We study the forested valleys, the traces of vanished glaciers contained in moraine fields, and Grande Glacier, a white-blue tongue of ice beginning at Laguna Torre and extending back into the Torre Range. Katrina and Rick speak very little on the summit, absorbing the sensuous spectacle and taking short videos and photographs. They marvel at the beauty they behold, though rarely uttering more than staccato phrases of joyful exclamation: "Oh!" "Unbelievable!" "Unreal!" Eventually, we start back down the ridgeline and arrive in El Chaltén around midafternoon, passing another dozen tourists. In all, the roughly eighteen-kilometer trip has lasted around six hours, a very common distance for a day hike. Later in the afternoon, we talk about the significance of the Loma hike, their expectations of El Chaltén, and the salience of the mobile body to trekking.

Tourists enter the PNLG with specific understandings of its significant attractions. Internet searches and guidebooks provide the initial delimitations of El Chaltén's place value as globally significant, producing a list of must-see experiences. At the station, rangers give informal talks of 20–30 minutes to tourists, which communicate key information about the trail system and the *no deje rastro* (leave no trace) rules of park conduct. In the process, rangers begin to incorporate visitors into the framework of ecotourism. Rangers confirm the sites of touristic distinction promoted by the guidebooks and impart logistical information. With only a few days allocated to El Chaltén, trekkers focus on two popular destinations: the Fitz Roy Valley trail to Laguna de los Tres and the Torre Valley trail to Laguna Torre. These are the key zones used to build the dramatic plotlines of alpine adventure for tourists.

Trekkers often rank their accomplishments according to the levels of difficulty they overcome to reach destinations. Katrina noted: "This is such a huge area, and you have two main trails. And then you have five to seven hidden trails that are literally hidden." Rick added: "It kind of keeps the trails secret for those who stay here a long time and make connections. . . . [That's] the adventure element that people come down to Patagonia for—because no one is going to be holding my hand. . . . [Sadly, most] people are here to find the views they've seen on postcards. To re-create the pictures they saw in *National Geographic*, or whatever." Rick and Katrina express the dominant opinion of Patagonia as a wilderness where one must heroically rise to the challenges encountered. The Loma trek provides an off-the-beaten-path experience to signal a deeper commitment to adventure than that of inexpert tourists who want only to replicate "postcard" images. For some, the appeal of having an anthropologist tag along to conduct research is the knowledge I possessed of these ostensibly "secret" destinations beyond the madding crowds.

Trekking is a kinesthetic form, or cultivated sense of movement (Merleau-Ponty 1981).[4] At its most basic, trekking is just a form of walking. But when walking is paired with an environment identified as alpine wilderness, tourists invest their movement with unique qualities. Leaving El Chaltén, trekkers ascend the trails that take them over foothills and drop them into alpine valleys. Beginning the physical work of the trek, tourists become attuned to their heart rate, breathing patterns, body temperature, muscular action, and a wide range of other sensations. These sensations are indexical signs used to adjust the body to changing terrain, weather, and elevation. Trekkers modulate their speed, gait, clothing, and rest in response. As they move through nature, trekkers often refer to an awakening of their senses. Entering a state of sensory activation, trekkers identified a phenomenological integration between body and world, but they had a very difficult time describing it precisely during interviews. I refer to this feeling as the sense of being with nature. To feel a sense of being with nature is to treat trekking not simply as a type of walking, but as a cultivated form of movement shot through with grander cultural meanings.

Trekkers draw upon different cultural frames to define this sensuous relationship between body and world found in being with nature. Katrina remarked:

"It's a meditative process. Your mind is free to do whatever it wants when you are hiking. That's all meditation is. It's just repetitive physical actions that you don't need to have your mind on, so that your mind can do whatever it wants. . . . It's funny. It's not like you get into some philosophical interview with yourself. You have one thought here and another thought there. . . . I'm really just thinking about nothing. I'm in a no-mind state." For Katrina, the embodied practice of trekking is one associated with an absence of the mind. Trekkers achieve a meditative "no-mind state" as they settle into the peripatetic rhythms of the body. Recovering a freedom of the imagination, Katrina defines this as cognitive play—"your mind can do whatever it wants." Others talked about recovering an authentic self.[5] As one Chilean trekker noted: "You become yourself again. . . . Here you find your true self." Indeed, most tourists represented the trek as a walk that involved some element of spiritual recovery, self-discovery, or self-transcendence. The authentic self and meditation are two cultural frames available to trekkers to describe the embodied sense of being with nature that they achieve while walking. Rather than simply appreciating the natural beauty that one might find in an urban park or private garden, the Patagonian wilderness calls forth a distinct type of reaction that is more radical in scope: the interrogation of the self and the dislodging of everyday forms of being in the world. At the so-called end of the world for Argentine and foreign tourists, who often live in global cities like Buenos Aires and Berlin, the Patagonian wilderness provides an adventurous ecotouristic escape from society and an opportunity to establish a spiritual connection with an environment that everybody agrees represented genuine nature. Unlike the derivative forms one finds in cities and agricultural zones, Andean Patagonia represents an ur-nature or universal standard against which to measure paler examples of the type. The capacity to be with ur-nature, however, entails a politics of class consumption that excludes all but the members of the upper-middle and upper classes living in Argentina and elsewhere.

Trekkers adorn their bodies in specific ways to enhance the feeling of being with nature. Indeed, trekking clothing and equipment reflect upper-middle-class tastes. The outdoor industry continues to create cutting-edge materials and fabrics that are expensive and inaccessible to most consumers. Advertising campaigns publicize the role of sponsored athletes in testing this gear. Trekkers equip their bodies with these signs of expertise, appropriate to challenging environments. This is part of the fantasy work of trekking: using technical gear to dramatize an encounter between adventurer and wilderness that—as it turns out—may not be quite as difficult as expected. Indeed, Katrina and Rick wore specialized boots, pants, jackets, and packs from outdoor companies like Arc'teryx, Mammut, and Jack Wolfskin. These products have a particular feel to them. The outdoor industry constantly seeks to engineer the lightest, thinnest fabrics consistent with insulating the body from the environment, thereby creating comfort with performance. Here corporate design intersects with trekking as a cultivated sense of movement. The outdoor industry has sought to elimi-nate heavy fabrics that dull the sensations of the body, allowing consumers to experience nature in its plenitude: to feel the winds ripple across one's torso while remaining warm, and the rain pelting one's shoulders and arms while remaining dry. Trekkers communicate class taste by wearing expensive gear that signals a commitment to technical expertise, as well as facilitating a sensuous tactility when moving through nature.

Trekkers sometimes face ridicule. One of the tacit rules of trekking is that it is a faux pas to use gear inappropriate to the environmental conditions. "Super gringo" is a local term of ridicule that identifies tourists who mismatch expensive gear with absurdly easy hikes. One morning, I was working with the park service on a trail outside the ranger station. A pair of trekkers walked past us, heading up the Los Cóndores trail—the easiest, shortest path in the park. The couple wore rigid mountaineering boots appropriate for climbing in the Andes, but completely unnecessary on a trail where most people wear sneakers. "That is a super gringo," the trail boss laughed. Their boots were so shiny and clean that we assumed they had never been worn before. Mountaineers also challenge trekkers. Alpinists often hike trails in sneakers or flip-flops, which has the effect of undermining the presumed necessity for trekkers to be wearing technical gear at all. Some alpinists display what they refer to as a "dirtbag" image in public. Wearing dirty T-shirts, athletic shorts, and tennis shoes, alpinists speed down the trails, passing trekkers who are decked out in designer rain jackets, trekking pants, and boots. Patago-nian alpinists wear brand-name gear in the mountains, but their dirtbag persona on trails pokes fun at the seriousness with which trekkers take their wilderness adventures. These critiques emerge within a public culture that places paramount value on trekking. Indeed, livelihoods depend on keeping tourists happy. How-ever, most residents and climbers are keenly aware of the bourgeois affectations of many tourists. Light mockery is one way for residents and climbers to draw attention to the excesses of the "fashion show," as one Hungarian trekker called it. In short, trekkers seek out the Patagonian wilderness to recover a sense of being with nature associated with having alpine adventures. They clothe their bodies in material symbols of bourgeois taste that enable more tactile, comfort-able, and pleasurable experiences of nature.

THE END OF THE TREK: POETICS OF THE SUBLIME

Trekkers arrive at their final destinations, or the dramatic denouements to their journeys. These endpoints are located on the border with the backcountry, where tourists cannot go unless accompanied by guides. After tourists labor for hours to reach their destination, they are rewarded by the *miradores* (sce-nic viewpoints)—sites of aesthetic grandeur and epiphany. These miradores are associated with experiences of the sublime. Tourists sometimes remark aloud on these experiences, emotionally overcome by the landscape.

Edmund Burke conceived of the sublime as "terrible objects" that are "productive of the strongest emotion which the mind is capable of feeling" (1990, 36). Immanuel Kant conceived of the sublime as judgments of taste that are universally binding. For Kant, the sublime referred not to objects in the external world, but rather to the sense experiences of fear and pleasurable pain provoked by the "might" and the "magnitude" of nature (1951, 99). The Kantian sublime involves "terrible objects"—tumultuous oceans and towering mountains—that generate an inspiring sense of spiritual elevation. Like Burke, Kant recognized that the more fearful these sights are, the more attractive they become. People may experience the terrible pleasure of the sublime as long as they do not come into close proximity to dangerous entities. Instead of the omnipresent danger experienced by climbers, trekkers experience a pleasurable sense of imagined vulnerability that comes from contemplating the scope and force of nature.

Patagonian trekking exposes the body to sublime nature, both as overpowering force (with its winds, storms, and arctic conditions) and the impressive scale of its physical forms (mountains, glaciers, and lakes). Dramatically envisioned, the trek involves a confrontation between the tourist adventurer and a potentially threatening wilderness. Clothing themselves in technical gear, trekkers signal their readiness to meet the challenges of an extreme environment containing manifold perils, such as gale-force winds, rapidly developing tempests rolling off the icecap, hypothermia, and exposure. There are numerous injuries inside the park every season that require medical attention and rescue operations, adding to a sense of physical danger. However, rangers and guides have worked to secure the trail system for tourists, particularly those with no outdoor experience, by giving out free maps, marking paths with bilingual signs, and widening trails to make them more comfortable for transit. Some— particularly seasoned backpackers—have found the trekking circuit to be disappointing. "The scenery is incredible," remarked a Welsh trekker, "but the difficulty is negligible. I had hoped for Alaska and got something else." This sense of disappointment about frontcountry trails facilitates the appeal of commercial tours into the backcountry.

The Loma trek, discussed in the previous section, is particularly well designed to provoke an experience of the sublime. On the final approach to the summit with Katrina and Rick, we ascended a steep set of switchbacks on the east side of the hill that entirely blocked our view of the Chaltén Massif. The horizon of sense perception narrows as one focuses on what is immediately in front: the dirt path, stones and ruts to avoid, and the slope into which one leans. The physical difficulty affects the body: one's heart begins to race, muscles feel exerted, and breathing becomes labored. But when one reaches the top, there is a dramatic revealing of the Torre and the Fitz Roy Ranges. One's perceptual horizon expands to take in the vivid panorama. At the summit, Katrina and Rick stood rapt at the spectacle before them, using words like "oh" and "unreal" to describe their intensified feeling of being with nature.

From positions of physical security, trekkers delight in the disorientation of the senses. Figure 2.3 depicts tourists climbing up from Laguna de los Tres to a precipice that drops off hundreds of meters to Laguna Sucia below. In the center is the Río Blanco Glacier. The grand chasm that opens up below, before, and above tourists creates a destabilizing feeling, a pleasurable vertigo that under- mines the sensory anchoring of the body—particularly one's balance. While some tourists shrink away from the precipice as nausea sets in, most revel in this destabilization as they admire the granulated icefall, the sounds of breaking gla- ciers, the snow reflecting intense sunlight, the feeling of winds surging across the mirador, and the verticality of the peaks that miniaturize the body.

Trekking poetics identify the alpine backcountry as a site of epiphany. At the two key destinations in the park, Laguna Torre (LT) and Laguna de los Tres (LDLT), I recorded the following statements made by seven trekkers:

1. Argentine tourist (LDLT): Fitz Roy is like a soaring cathedral that puts Notre Dame to shame.
2. Chilean tourist (LT): The mushroom ice on Cerro Torre seems to hang there, ready to avalanche.
3. Argentine tourist (LDLT): The beauty here is lethal.
4. Canadian tourist (LT): Words fail what I'm feeling right now. It's so amazing.
5. Australian tourist (LT): This is the most spectacular mountain range in the world.
6. American tourist (LDLT): This is so unreal, this place—just unbelievable. Haunting.
7. Argentine tourist (LDLT): We're all so painfully small here. The mountains, glaciers—they're enormous.

These statements offer various permutations on the alpine sublime, creating spiritual elevation that distinguishes sacred nature from quotidian life. The first and fifth trekkers established the absolute or comparative value of the Chaltén Massif through reference to other mountain ranges or architectural wonders, while the fourth and sixth identified the ineffability of the experience, and the second and third invoked the rhetoric of terrible objects. The seventh identified the feeling of encompassment, as the sheer magnitude of the wilderness radi- cally eclipses the body, rendering it tiny by comparison. The speakers' tones communicated feelings of awe, reverence, and amazement.

FIGURE 2.3. Tourists hiking to the promontory across from Río Blanco Glacier (photo by author)

Trekking generates an aesthetic community through a shared encounter with the alpine landscape. Gathering around select destinations, people photograph the same objects, enjoy the scenery, and communicate experiences of epiphany. Rather than simply establishing a solitary relationship with nature, trekking also involves a shared sense of camaraderie at having been affected by the same grand nature. At the miradores, tourists articulate their heightened senses of being with nature through the poetics of the sublime, focusing on the magnitude and might of objects and forces within the Patagonian wilderness. Whether shared aloud or kept to oneself, these sublime experiences help create a kinship of aesthetic sentiment among foreign and domestic tourists that transcends language barriers. The experiences become the basis of the symbolic capital that is captured by affluent tourists pertaining to El Chaltén as a branded place. The abstract signifier "national trekking capital" gains concrete meanings through tourists' experiences of hiking trails and standing at the miradores to see firsthand this stunning, vivid, and inspiring alpine landscape. This symbolic capital—sought by bourgeois tourists as testament to their aesthetic taste—becomes the strategic point of action for the tourism industry, as it seeks to open up and commoditize access to high-value destinations.

THE COMMERCIAL GUIDING SECTOR AND BACKCOUNTRY EXPERIENCE

My first encounter with the commercial trekking sector in the PNLG took place in 2006, as I began my fieldwork. El Calafate is a tourism town and the major port of entry to the PNLG, with an international airport that hosts daily flights to and from Buenos Aires. Most tourists heading to El Chaltén fly into El Calafate and take the two-hundred-plus-kilometer bus trip to the northern section of the park. While the northern zone is geared toward trekking, the southern zone is set up mainly for commercial tours to the observation decks at the front of Perito Moreno Glacier, boat trips through the fjords of Lake Argentino, and ice trekking excursions. Staying at a hostel, I signed up for what the receptionist called the "classic adventure" excursion in the El Calafate zone: the "mini-trekking tour" onto Perito Moreno Glacier. This two-hour-long ice trek is the most popular option for active tourists. Throughout downtown El Calafate, images of glacier trekking and ice climbing are ubiquitous. Most images depict Perito Moreno Glacier, showing happy, white tourists wearing crampons and wielding ice axes. The key motif in this tourism hub is mountaineering and extreme nature, communicated by the images adorning storefronts, pamphlets, street signs, and posters. These advertisements invite tourists to imagine themselves as alpinists risking death in the vertical wilderness.

A charter bus picked me up early in the morning and drove a group of twenty of us to the national park, about fifty kilometers to the west. We got off the bus and spent a couple hours walking the observation decks in front of Perito Moreno Glacier before taking the bus to a nearby dock. Boarding a small boat with other tourists, we cruised across a narrow channel for a close-up view of the glacier, which rose some seventy meters out of the water. The boat motored back and forth while tourists hugged the rails of the vessel and snapped pictures. The constant wind buffeted the deck. Giant tongues of ice broke free from the glacier and calved off into the lake. People exclaimed with glee with each new addition to the flotilla of icebergs.

We disembarked near the perimeter of Perito Moreno Glacier. Divided up into Spanish- and English-speaking groups, we stopped at an alpine chalet adorned with maps and photos of the area and then continued down a forested trail to a beach at the edge of the glacier. Carlos Arce, the head guide, gave a ten-minute talk on the history of the Southern Patagonian Ice Field: its formation, its mass balance dynamics (the gain or loss of ice based on accumulation and ablation), its recession since the end of the Pleistocene, and the threat posed by climate change. We then walked to an equipment station where the guides strapped well-worn, eight-point crampons on our feet. On a vacation from her work in the financial industry, Grace Sen, a young Singaporean woman, was perturbed, having come in sneakers and ankle socks. The guides passed out crampons and thin gloves, but not boots or socks. "Given what we're paying, you would think that they would give us better equipment," noted Grace, who was excited about the trip but concerned about the cold. Once we had our gear on, Carlos brought us onto the glacier, introduced the assistant guides, and gave us a five-minute demonstration, showing us how to walk uphill, downhill, and on flat terrain with crampons. "If you go off on your own, you will endanger yourself and other people," Carlos warned. The language of risk vigilance was constant during the trek, as the guides identified key sections as dangerous.

Carlos took us down a well-trodden path. Tourists quickly lost all sense of geographic orientation. After five minutes of walking, we stopped to take pictures. The guides showed us the first real danger of the journey: invisible pools of water hidden under a thin layer of ice. The oohing and aahing of the tour group's members soon gave way to quiet seriousness as each of us took a turn stepping over a crevasse, with the guides holding our hands. We continued to pick our way through the labyrinthine ice field, gaining an intimate perspective on something that most tourists see only from afar on the observation decks. The exhilarated participants communicated the sublimity of the experience to one another during rest periods, through smiles and finger wagging at novel ice formations. Even Grace overcame her skepticism, commenting that "this is beyond what I could have imagined." Over the course of the trek, tourists developed a kinesthetic sense for how to use crampons—that is, how to widen and shorten their gait to grip the ice with their spikes. Many people fell at least once as they awkwardly tried to traverse 30-degree slopes, but doing so soon became routine.

The trek finally came to a celebratory culmination. The guides brought us into a large opening where they used their ice axes to cut chips off the glacier. A couple of bottles of whiskey materialized. They passed out cups filled with spirits and glacial ice. Following a series of toasts, we deposited our gear at the equipment station and walked back to the chalet where we waited for the boat. Huddled in the warm shelter, the tourists reflected on the significant dimensions of the trek and talked about what was to come. Some were headed for El Chaltén to go trekking. Grace was staying in El Calafate to take the boat trip through the fjords. Others were taking a bus to Chile en route to Torres del Paine National Park.

The commercial guiding sector has profited immensely off tourists' desires for direct experiences of glaciers. In the southern zone of the park, the industry opened up Perito Moreno Glacier to the mini-trekking tour just described. In El Chaltén, the industry began by offering guided tours of the park's frontcountry, which soon gave way to glacier treks. The easier treks—onto Viedma Glacier and Grande Glacier—were similar to the mini-trekking tour. However, an enterprising business opened up an even higher-risk option, the icecap traverse. The traverse provided a weeklong excursion onto the Southern Patagonian Ice Field to see the hidden western aspects of the Chaltén Massif. This very costly and physically difficult circuit became the apex of the adventure tour options in the PNLG.

The commercial guiding sector positions tourists within a hierarchical field of adventure options. In the southern zone of the PNLG, the industry markets the ice trek as a premier adventure by constructing an opposition between active agents and passive observers. The daring ice trekkers represented in advertisements—mostly young, white, and of ambiguous nationality—emerge against the tacit background of the passive tourists who only visit the observation decks above Perito Moreno Glacier. Rather than merely gazing upon a sublime spectacle, the mini-trekking tour invites consumers to place value on the other bodily senses, especially kinesthesis and touch. In El Chaltén, the industry works to distinguish frontcountry trekking on the primary trail system from adventures in the backcountry. With tourism massification and ongoing efforts by rangers to create easier trails, some trekkers express disappointment at the lack of difficulty and danger. The guiding sector has capitalized on this disappointment and the desire for hardcore adventure among the majority of tourists.

The commercial guiding sector intervenes into the alpine sublime by creating new vehicles of desire for wilderness adventure. Recognizing that tourist fantasies about Patagonia involve heroic engagement with danger, the industry has worked to identify the glaciated backcountry with the sublime. Rather than the stationary sublime associated with standing at a mirador, the ice trekking tour involves the mobile sublime, or the ongoing sense of sensory destabilization as the group moves across the glacier. Indeed, the trekking industry deposits tourists in environments for which they entirely lack the necessary competencies. With guides providing mobile security, tour group members are free to delight in their imagined exposure to physical danger. The trek also sells the experience of using technical tools of exploration: crampons, helmets, and—in some cases—ice axes. Part of the thrill of the glacier trek is the disorientation that comes from not knowing how to use crampons or navigate safely from point to point, and the fears of hidden crevasses. The glacier trek is centrally connected to the commodification of the high-risk imagery of mountaineering, selling the experience of what it is like to be an alpine explorer for the day. At the basis of this enterprise is the territorial monopoly that the industry has over the backcountry. The tourism industry develops its rentier position by controlling spatial access to park destinations.

PLACE-MAKING DISCOURSES

Trekkers congregate to talk, share photos, and tell stories after returning from the park. These place-making narratives sometimes take the form of testimonials, encouraging or dissuading others from visiting a destination or taking a tour. They might also offer comparative evaluations of the PNLG in relation to other parks around the world. Sitting at a table at Estancia Verde Hostel, Sam Matthews-Johnson, an Australian doctor, discussed his reasons for visiting Patagonia: "I knew about the Andes and how remote and beautiful everything was here. A friend of mine went on an Antarctic cruise from Ushuaia and told me about it [Patagonia]. And a couple of months before that on a rock-climbing website people were talking about it. Everybody just made it seem like it was the best possible trekking experience you could have, and I was like, okay. Why shoot for anything less than the coolest thing available?" A seasoned trekker, Sam had spent four days in El Chaltén and over a week in Torres del Paine in Chile. His narrative reflects a central concern of bourgeois travelers: to seek out the highest-value adventure experiences around the world. As he put it, "Why shoot for anything less than the coolest thing available?" Indeed, he has pursued trekking experiences in alpine environments around the world. His Patagonian trip provides creative fodder for the fantasy work of envisioning the next journey, as it does for tens of thousands of other tourists each year. These narratives feed into the global dissemination of the Chaltén place brand, facilitating the ongoing expansion of tourism. Returning home, these tourists communicate these experiences, recruiting futures waves of adventure trekkers in pursuit of symbolic capital and the aesthetic distinction it affords upper-middle-class consumers. These repatriated narratives about the El Chaltén zone allow prospective tourists to connect the Patagonian landscape with—and compare it to—other locales within the global category of alpine environments.

Argentine tourists did not just position the Patagonian landscape in a global class of complementary environments; they also drew attention to its world-class status. One representational frame that bound Argentine tourists and local residents together was a discourse of landscape ranking in which El Chaltén was touted as one of the most spectacular destinations in the world. Travel guide-books and foreign tourist narratives worked to stabilize this aesthetic judgment, which provided Argentines with a great sense of pride. For older Argentines, the El Chaltén zone had another layer of meaning linked to geopolitical conflicts with Chile. During the 1990s, El Chaltén came to public attention during these disputes (see chapter 8), which prompted state action to defend the zone (Sopeña 2008). Through travel to the PNLG, this older group of Argentine citizens per-formed a long-standing patriotic duty to visit and enjoy the aesthetic splendor of a national landscape nearly lost to the Chileans.

These place-making discourses hide much about the social and cultural condi-tions that underpin trekking and ecotourism. James Carrier and Donald Macleod's (2005) notion of the ecotourism bubble refers to this abstracting of consumers from the sociocultural contexts and ecological impacts of the industry. Tourism has precipitated the rapid urbanization of El Chaltén, which has stressed its water-treatment and waste-disposal infrastructure and generated growing social tensions between permanent and seasonal residents. However, trekkers remain oblivious to their impacts on this locality. Moreover, the class exclusivity of Patagonian ecotourism rarely enters trekking discourse. Nonetheless, one Argen-tine tourist, Sonia Paz, remarked:

> It's not that they [most Argentines] undervalue Chaltén. Rather, it's that this is beyond the means and classic habits of Argentines. It's expensive to come here, and it's not part of the classic tourist places for Argentines. Middle-class Argen-tines go to accessible places that are traditional tourist destinations: Bariloche or the coast. Your typical Argentine is not going to come somewhere exotic like here for ten days, especially if they have a family—children or grandparents. . . . But the same is true for the average foreign tourist here: they also are not classic tour-ists, but people who really want to be in the mountains, whether trekking or climbing. And so you don't find your typical Argentine or your typical European here.

Sonia's statement draws attention to national tourism patterns, which concen-trate mass tourism along the Atlantic beaches, as well as—increasingly—Bariloche in northern Patagonia, which has become a hub for youth tourism. As northern Patagonia has gradually been pulled into the orbit of mass tourism, southern Patagonia has become more tightly associated with alternative ecotravel. Even within the PNLG, there is a dialectic of mass versus alternative travel: El Calafate is associated with more commercialized forms of tourism, while El Chaltén has claimed the mantle of an alternative destination for more ecologically conscious travelers. As a flexible market logic, ecotourism operates within a nested, shifting set of dialectical oppositions between mass and alternative travel. These oppositions depend upon an ever-changing set of classed consumption practices. Southern Patagonia remains a site of alternative tourism that is not only beyond the "classic habits of Argentines"—as Sonia notes—but also beyond their "means." The green economy is grounded in global tourism, but of a highly exclusionary kind. For the vast majority of people in the global south and global north, the cost of vacationing in southern Patagonia is prohibitive. The aesthetic community created by ecotourism is a highly exclusive club that creates a kin(g)ship of sublime sentiment.

Patagonian ecotourism is a mutating discourse of alternative travel to and within pristine nature that is ideally but not always associated with the presence of an indigenous, non-Western other. In the Northern Patagonian Andes, there are various Argentine and Chilean parks—Lanin, Nahuel Huapi, and Chiloé— within whose borders tourists may encounter small Mapuche communities, whose members engage in livestock farming and provide tourism services (Martín and Chehébar 2001; Oltremari and Jackson 2006; Miniconi and Guyot 2010). In the Southern Patagonian Andes, indigenous communities were decimated by the military, diseases, and settler-colonists and almost entirely pushed outside of areas designated for national parks (Navarro Floria 1999; Bandieri 2005).[6] In Patagonia, then, the ecotourism industry is dominated by nonindigenous Argentine and Chilean settler communities and tourism companies. Thus, Patagonian ecotourism more closely approximates popular ecotourism destinations in Costa Rica—such as the Monteverde Cloud Forest Reserve and Arenal National Park—than sites in the Ecuadorian or Brazilian Amazon run by indigenous communities. In El Chaltén, the ecotourism industry is structured by a double logic of non-Western otherness. Ecotourism celebrates and commodifies the discourse of the vanished presence of the Aonikenk people who once inhabited the zone. Entrepreneurs use the figure of the so-called heritage Indian—proud, romantically primitive, and tragically absent—to sell the cultural patrimony of El Chaltén, but in a way that does not foreground the state violence visited upon indigenous societies. Local commercial spaces situate wilderness adventure imagery within a sanitized indigenous history focused on horseback riding and the bola—a throwing weapon composed of connected cords with weights at the end that was used to hunt animals while the rider was mounted. Visitors can buy T-shirts, posters, postcards, and books of photographs depicting Aonikenk material culture, aesthetic designs, and masculine equestrian prowess. This horse- and male-centered discourse of the heritage Indian is the historical basis for the second aspect of the double logic of non-Western otherness, the Patagonian gaucho. These horsemen represent (to tourists and residents alike) the vanishing agrarian society in Patagonia focused on the estancia and the tending of livestock herds on the range. In El Chaltén, the rise of the ecotourism industry has fundamentally marginalized livestock farming as a productive activity, since it is associated with environmental degradation and forms of land use antithetical to the fantasy of virgin wilderness. However, gauchos and estancias have been repurposed for heritage tourism to celebrate a vanishing masculine, frontier ethos. There are a few estancias in the zone that have moved away from livestock farming and embraced heritage tourism, allowing visitors to stay at hotels, eat traditional Patagonian food, watch sheep being sheared, and go on horseback riding tours with gauchos. Moreover, El Chaltén's residents keep gauchos at a distance, since they are thought to be wild, heavy drinkers, frequent visitors of the local brothel, and always armed with a knife. Gauchos have come to occupy the savage slot of the non-Western other typically reserved for indigenous populations within the ecotourism market.

THE ALPINE SUBLIME

Trekking risk subjectivity is fashioned through the pursuit of sublime adventure. Rather than confronting existential peril in the mountains like climbers, trekkers seek novel experiences in the horizontal terrains of the PNLG, hiking its trails and taking commercial tours of the backcountry. From faraway cities like New York, Barcelona, Buenos Aires, or Sydney, tourists construct fantasies about Patagonia that are worked upon and reshaped after arriving in El Chaltén. In the process, trekkers construct and take back home diverse experiences of the alpine sublime: the embodied experiences of being with nature, the poetic elaborations on the might and magnitude of Patagonian wilderness, and the mobile exploration of glaciers. They situate these trekking adventures within the historical framework of the vanished heritage Indian and the vanishing gaucho, figurations of non-Western otherness.

Trekking and mountaineering work together to create the sphere of tourism consumption that defines the green capitalist economy. A historical force for constructing a meaningful framework of action pertaining to the alpine landscape, mountaineering has created the context of high adventure for trekking tourism to flourish in the trekking capital of Argentina. Local businesses use mountaineering imagery to commodify the park and market guided tours, inviting trekkers to envision themselves as alpinist explorers for a day. Progressively opening up new zones in the park to commerce since the 1990s, the guiding sector has played a seminal role in stimulating tourist fantasies about backcountry adventure that capitalize on the modest disappointment felt by some expert trekkers, who see the frontcountry as too safe and too comfortable. Thematizing the body in nature, the risk subjectivities of mountaineering and trekking exist in productive tension with one another, creating distinct tourist positions within the theater of alpine adventure. The title of this book refers to the alpine sublime as the master image-experience of Patagonia within the global tourism market. However, this commodity aesthetic depends upon a robust sociopolitical infrastructure—including workers, entrepreneurs, and park service staff members who labor to produce and stage alpine adventure. The remainder of this book moves beyond the consumer market and the fetish of the alpine sublime to examine the backstage politics of the ecotourism industry.

Mountaineering and trekking provide a vantage from which to understand the Kirchnerist neo-developmental approach based on aggressively expanding the exploitation of natural resources, whether in the agro-extractive sector or the ecotourism industry. The local green economy has more than doubled its consumer market under the Kirchner-Fernández regimes, reflecting a dynamic that is similar across the federal protected-area system as a whole. This has resulted in the arrival of more mountaineering expeditions and the massification of the trekking market. Moreover, the green economy has turned on a strategy of identifying and fixing the symbolic capital—of place, region, and nation— through branding efforts. With increasing numbers of arrivals, the tourism industry has developed the place brand of El Chaltén in concert with the concrete activities of visitors. Mountaineering and trekking establish the local meanings of the alpine landscape within the long-standing political project to aestheticize the supposed Patagonian desert. The Kirchner and Fernández administrations have overseen the stronger integration of national alpine nature into the global consumer economy. Their ecotourism success, however, draws attention to a contradiction within post-neoliberal politics: progressive capitalism relies on fostering a highly classed form of consumption. Only affluent Argentines and foreigners have the economic means to travel to El Chaltén (and similar destinations) to contemplate and delight in an environment that has become iconic of the nation.

PART 2　THE SPHERE OF SERVICE PRODUCTION

3 · *COMERCIANTE* ENTREPRENEURSHIP
Investment Hazard and Ethical Laboring

During the 2009–2010 season, Raquel Ibañez talked about opening her own hostel. She explored the possibility of taking out a loan from her boss, Manolo Artigas, though this never came to fruition. She eventually left El Chaltén and settled in Córdoba with her husband, Ricardo, where they worked for a few years and devised a plan to return to Patagonia. In 2013, she became a member of the entrepreneurial middle class as a *comerciante* (small-business owner):

> Ricardo was the driving force for this idea and to sell all our things to rent a hotel. Within a month Ricardo had sold our cars, our land, and all our material possessions, from the most dispensable to the most indispensable. . . . And so began the dream of running our own hotel. . . . In my experience I had always been a seasonal laborer and worked hard. But with the hotel, the strategy changed dramatically: as comerciantes (not the owners but the renters of a hotel) we work all the time. My workday begins at 6:00 A.M. and ends at 12:00 A.M. every single day of the tourism season. A boss like me needs to be working all the time, dealing with all the details, and being there for the clients, the employees, and in general. My work commitment is stronger than ever, since it's for me—for myself. After working eight hard years in a travel agency in Chaltén for another person, I know that the effort I put into my own business is at an even higher level. As a comerciante in El Chaltén, I feel that I work at 100 percent capacity and have no time to do any more.

Raquel identifies two difficulties involved in becoming an entrepreneur. First, the opening of a business requires a sizable capital investment to rent (or buy) an existing property and have enough cash on hand to make renovations, acquire supplies, and pay wages long before the business turns a profit. Second, comerciantes work just as hard if not harder than seasonal workers, in her esti-mation. Raquel puts in eighteen hours every single day during the tourism sea-son. In El Chaltén, the tourism industry entails two social classes: the scores of entrepreneurs who own businesses (hotels, hostels, bakeries, restaurants, and so on), and the hundreds of *golondrinas* (seasonal service workers) who travel to the area during the season. A golondrina is a Patagonian swallow. Seasonal work-ers are thus figuratively called golondrinas to draw attention to their migratory status, returning in the spring and leaving during the fall. Entrepreneurs com-press their annual earnings into the lucrative months from October to April, shutting down during the austral winter.

Raquel's business operates within an ecotourism industry based on the cre-ation and perpetuation of a semiotic estate. An estate is a vast property owned by a landlord—one might imagine an aristocrat or a land baron. National parks, however, are estates of an unusual kind since they are controlled directly by park administrations and indirectly by the tourism industry. Moreover, these national park estates are wedded directly to the semiotics of place: how destinations are represented as having unique place brands within the global tourism industry. In the context of El Chaltén, the semiotic estate refers to how entrepreneurial capital and the conservation state work to control the symbolic monopoly over place branding and the territorial monopoly over the national park. Entrepreneurs and park rangers have worked to improve the park and create an ideal alpine wil-derness to attract more-affluent customers. Since the 2000s, this public-private alliance has poured resources into the park to shift the customer base away from young backpackers traveling on shoestring budgets and toward affluent tourists willing to spend greater sums of money. Moreover, the local *Cámara de Comercio* (Chamber of Commerce) has worked closely with the park service to promote place branding. The branding campaign identifies the uniqueness of the alpine landscape and of the experiences that tourists can have. The conservation state exercises a direct monopoly over territorial access to the park, with the capacity to charge—or not charge—users and extract ground rents. Park users include tourists and guiding companies. By paying user fees, entrepreneurs (and the guiding sector in particular) gain indirect control over the park. As a result, guiding companies enjoy a subsidiary stream of rent beyond what the park ser-vice makes. Companies set prices for their tours in ways that reflect not only their labor costs (for guides, porters, and office staff members) and the owners' profit margin (since they risk their capital), but also their position as landlords. In other words, the guiding sector has the power to inflate prices and extract rent because they are licensed by the state to commercialize the park. Beyond the guiding sector, there is an urban sector linked to gastronomy, hospitality, retail, travel, and construction that includes business owners like Raquel. The urban sector works to support park tourism but does not have a territorial monopoly akin to that of guiding companies or the conservation state. Instead, the urban sector makes use of its spatial proximity to Parque Nacional Los Glaciares (PNLG) and inclusion within the brand image of El Chaltén.

Though ecotourism is based on rentier capitalism, entrepreneurs do not explain their success as the product of a monopoly position. Instead, entrepreneurs like Raquel formulate market discourses that valorize competition, ethical laboring, and business solidarity as the rationale for growing accumulation. As a result, the rentier logic to ecotourism becomes visible only in a fragmentary way.

TOURISM ENTREPRENEURS

Since the 1990s, people have migrated to El Chaltén to establish new lives and open businesses within the ecotourism industry. Like golondrinas, most entrepreneurs have come to the area from Argentine cities such as Buenos Aires, Rosario, and Córdoba. Though some brought start-up capital, many worked as golondrinas to save enough money to open a business. The slow pace of business expansion during the 1990s gave way to a rapid diversification with the start of the ecotourism boom under President Kirchner. The entrepreneurial class sells services and goods to growing masses of tourists and has established partnerships and trading relations among business owners. This capital-owning group has increasingly accumulated wealth and become the dominant pillar of a robust middle class in El Chaltén that includes public-sector professionals like rangers and teachers. This middle class is predominately white and presents itself as culturally associated with metropolitan zones like Buenos Aires. Unlike the more racially diverse population of golondrinas, many entrepreneurs trace their ancestry to Mediterranean Europe, with some holding dual citizenship in countries in the European Union.

El Chaltén's entrepreneurs have faced a number of difficulties as a result of the Great Recession. The vast majority of entrepreneurs are comerciantes: small-business owners who typically run one enterprise, work at their own establishment, and employ fewer than thirty workers. During the 2008–2009 season, comerciantes experienced the growth of uncertainty as the Argentine economy went into recession. Dependent on affluent travelers from Argentina, the United States, and Europe, comerciantes feared a large reduction in the number of tourists. Luckily, the downturn was not as severe as anticipated. Under President Fernández, the green economy entered a phase of ecotourism consolidation that registered more modest growth amid national economic problems such as high inflation, sovereign debt repayment, and sharp devaluations of the peso. Beyond global and national scales of risk, comerciantes have faced threats from within the entrepreneurial class. There is a small set of *empresarios* (big-business owners) who run multiple businesses and employ scores of workers. Empresarios are the privileged fraction of the entrepreneurial class. Comerciantes have increasingly viewed empresarios as having a stranglehold on the most lucrative sectors of the green economy—like park concessions and use rights—and as excluding the majority of business owners from crucial opportunities. Equally troubling is the fact that empresarios—as well as a growing group of landlords—have moved out of El Chaltén, cutting the social and moral ties of trust that bind entrepreneurs together. This foreshadows a growing division of entrepreneurs into a middle-class majority of comerciantes and an upper-class minority of wealthy, powerful empresarios and absentee landlords. In the face of these concerns, comerciantes established the Cámara de Comercio to represent their interests, created microcartels to fix prices and recommendation networks, and embraced rental housing as a secondary way of generating income.

Comerciantes have articulated a unique position within the Patagonian risk society by engaging the threats and opportunities posed by empresarios, golondrinas, and the Kirchner-Fernández administrations. I examine their relationship to workers in the next chapter, and here I focus on intraclass and governmental factors. Comerciante subjectivity is constituted through an engagement with investment hazard. Rather than the body-nature relationship experienced by tourists, entrepreneurs instead thematize risk within the socioeconomic world of ecotourism premised on a drive to accumulate capital that is linked to a moral commitment to laboring. Comerciantes emphasize a laboring culture whose values of hard work, frontier self-reliance, residency in the village, and intraclass solidarity distinguish them from an emerging upper class solely interesting in making money. After discussing the political culture of Kirchnerismo, I investigate the entrepreneurial commitment to laboring, competing visions of the market, and ongoing struggles with empresarios and absentee landlords.

THE POLITICAL CULTURE OF KIRCHNERISMO

The Kirchner-Fernández administrations have fashioned the political ideology of Kirchnerismo as a way to justify changes made to the national economy, social welfare, and natural resource exploitation in the aftermath of neoliberalism. Citizenship is a key aspect of this ideology. The Kirchners have centrally framed themselves as the twenty-first-century standard-bearers of Peronism—an Argentine political movement associated primarily with the first administration of President Juan Perón (1946–1955). The oligarchic class that dominated Argentina following the civil wars of the nineteenth century advanced a constitutional order based on classical liberalism and individual liberty (Faulk 2013, 30–36). Following World War II, Peronism introduced a political ideology that radicalized the demand for social justice. As Daniel James has argued, "Citizenship was not to be defined any longer simply in terms of individual rights and relations within political society but was now redefined in terms of the economic and social realm of civil society" (2001, 16). The Peronist constitutional reforms of 1949 sought to protect the "collective good of the people" through a long list of rights given to "workers, the family, children, and the elderly" (Faulk 2013, 36). During this period, the unionized working class benefited from the expansion of welfare and benefits programs connected to formal employment. This established a set of social rights that became the basis for popular understandings of labor-based citizenship (Lazar 2012).

Following Peronism, the national categories of *blanco* (in this sense, meaning "formality") and *negro* (meaning "informality") became identified with the presence or absence of workers' rights and benefits such as social security, paid vacation, sick leave, and subsidized health insurance. Subsequent governments began to chip away at Peronist labor-based citizenship that idealized formal work as a pillar of inclusion in the body politic. During the military dictatorship (1976–1983), the government began the tentative process of transforming the economy through "privatization, deregulation, and deunionization" (Shever 2012, 10). During his term in office (1989–1999), President Carlos Menem implemented a series of reforms that weakened labor laws and reduced the number of public-sector jobs, provoking the rise of unemployment and underemployment (Whitson 2007a, 123). The relatively low levels of informality in the workforce during the 1970s (20–30 percent) ballooned to 45–55 percent of the working population by the end of the 1990s, as deregulation and labor flexibilization transformed the economy (Whitson 2007b, 2918–2919). The Kirchners faced a dire situation of growing informality, unemployment, and poverty after the national crisis of 2001–2002. As a political ideology, Kirchnerismo signaled support for welfare programs, union power, and wage protections to rebuild the nation (Grugel and Riggirozzi 2012). Drawing on the Peronist legacy, the Kirchners advanced the ideal of labor-based citizenship to promote greater inclusion of citizens in the post-neoliberal social state.

Regional and local conditions shape how the political ideology of Kirchnerismo is interpreted and incorporated into everyday social life. In El Chaltén, the personal connections that residents have to the Kirchners are vital to how they perceive Kirchnerismo. Residents have supported Kirchner and Fernández for over two decades as provincial and national politicians. The El Chaltén electorate is typically friendly toward the Kirchnerist center-left wing of the Partido Justicialista. Though ascribing legitimacy to Kirchnerismo and the political agenda of green productivism, residents also identify "Cristina" and the late "Néstor" as individuals with a personal interest in the green economy.

The Kirchners not only visited the village frequently in the 1990s and early 2000s, but they also have invested their own capital in the green economy, owning hotels and real estate in El Calafate and El Chaltén. Residents of El Chaltén distinguish between "los Kirchners" as individuals and Kirchnerismo as a political ideology. According to residents, los Kirchners had a personal incentive to adopt protourism policies once they ascended to the presidency. Moreover, los Kirchners built a formidable political patronage machine in Santa Cruz (P. Lewis 2009, 153–154). According to many residents, los Kirchners used their presidential power to channel state money and public works contracts to provincial allies, enriching themselves during their time in office. Chaltenenses have thus formulated a response to post-neoliberal politics that highlights a double state marked by ambiguous governance. The Kirchners personify a federal state that is doubly defined by a legitimate progressive agenda and by illegitimate networks of corruption associated with the exercise of personalized power. Residents view Kirchnerist governance as highly ambiguous and are uncertain how to distinguish between its licit and illicit dimensions. Corruption is not entirely a bad thing for residents. The village has benefited from having local politicians in office, reaping the rewards of lavish public works projects initiated in Santa Cruz. However, residents recognize that los Kirchners see the economic potential of the local ecotourism industry. This interest imputed to los Kirchners has created a realm of shadow politics lurking behind the scenes of everyday life, which residents strain to see clearly.

Chaltenenses have embraced labor-based citizenship. They have creatively adapted the categories of labor-based citizenship, such as formality and informality, to local conditions. In the process, they have constructed a mode of local citizenship—of sociopolitical inclusion in the community—based on the ideal of becoming members of the propertied, formalized middle class. Registering their businesses legally with the government, entrepreneurs enjoy a formalized employment status that most of the golondrinas they employ do not have. Indeed, most workers labor in informal employment situations. Beyond this, residents seek to become property owners. This involves applying for a land grant to the Consejo Agrario Provincial, the provincial state agency that administers the distribution of public land to people who have established residency in the village. The agency sells this state-owned land at a very reduced price to the few who receive grants each year. For residents, the land grant is a visible sign of state recognition that formalizes their long-term contributions to making El Chaltén a successful tourism destination. The formality-informality division thus pertains to both property ownership and employment status. Amid the uncertainties of post-neoliberal politics, Chaltenenses have aspired to achieve local citizenship based on entering the formalized middle class.

LABORING *A PULMÓN*

Alejandra Dos Santos steers her minivan up the driveway outside of Hostel Cerro Solo. Alejandra has a business degree, is from an upper-middle-class family, and—like many comerciantes—hails from Buenos Aires. She established a very successful restaurant but had a falling out with her business partner, who bought out her share. Using this capital, she opened the hostel and has gradually built up the business. With the arrival of satellite internet in the mid-2000s, she was one of the first to recognize the potential of online reservations and consumer review sites like TripAdvisor. Working six days a week throughout the season, she earns enough money to go traveling during the off season. With over a decade of business ownership and accumulated capital, she does not have to work quite as hard as someone like Raquel Ibañez. Alejandra and I walk inside Hostel Cerro Solo to talk about her enterprise.

Comerciantes distinguish themselves from empresarios along the lines of power, profit, and ethical integrity. To call a comerciante an empresario is to invite a sharp retort, since the figure of the empresario is associated with unethical accumulation. Alejandra notes:

> The same lie exists here as in the rest of the world. We are all the same, but some of us are more equal than others! So said George Orwell. Today there is a lot of inertia. There are those who have a hotel, have a travel agency, and have a bus company and are going to have much more power and capacity to market their services, or to decide that they're all booked up, and send it [business] elsewhere. Those who were disposed to [support] Manolo Artigas, to offer commissions . . . well, Manolo could dictate which hostels were full and which ones not, because if I were disposed to give my 10 percent to him, I would be full, because when people arrive on a windy night, and they're full, they will say, no, wait, I'll call to see who is open and sell you a voucher. If I were disposed to give you 10 percent of my profit, because I have small margins, I would be full. But I have a much smaller margin.

With characteristic wit, Alejandra identifies the entrepreneurial class as divided into those who own one business and those with multiple businesses. By having a consortium of companies, an empresario—like Manolo—achieves greater levels of market capture, which facilitates larger profits and power over other businesses. Manolo's hostel, Estancia Verde, often has significant overflow because his bus company drops passengers right outside the front door. If Alejandra had higher margins, then she could afford to pay the 10 percent "finder's fee" to Manolo for sending his overflow her way. Quoting Orwell's *Animal Farm*, she draws attention to the falsity of the narrative of market equality. Alejandra's contempt for empresarios has much to do with their business ethics: the exploitive tactics they use to rob small-business owners of their profits.

Comerciantes have articulated a discourse of market individualism. Continuing her rumination on tourism, Alejandra notes:

> We are all occupied with making money. When the time comes to make money, we're all concerned just with making money. Me included. I include myself in this critique. In October and September when not many people have arrived yet, you say, "Oh, I'm opening; oh, I'm opening; I need to open." Then the other months you say, "Oh I'm working, I'm working." And then by May I'm gone. There is no social cohesion. *There is no social cohesion.* There is no society. There are a ton of individuals who just want to milk the cow. This is the biggest problem: that the majority of people aren't creating a future here.

Her statement frames the market as an asocial space of self-interested individuals trying to accumulate as much money as possible. As capitalists who espouse an ethic of hard work, comerciantes focus chiefly on what Alejandra euphemistically calls "milking the cow"—that is, squeezing every last drop of profit from their businesses. However, she gives a historical context to this perspective: "Ten years ago we were so isolated that we had to depend on and look out for each other." In the 1990s, when residents traveled to the nearby town of El Calafate to access its supermarket or gas station, they called up a dozen or more people to see what they needed. According to Alejandra, residents had created a community, but their solidarity had weakened as the green economy expanded. With growing numbers of residents, the pueblo has begun to fracture along class, racial, and ethnic lines. Alejandra articulates a discourse of market individualism that is simultaneously a historical commentary on the differences in El Chaltén between the mid-1990s and the late 2000s. Green productivism has stimulated the rapid expansion of tourism consumption and entrepreneurial opportunity, leading to the multiplying of businesses in the pueblo and growing stratification.

Market individualism is also used as a comparative framework to distinguish El Chaltén from other towns in Santa Cruz. Estela Cambiaso contrasts the "self-sustaining" and robust private sector in El Chaltén from the situation in other villages and cities in the province that had "70, 80, or even 90 percent public-sector employment." She added: "The background of the people is what makes them compete. In this pueblo there are many tactics that people use because they're not people from small pueblos. These are city folk. These are *business people* [spoken in English]. In greater or lesser measure. To shit on others, or to be shat on oneself. They are people who have a mentality that's much more anonymous and much more urban." Estela's statement identifies the market as saturated by a Hobbesian spirit of the *bellum omnium contra omnes* (the war of all against all). This dog-eat-dog ethos—to "shit on others, or be shat on oneself," as she colorfully phrases it—paints a picture of a hypercompetitive market of business-savvy individuals. For Estela, this ethic is a product of the metropolitan environment from which most residents come, Buenos Aires. The subtext to Estela's point is that El Chaltén is wealthy, white, market-friendly, and middle class because it has a *porteño* (people from Buenos Aires) settler culture, which is distinct from the surrounding racially and ethnically marked Patagonian society whose members are dependent on public-sector jobs and handouts from the Kirchnerist state.[1]

Market individualism enables entrepreneurs to extol the value of laboring *a pulmón*. This idiomatic phrase means "by lung" or "by sheer will," though the Americanism "by the bootstraps" captures the spirit of the phrase. Violeta Marconi remarked: "Getting money from the bank would be beautiful, but here, no, that doesn't exist! Investment capital comes from your own pocket! Or from your parents or sister. Here, almost no one has access to credit. Here it is a pulmón." Rather than rely on public-sector jobs and the Kirchner-Fernández patronage machine, El Chaltén's middle-class entrepreneurs have flourished—according to residents like Violeta—because of their self-reliance and capacity to act a pulmón. Throughout the 2000s, there were no local banks or formal sources of credit. While the absence of credit is a barrier to capitalist expansion, this lack also enables comerciantes to frame business success as theirs alone, completely independent of any help from the state or banks.

The discourse of market individualism and laboring a pulmón intersects with the frontier history of El Chaltén. The legacy of the pioneers is communicated through public signs, commemorative plaques, and oral histories that refer to the first generation of settlers to displace the Aonikenk people and transform the zone through livestock farming. Since the creation of El Chaltén in 1985, a new pioneer generation has settled in the area to carve out a living in the face of climatic hardship and the lack of services. Entrepreneurs are representatives of a new pioneer ethic based on austere living, prudence, hard work, and a commitment to the "duty" to save—the last item being the cornerstone of capitalism for John Maynard Keynes (1920, 17) and Max Weber (2004). El Chaltén becomes a space of heroic individualism and risk taking, where frontier capitalists meet the challenges of globalization.

Entrepreneurs like Alejandra have become local representatives of labor-based citizenship. These entrepreneurs have created legal businesses in which they have a licit employment status in the eyes of the Argentine state. The everyday actions involved in running their businesses constitute a kind of formalized labor. Entrepreneurs also generate the revenues that allow them to pay federal taxes to support the health care and social security systems, create jobs, and save enough money to take vacations and reinvest in their businesses. El Chaltén's entrepreneurs are icons of self-reliance in building a robust, white, middle class composed of residents not native to Patagonia. This autonomy allows comerciantes to distinguish their virtuous profiteering from the dependency, corruption, and patronage fostered by los Kirchners. At this juncture, entrepreneurs have a positional understanding of Kirchnerismo that focuses on the personalized state, rather than the political state that residents have electorally supported in the past. Ironically, though, entrepreneurs have depended for their success on Kirchnerist green productivism and the national commitment to ecotourism.

MARKET SOLIDARITY

Claudia Soto hands me the maté gourd as she smokes a rolled cigarette. Speaking quickly with a percussive cadence to her voice, she reflects on the investment climate in El Chaltén at the beginning of the 2009–2010 season. The co-owner of Hostería (meaning a bed-and-breakfast) Nunatak Viedma, Claudia has spent well over a decade in El Chaltén and experienced the tumultuous transition from the neoliberal Menem government to the post-neoliberal Kirchner-Fernández administrations. As an early resident of the town, she received a land grant from the provincial state long before there were any worries about land scarcity. She built a lovely, alpine lodge–style house on her property, as well as a set of cabins to rent to tourists. Not just a thriving businesswoman, Claudia is a property-owning, middle-class resident and thus embodies the ideal type of citizenship that newly arrived entrepreneurs (and golondrinas) have sought to attain. Claudia draws attention to the strength of the tourism market, but also to the lack of competition that exists in El Chaltén:

> Those who fail, fail because of personal reasons, in that Chaltén is not really interesting to them anymore as a place to live. There is a very high cost of living and a high cost of consumption for a family throughout an entire year.... But in general, who tries, who works, will make lots of money because, of course, you also spend tons of money, like I said before. But here there is a very strong market. No, there are not many businesses that go bankrupt, or, at least, thanks to the market.... The market resists a lot.... But we have bad faith with respect to the market, because it still allows us to be delusional.... There are very high external risks. I think the biggest risk is to believe that there is no limit to the chicken that lays the golden eggs. And the limit is very close.

Contrary to the discourse of hypercompetitive market individualism, Claudia argues that bankruptcies are infrequent and that people who close their businesses do so for "personal reasons." With the end of the ecotourism boom, however, Claudia identifies the "very high external risks" that exist—the foolish belief that tourists will continue visiting El Chaltén without any regard for the growing cost of business and escalating national inflation. Her statement highlights the increasing sense of risk exposure faced by comerciantes as capital investors during a period of socioeconomic transition.

To mitigate economic risk and ensure the social power of the comerciante majority, entrepreneurs formed the Cámara de Comercio. Until recently, El Chaltén had a Comisión de Fomento (Development Commission, or local administrative council) whose members were appointed by the governor, since the town had not yet met the minimum population requirement to become a municipality. Not the relatively weak Comisión de Fomento, but the Cámara de Comercio, the most organized civic group in town, has long been the real seat of social power. The Cámara has organized a united front of entrepreneurs to promote tourism development, coordinate the branding and marketing of the village, and make decisions about any social issues and public policies that might affect the local economy. Open to any entrepreneur, this body provides an important forum for comerciantes to promote an economic agenda that includes and represents the voices of the majority fraction within the entrepreneurial class. This provides a check on empresario power. The Cámara also allows entrepreneurs to act against other social groups, respond to political events, and intercede in the distribution of natural resources.

Entrepreneurs have also promoted an informal labor market in hiring golondrinas. As petty capitalists, entrepreneurs have fostered a "strong market," as Claudia called it, by using informal employment to cut labor costs and benefits, negotiating contracts one-on-one with workers, keeping some revenue streams off the books, and undermining unionization to shore up their bottom lines. The golondrina class bears the brunt of this process of transferring investment risk away from the capitalist class. Indeed, Claudia is one owner who employs golondrinas informally to protect her profit margins. Though informal employment is widespread, some entrepreneurs like Raquel Ibañez have resisted this practice and instead hired on formal workers. As a former golondrina, Raquel knows all too well the stigma associated with this status. She rejects the practice of informal employment and cites considerations of morality and social justice.

A discourse of market solidarity exists among entrepreneurs, contradicting the market individualist perspective. One business practice that exists in El Chaltén is the creation of microcartels. Rather than seeing competition as a natural and ontological condition of the market, some comerciantes have moved to create a system of price-fixing. Claudia draws attention to the difficulties of this strategy among her *compañeros de rubro* (market-sector partners):

I think that people today are still loyal because the market allows it.... In January it doesn't hurt me to be consistent with my pricing. When it does hurt me is in October when I don't have any reservations yet. When I don't have even one cent. Or at the end of March when I have rooms open. And rather than take loss after loss, I would prefer to sell them for 120 [pesos] rather than the 280 that's advertised. It's very difficult to be consistent, and I know a lot of people who aren't. It's very easy to be disloyal to your compañeros de rubro.... You try to respect the tariff that's published on the internet, and someone else sells the same service for one-third the price. I think they're isolated, these cases. But I don't think it's because of something ethical or moral, but because the market isn't so demanding. If there was more time in October or more time in March, then I think we'd be trashing each other a lot more. I don't think we're such good people or so consistent.

One way that some entrepreneurs cooperate with one another is by forming microcartels to fix prices for goods or services within the same subsector. Claudia deals with compañeros de rubro associated with the hostería subsector. On the whole, group solidarity is strong, with few deviations from the prices for rooms agreed to at the beginning of the season. Price-fixing is a collective strategy taken to maximize profit by avoiding the "internal class disputes" and the "bloody struggle of competition" often found among petty capitalists (Gramsci 2000, 40), while inflating prices to the level that affluent consumers will pay. Nevertheless, Claudia argues that the reason why her compañeros de rubro maintain their united front is not "moral" but that the market is still very strong. If the market were to contract precipitously, then this mutual aid network might begin to fragment.

The recommendation is another dimension of market solidarity. Though microcartels exist in various subsectors, there are entrepreneurs like Raquel Ibañez and her husband who work independently in terms of setting prices. Despite their autonomy, Raquel notes that solidarity also manifests itself through the passing along of information and clients. Indeed, a key portion of her job as a hotelier is to recommend specific tour companies, restaurants, and internet cafés. In sending clients to other comerciantes, Raquel establishes relationships of trust and reciprocity that have provided her with new customers, as other owners have recommended her business to tourists.

Market solidarity emerges against the backdrop of global investment hazard. Contrary to the rhetoric of market individualism, entrepreneurs have organized the market as a domain of mutual aid to enhance consumption receipts and mitigate the socioeconomic risks deriving from the end of the ecotourism boom, the fallout from the global financial crisis, and the growth of national inflation. Mateo Lis, who participates in a microcartel, remarked about the inflation forecast:

For me it's really difficult to anticipate things with the level of inflation we have. With such variation it's very difficult to foresee the margin of personal loss that I will have. If I anticipate 40 percent inflation and I don't think the market can support a 40 percent rise in prices to offset inflation, then I have to figure out how much I'm willing to lose in my business. I try and figure out how much the market will take and I risk it. . . . [We] look for 10, 15, 17 percent increases every year, understanding that at minimum inflation is rising at 30 percent per year, and understanding that every year our capacity for generating profits through reinvestment is declining.

High inflation is viewed as one of the key conditions of Argentine post-neoliberal politics for El Chaltén's entrepreneurs, particularly under President Fernández. Mateo identifies inflation as around 30 percent per year during the 2009–2010 season, but he also observes that the market supports only a 10–17 percent increase each year, resulting in a falling rate of profit. For entrepreneurs, the national inflation index is an economic domain associated with the taint of impropriety (Richardson 2009, 250). The Instituto Nacional de Estadística y Censos (INDEC; the National Census and Statistics Institution of Argentina) is the state agency charged with gathering and publishing statistical information. However, Chaltenenses and many other people throughout Argentina came to believe that INDEC was cooking the books—misrepresenting the inflation rate in the country under the direction of the Kirchners to decrease the cost of servicing the national debt and government bonds indexed to inflation. INDEC thus became a sign of Kirchnerist corruption and ambiguous government, since comerciantes were unsure of the degree to which the agency's numbers diverged from an accurate measure of price increases. Opposition politicians and academics began publishing alternative inflation reports. In the context of opaque numbers, comerciantes like Mateo have tried to anticipate what inflation will be and to set prices as high as the market and their compañeros de rubro will allow.

Comerciantes give voice to two distinct market discourses: a narrative of market individualism based on laboring a pulmón and social distinction from surrounding provincial spaces, and a discourse of market solidarity grounded in collective action by the Cámara de Comercio, microcartels, and recommendation networks. Entrepreneurs have asserted tighter control over labor markets to contain costs and curb competition among compañeros de rubro, consolidating social power within the pueblo.[2] In the process of dealing with investment risks, entrepreneurs have developed a situated understanding of Kirchnerismo that draws attention to ambiguous governance and state corruption within the production of statistical knowledge about the national economy.

EMPRESARIOS AND THE LAKE VIEDMA
CONCESSION GRAB

El Chaltén has witnessed the emergence of a small group of empresarios that controls multiple companies and has distinguished itself from the comerciante majority. Manolo Artigas has long been known for his travel agency, bus line, internet café, and hostel. Since the 2008–2009 season, he has opened a discotheque, budget hotel, and luxury hotel. Manolo is unusual among empresarios in that he lives in El Chaltén, and he has become a leader in the Cámara de Comercio and participates in the social life of the community.

Despite Manolo's relatively positive image among residents, some people suspect him of corruption. He seems to possess an almost magical ability to multiply his capital and expand his business consortium. Given the uncertainty about how he was able to expand his local empire so quickly, some comerciantes have turned to narratives of corruption. One said: "I have seen Manolo entertain members of the Agrarian Council at Hostel Verde, giving them free meals and drinks, and free rooms for the night when they come through Chaltén. Why do you think he never has any problem getting land when he wants it? He . . . probably gives them money on the side. That's why he's been able to grow his business as quickly as he has—because he gets as much land as he wants, while the rest of us fight over scraps." This comerciante identified bribery of the provincial officials working with the Consejo Agrario Provincial (CAP; Provincial Agrarian Council of Santa Cruz) as the likely reason why Manolo has gained so much land. This malfeasance has come at the expense of comerciantes, who do not have the largesse to buy political favors. The ascription of corruption to Manolo equally implicates the CAP and the provincial government, which residents viewed as tainted by the Kirchnerist patronage machine.[3] The CAP becomes associated with the same backroom deals and shadow politics linked to los Kirchners. As investors in the green economy, los Kirchners are the biggest empresarios imaginable, since their business consortium intersects with the awesome power of the federal state. According to entrepreneurs, this personalized state interest in the green economy has sent large amounts of federal money to the province to improve tourism infrastructure through public works projects (such as highway construction). However, the same interest also exposes the people of El Chaltén to the more nefarious intentions ascribed to los Kirchners. This creates the sense that there are invisible political powers operating behind the scenes of everyday life. The magical ability of an empresario like Manolo to multiply his capital becomes an object of speculation and fascination for residents who suggest that the invisible power of los Kirchners must certainly be involved for this situation of growing inequality to make sense.

Though Manolo is relatively well regarded, residents view Francisco de la Vega as a devil. Vilified during a land dispute in 2000 (see chapter 7), Francisco had a second fall from grace a few years later. An Argentine mountaineer, Francisco traveled to the El Chaltén zone in the 1980s and 1990s on climbing expeditions. One of the first residents of El Chaltén, he played a key role in creating the commercial guiding sector, working with the park service to establish the first tours. He became co-owner of Torre Expediciones, a commercial guiding company, and Patagonia Salvaje, a boating firm that runs tours on Lake Viedma to see Viedma Glacier. In El Calafate, one company has a monopoly on the ice-trekking tour of Perito Moreno Glacier, and another firm has rights to the boating tours of the fjords connected to Lake Argentino. Patagonia Salvaje acquired the monopoly concession to the Lake Viedma boating and the Viedma Glacier ice-trekking and ice-climbing tours. The only such concession that exists in the northern sector of the PNLG, this has helped Patagonia Salvaje—and Torre Expediciones, its sister company—move to the head of the pack among tourism firms. Like other companies in the guiding sector, Patagonia Salvaje enjoys an indirect territorial monopoly over park destinations.

There is a history of corruption associated with the Lake Viedma concession that colors residents' perceptions of Francisco in particular and empresarios in general. Marcela Barros, one of the park rangers who witnessed Patagonia Salvaje gain a monopoly, noted:

> That concession came out surreptitiously. It came about illegally. . . . They just appeared one day on Lake Viedma with . . . an authorization from the national park service to develop an experimental activity. And all the activity like that has to be made through a concession with an open bidding process. When you have the possibility of developing a commercial venture like this, you're going to have many people interested in doing so because it's a great business. You need to give everyone the opportunity to apply for the concession. Ten or twenty businesses might make offers, and the best one in terms of fitting with the national park service will get it—that best suits the interests of the national park service. In this case, this business had a direct permit from the central office in Buenos Aires.

Marcela identified this concession grab as part of a wider history of malfeasance in the PNLG by empresarios. According to administrative law, the National Parks Administration of Argentina (Administración de Parques Nacionales, or APN) must open up a concession to bidding by multiple parties. However, the APN instead granted a permit to Patagonia Salvaje. Moreover, this permit came from the very top of the APN, originating with federal administrators in Buenos Aires. A high-level APN official corroborated the illegal nature of the concession, observing that "through the influence that they [Patagonia Salvaje's owners] had in Buenos Aires at the time, they were granted a permit." The official noted that the local rangers and the regional land managers had opposed the concession, chaffing at how empresarios had circumvented their authority over sustainable development by using personal networks of influence. The official continued: "After two or three years, there was a bid. . . . It began as an irregularity through influential sources, but then it was normalized. There was a bid, and they [Patagonia Salvaje] won the bid."

The Lake Viedma concession grab had key impacts on comerciantes, residents, and park rangers. Rangers recognized their lack of power in the face of APN administrators' authority. Though the ranger corps and land managers opposed the permit, APN administrators overruled them and then regularized the concession after the fact when Francisco and his partners won the bid. Moreover, it showed rangers that corruption exists in the conservation state, making them cynical about the political influence wielded by empresarios. For residents, the grab confirmed their suspicions that the entire conservation state was corrupt, which lumped local rangers together with the federal administrators at fault. Moreover, it showed residents and comerciantes in a very concrete way that corruption and illegality exist at the interface between commerce and the federal state. Associated with the taint of unethical accumulation, empresarios in general came under suspicion by members of the public. Seen by residents as a devil, Francisco left El Chaltén and moved to Buenos Aires, returning only a few times each season to check on his businesses.

The process drew attention—if only in a limited fashion—to the rentier logic of the ecotourism industry and the drive to consolidate a monopoly position over access to park destinations. What became visible were not the widespread actions of the conservation state and entrepreneurial capital to control the semiotic estate—that is, to consolidate hegemonic power over park territory and the semiotics of place branding. Instead, the Viedma concession grab highlighted one particular case of corruption bound up with the struggle by an individual company to monopolize access to a specific destination inside the park. Rather than delegitimizing the system of capital accumulation, the local politics surrounding this concession demonstrated a public attempt to isolate and excise the personalized connections that could corrupt the system. People did this by stigmatizing Francisco.

THE ABSENTEE LANDLORD THREAT

"Put it on my tab," says Domingo Bridges to the clerk at the hardware store. The clerk takes out a notebook full of names and numbers representing the outstanding amounts owed by residents to the store. She adds the cost of the construction materials to Domingo's account. Like many villages, El Chaltén has a credit economy based on personal connections and social trust that allows residents to pay down their tabs when they receive income. Domingo and I grab the supplies and walk down the street to the new house being built by his girl-friend, Maria Elena Salinas. We then set to work on fixing and caulking the windows. As a recent recipient of a land grant from the CAP, Maria Elena has become a fully recognized citizen. She is a permanent resident, property owner, and member of the middle class—joining Domingo, who had received his land two years before. Both she and Domingo are not entrepreneurs, but unionized public-sector employees with formal employment status. Though outside the social world of comerciantes, Maria Elena represents a new source of entrepreneurship among residents: the building of rental houses and apartments. Whether comerciantes or public-sector professionals, middle-class landowners have recognized the deficit of housing that exists, the supplementary income that can be earned, and the growing demand among seasonal workers and tourists for rental units.

The house is the material sign of a homeowner's social ties to the community. Many homeowners build their houses by hand, conjuring up a sense of frontier life among this new set of pioneers. Neighbors, friends, colleagues, and acquaintances contribute time, effort, and expertise to the construction of the home. The work party is a vital source of free labor; for example, Maria Elena and Domingo each enlisted the support of about a half-dozen people. The expectation is that the couple will help each member of their work parties in turn, at some point in the future. The home has two primary sources of value. First, it is private property that has exchange value on the real estate market. Second, the house has social value grounded in reciprocity. Given the difficulties involved in getting a land grant, many residents view the home through the lens of social value: it is a sign of having made it in El Chaltén, becoming recognized formally by the state as a legitimate citizen. Though few would dream of selling their property, homeowners have taken note of the shift toward building rental units alongside their primary residence.

Maria Elena and Domingo have agreed to live at Domingo's bungalow so that they can rent Maria Elena's new home to tourists. Domingo remarks: "The idea is to fix the place up as quickly as possible so that we can rent it, whether to tourists or locals—or maybe some climbers. I lent Maria Elena a lot of money to build her home, and so that money would come back to me with the renters. . . . I think 1,500 pesos [$350] is a pretty reasonable price [per month]. The rental housing here is so expensive, it's so commercial, and I don't want to be part of that. I'd prefer to know the people who would be living here, charge them a reduced rate per month, with the idea that they'd be good caretakers for the place." The rental housing market is very expensive, with prices often triple or quadruple what Domingo suggested. His statement reflects the ambivalence of some new landlords, who do not want to be publicly seen as profiting off a residence built in the spirit of reciprocity. Instead, a fair price is all they seek—in this case, one that will generate enough revenue for Maria Elena to pay her debt to Domingo.

Others are far less worried about the commercial dimension of a rental contract. Claudia Soto has built rental units behind her home, contracting with informal manual laborers rather than enlisting the support of a work party. She has become a landlord in addition to running the hostería:

> So I've expanded my business from the hostería to having four apartments behind my house. And so I'm making more than double what I was before, which is great, but I'm also working not quite double what I was before. I can rent these out to climbers, or to Argentine families coming here on holidays, and make a lot. I have the commitment, you know, but it is all worth it to give me greater freedom. Why make the effort if you can't enjoy the freedom? And sure, tourists will complain about this or that, about showers, or the bed, or what have you. It's all my own, unlike the hostería [which is co-owned]. We have a rental agreement that's coming due soon [on the hostería]. So if the owner decides to raise our rates beyond what's possible, I can say "ciao," and I know I'll be fine with just the apartments. Or I can just leave town altogether and rent out my apartments and this house, and make loads of money, and live off the rents. I could go to Baja California or Spain or Brazil and be perfectly fine, and come back here only once in a while during the summer.

As Claudia notes, rental units allow entrepreneurs to diversify their businesses and generate greater returns. She and her business partner are exposed to the whims of the landlord who owns the physical structure and land on which Hostería Nunatak Viedma sits. To build, own, and rent a unit is a strategy of financial hedging that allows Claudia to walk away—if necessary—from the hostería and simply become an absentee rentier: a landlord who lives off rental income.

Claudia articulates a growing option for some businessmen and businesswomen that is threatening to comerciantes. She fantasizes about living a rentier lifestyle abroad on the beaches of Mexico, Brazil, or Spain. A small but salient set of entrepreneurs have sold their businesses but maintained ownership over real estate. Living off the rents generated by their properties, this group of rentiers has renounced their residency in El Chaltén. The figure of the absentee landlord contradicts the ethical value placed on laboring a pulmón by comerciantes. This figure is morally threatening to the community, because its existence indicates a pathway open to comerciantes and empresarios to remove themselves from the social and moral bonds of trust and solidarity that bind the entrepreneurial class together. Many empresarios have renounced local citizenship—which includes permanent residency in the community—and moved elsewhere.

INVESTMENT HAZARD AND MORAL LABORING

The risk subjectivity of entrepreneurs—such as Raquel Ibañez, Claudia Soto, and Alejandra Dos Santos—emerges out of concrete experiences of investment hazard related to local, provincial, national, and global conditions. Entrepreneurial subjects govern their capital investment in ways that emphasize a commitment to remaining permanent residents, laboring a pulmón as the newest wave of Patagonian pioneers, engaging in market competition but also acting in solidarity with other comerciantes by making recommendations, fixing prices, and organizing through the Cámara de Comercio. In the process of engaging investment hazard, comerciantes position themselves socially by foregrounding their ethical laboring. This distinguishes them from the absentee landlords and empresarios who have left El Chaltén and cut the social bonds of trust among members of the entrepreneurial class.

These business practices—organizing the Cámara as a force to represent the majority comerciantes, creating microcartels, and turning toward housing rentals as a secondary source of income—are key ways to consolidate the social power of capital over the pueblo that work in concert with the state-capital alliance to control the territorial and place branding dimensions of the semiotic estate. Rather than understanding the ecotourism industry as dominated by a rentier logic, though, comerciantes have imaginatively rendered their world in terms of intraclass competition and the risking of capital investment. The rentier logic of ecotourism appears in fragmentary ways: the actions of empresarios like Francisco in grabbing a park concession, the absentee landlords whose existence contradicts the value of entrepreneurial moral laboring, and the shadowy realm of Kirchnerist politics in which favored empresarios are granted land. Comerciantes articulate the dangers associated with the emergence of an upper class of business owners who exploit the less capitalized majority and increasingly capture key sectors of the ecotourism economy.

Entrepreneurs provide a clear point of entry into understanding the representational pluralism of post-neoliberal politics. The political culture of Kirchnerismo generated by residents underscores a double state of ambiguous governance. The Kirchnerist state is doubly defined by a legitimate center-left political agenda but also by the personal interest that los Kirchners have in the green economy by virtue of their political history and family investments. The corruption and illegitimacy that taints los Kirchners has affected local perceptions of empresarios, whose wealth is rumored to be linked to the Kirchnerist patronage machine in Santa Cruz. As they work to create solidarity and limit intraclass competition, comerciantes face the global investment hazards stemming from the Great Recession, uncertainty surrounding flows of foreign tourists, the economic downturn in Argentina, and ambiguous governance associated with national inflation. Green productivism has facilitated the rapid expansion of the entrepreneurial class and generated income that is unevenly distributed. What troubles comerciantes is the expanding inequality among the owners of capital. Comerciantes have embraced a sense of local citizenship that places value on living locally and working to spread and diminish risk across the market. The capitalists increasingly marginalized from this moral form of labor-based citizenship are those who have left town, largely severed their social ties, and increasingly treated the village as a cash machine.

4 · *GOLONDRINA* LABORING
Informality and Play

Hostel Lago Viedma was one of the budget options for housing in El Chaltén. Owned by investors who lived in the nearby town of El Calafate, the establishment contained a dozen rooms furnished with bunk beds, as well as a small plot of land for camping. Many seasonal workers—called golondrinas because, like the Patagonian swallow they are named after, they migrate annually to the region—had pitched tents outside the hostel, using the common area inside to cook meals and socialize. As the 2008–2009 season entered its final months, the crowd of golondrinas began to shrink to just a handful. Many had already left El Chaltén, disappointed with their meager earnings—though not entirely surprised, given the turmoil and uncertainty precipitated by the Great Recession. Some of these young adults returned to their family homes in Buenos Aires, Córdoba, Rosario, and Salta. Others had departed for Andean destinations like Mendoza and Bariloche, hoping to work in the ski industry.

Patricio "Pato" Chavez was comanager of the hostel, along with his friend Ricardo Mendoza. They decided to remain in southern Patagonia during the off season, assisting with the construction of a hotel north of El Chaltén. Pato and Ricardo had helped a small group of friends who were still living at the hostel. Rosita Camargo worked at a laundry around the corner, while El Morocho Montemayor was a porter who took day jobs with various commercial guiding companies. He carried loads for tourists and helped the head guides by pitching tents, tending camp, and cooking meals. A novice mountaineer, El Morocho had ascended Aguja Poincenot the previous year. Both he and Rosita were informal workers. Pato had hired them on the side, having them buy supplies, clean up after meals, and tend the front desk when he or Ricardo took a break. "It's been a hard, hard year," Pato remarked one evening. "It's not much, but people are suffering. So I've tried to give them some work, so they can camp here for free." Rather than hiring the two as formal employees, Pato framed the exchange as a gift. He and Ricardo did not actually need any more workers, but he felt obligated to help out his friends when he could, subsidizing their housing for a few hours of work per week.

Pato had a similar arrangement with Griselda and Jorge Cundin, a mother and son from Comodoro Rivadavia, an oil city on the Atlantic coast. Griselda was in her sixties and suffered from heart and lung problems. In his late thirties, Jorge had first come to El Chaltén in the early 1990s to protest the Chilean attempt to claim sovereignty over the Lake del Desierto area just north of the pueblo. He had left and then returned to El Chaltén in the early 2000s to work as a seasonal laborer, eventually convincing his mother to move to the pueblo. Griselda and Jorge were some of the few tourism industry workers who stuck around the village during the winter, when most of the remaining residents were business owners and state employees like teachers, police, and rangers. Like his mother, Jorge suffered from medical problems, but his were caused by falling off a boulder while rock climbing. With only two doctors at the small clinic in town, Jorge and Griselda had a very difficult time receiving adequate medical care. Pato had offered them a private room to keep Griselda out of the cold, in exchange for informal help around the hostel. Jorge cobbled together odd construction jobs around town to earn a meager income. Informal work arrangements in exchange for housing and other goods like the ones Pato and Ricardo doled out to their friends began to multiply throughout El Chaltén's service economy as Argentina entered a recession and the forecast for the future remained gloomy. Though the tourism market had begun to recover—albeit slowly—by the following year, the golondrina service class faced increasing socioeconomic barriers that constrained their upward mobility.

SERVICE WORKERS

Each October, hundreds of workers arrive in El Chaltén for a season that lasts until the following April. The service class increases the population of El Chaltén by approximately one-third, drawing people from Argentine cities and neighboring countries like Paraguay and Chile. Unlike some tourism markets in northern Patagonia, such as Bariloche in Argentina and Pucón in Chile, there are very few Europeans or Americans working there. Consisting mostly of Argentine men and women ages 18–35, the service class is a social group whose membership is defined not only by workplace identities and the need to sell labor power for wages, but also by socialization outside of work. El Chaltén offers higher wages relative to other parts of Argentina, as well as the potential to apply for land, a long-standing benefit granted by the government to citizens willing to relocate to remote areas of Patagonia. Part of the allure of El Chaltén is the well-trodden path that residents have followed. Beginning as seasonal workers, some have moved up the social ladder to open their own businesses, acquire land, and establish a foothold in the burgeoning middle class. Many golondrinas have aspired to become permanent citizens of El Chaltén, a dream that seemed increasingly likely during the heady days of the ecotourism boom under President Néstor Kirchner. However, the slowing rate of economic growth under President Cristina Fernández de Kirchner presented many challenges for golondrinas, and their hopes for upward mobility began to fade.

Golodrinas draw attention to the positionality of labor within the Patagonian risk society through their exposure to the social power of entrepreneurial capital and the conservation state. Service worker subjectivity has emerged through experiences of socioeconomic marginalization and precarity exacerbated by the Great Recession. Facilitated by green productivism, the dream of Patagonian frontier opportunity had recruited growing numbers of workers to the zone. With the end of the ecotourism boom, though, golondrinas articulated a growing set of problems—inflation, land scarcity, the escalating cost of living, informal employment, and diminishing access to public resources—that raised socio-economic barriers to their upward mobility into the formalized middle-class citizenry. In a context of diminishing opportunity, golondrinas increasingly made a virtue out of their own seasonality, embracing the aesthetic freedoms of play (Schiller 1982) in work and leisure spaces. After discussing national labor politics, I examine the risk subjectivity of service workers bound up with the loss of free housing in Camp Madsen, the dream of Patagonian opportunity, the difficulties faced within an informal labor market, and the new meaning that the youth culture invested in play.

THE POLITICS OF LABOR

Kirchnerist green productivism has promoted ecotourism-led development based on expanding the permanent and seasonal populations at Patagonian destinations, accelerating capital accumulation, and growing employment. Green productivism is only one part of a wider national strategy to promote a new form of capital accumulation and social inclusion based on overcoming the contradictions and conflicts associated with neoliberal reforms. In the face of escalating informality, unemployment, and poverty, the Kirchner-Fernández regimes have advanced a neo-developmentalist strategy to expand welfare programs, increase union power, and institute wage protections to rebuild the nation. Kirchnerist post-neoliberalism has affirmed a "commitment to welfare" and social justice that places the state especially "on the side of the working class, the lower middle class and the poor" (Grugel and Riggirozzi 2012, 9–10). Under the Kirchners, poverty and extreme poverty fell sharply, while unemployment declined from 18.4 percent in 2002 to 8.0 percent in 2010.[1] Increased spending on social programs and public subsidies for food, transportation, and energy provided cash transfers to the poor and real wage protections for workers (Calvo and Murillo 2012, 151–152). However, the Kirchner-Fernández administrations made only partial gains in reducing entrenched levels of informal laboring, which declined from 50 percent in 2003 to 35 percent in 2010 (151).[2]

The neo-developmentalist paradigm places key limitations on the capacity of the government to deal with entrenched informality. Rather than a socialist strategy of nationalizing entire industries and expanding the public sector to provide jobs for the unemployed and the informally employed, the Kirchners have relied on the more modest, mixed approach of safety-net programs, subsidies to support domestic consumption, and rapid economic growth. To limit inflation and maintain Argentina's competitive position, the Kirchner administrations have sought to slow wage growth in two ways. First, the administrations have brokered sector-wide pacts with affiliated unions and industrial capitalists to raise wages for relatively well-off formal workers in an incremental fashion (Etchemendy and Collier 2007). These formal workers, who represent a minority of the labor force, are the core representatives of the Kirchnerist drive to promote the notion of labor-based citizenship. Beyond these formal workers, however, there is still a substantial population of informal workers who have been segmented out of these corporatist pacts—between the state, capital, and unionized labor—and are compelled to negotiate directly with employers. Though the state has not intervened directly in their wage negotiations, informal workers have benefited from national minimum wage increases, real wage protections, rapid economic expansion, and social programs to support lower-income families with children.

The green productivist agenda has facilitated employment opportunities for growing numbers of workers in ecotourism destinations. Green productivity rises as informal laborers are put to work building a formalized economy that includes business owners and people in the unionized public sector, such as park rangers and teachers. This situation draws attention to another contradiction within postneoliberal politics: a tiered system of citizenship that divides formalized from informalized workers. Though attempting to promote greater social inclusion for Argentine workers around the ideal of labor-based citizenship, the Kirchner-Fernández administrations have pursued policies more focused on economic growth, which have made only partial progress in diminishing informality. In El Chaltén, this formal-informal divide manifests itself primarily along the boundary between the middle class and the service working class. Despite the Kirchnerist post-neoliberal vision of greater social inclusion and equity, the El Chaltén service class has become representative of the limits of this ideology, bearing witness to persistently high levels of informality in certain industries and the national conditions of tiered citizenship.

CAMP MADSEN

Green productivism and the ecotourism boom created a raft of new jobs in El Chaltén, but urban development failed to keep up with the growing number of seasonal workers. Many of them moved into Camp Madsen, a free public campground located at the northern edge of El Chaltén, inside the boundaries of the national park. Since there were no restrictions on the length of stay, workers lived in Madsen throughout the season. However, the park service closed Madsen during the austral winter of 2008. Coinciding with the beginning of the global financial crisis, the 2008–2009 tourism season proved tumultuous for workers, who anticipated staying at Madsen for free. Instead, they had to move into town, where there was already a shortage of affordable housing. Many landlords prioritized short-term rental contacts with tourists over seasonal rentals for residents. Some golondrinas rented houses or apartments, while others stayed at private campgrounds or budget hostels like Hostel Lago Viedma. A few lived at their sites of employment, paying rent to their bosses. As a consequence, many workers reported spending between one-quarter and one-half of their wages on housing.

Camp Madsen was the social center of a service class that espoused countercultural values. Madsenitas (residents of Madsen) created a tent village where people lived and shared meals, establishing an alternative space to mainstream Argentine society. According to Fernando Irrazábal and Luis Soto Jr.:

> Madsen marked one of the most important moments in El Chaltén, when the demographic explosion happened and there was work for everyone.... For the "Madsenita," Chaltén was another reality, as if it were El Calafate. It spoke a different language, had its own laws and rites.... Companionship,... cleanliness, respect for one's neighbor and good vibes.... Some with their artisan goods, others with a guitar, yoga areas, the smell of joints mixed with *tortas fritas* and when one had the time you took a trip to the pueblo to visit a friend, to drink a few rounds of *mate* in someone's house and work on your tan, or you stayed in your tent reading a book.... A few visited the camp only to find an assistant guide or see some gringo selling their climbing gear, but in this place there were clinics on slacklining, English, Portuguese, bouldering and in the final years, light construction.... In the year 2008 by decree of the park service, they shut the camp because of a lack of resources to govern it in an efficient manner and El Chaltén lost even more authenticity. (2009, 36–38)

Irrazábal and Soto highlight a number of key aspects of Madsen. First, it existed as a site of alternative sociality—defined by solidarity and horizontal ties—situated in opposition to El Chaltén, "as if it were El Calafate." This refers to how Chaltenenses define their community: as a remote, bohemian, mountain village differentiated from El Calafate, which is seen as hypercommercialized and mainstream. Irrazábal and Soto imply that Madsenitas view El Chaltén in a similar fashion. Second, these alternative residents speak "a different language" expressing a culture of sharing, trust, respect, and *buena onda* [good vibes]. This culture manifests itself through shared pleasures of the body associated with yoga, music, drugs, and food. Members of this alternative society help each other advance their social position, with clinics on foreign languages and even light construction. Third, Irrazábal and Soto identify the closure of Madsen with a loss of "authenticity" for El Chaltén, an opinion echoed by many former residents of the camp.

Madsenitas embraced the romanticism of precarious living. The service class congregated in their own *villa* (settlement), which became a material sign of difference with respect to El Chaltén: a public embracing of seasonality, improvised housing, and constant turnover. Many seasonal workers tried to gain permanent residency status, which would enable them to apply for a land grant to build a home. However, Madsenitas were keenly aware that Chaltenenses viewed Madsen as an aesthetic eyesore that devalued the local brand. Sensitive to this scorn, many Madsenitas saw the tent village as a space of youthful play in relation to the older, more conservative El Chaltén. Rather than viewing Madsen as a collection of substandard dwellings that lacked running water, electricity, and central heating, camp residents placed value on the rigors of tent living in closer contact with nature. There was a double freedom in this: not only was it monetarily free, but it also facilitated a "carnivalesque" liberality (Limón 1994, 139) that was frowned upon in mainstream Argentine society. Participating in drum circles, communal dinners, casual sex, and drug use, residents blended youthful hedonism with outdoor living.

For some Chaltenenses, Madsen introduced an unseemly association between El Chaltén and a shantytown (Auyero 2002; Auyero and Swistun 2009). The visual precarity of Madsen—a settlement lacking public services—bore a superficial resemblance to metropolitan shantytowns, stoking the fears of some business owners that things would get out of hand. However, Madsen was under the jurisdiction of the park service. The Cámara de Comercio began to press the rangers to shut it down.

Though there were dissenting voices, the park service turned against Madsen. According to rangers, there were growing incidents of petty crime, such as the stealing of tourists' belongings. Some rangers voiced dissatisfaction about the amount of time they had to devote to policing and ensuring that conditions in the camp were sanitary. A ranger named Mateo Lopez supported the closure:

> The Cámara de Comercio asked the national park service to close Madsen because this place was . . . a petri dish. . . . The doctor wrote the letter and referred to this term, petri dish, because the people in this place slept in tents, and there

were cold nights, and many people had to go to the clinic with pulmonary problems, with bronchitis, and this generated an infectious situation in the camp. And
after the Cámara de Comercio asked for this, the national park service accepted
it. The job of the national park service is not to provide housing for people of the
town, but rather to give opportunities to people who come here as tourists. They
shouldn't have to take responsibility for the problems of the pueblo. So the pueblo
asked for it, and the national park service accepted it and closed it [the camp].

Mateo's statement draws attention to the opinion, voiced by many rangers and
business owners, that the mission of the park service is not to solve the local
housing crisis. Instead, the park service provides other social goods to residents,
such as conserving the ecological conditions of production that facilitate ecotourism. However, a set of social forces—the park administration, the majority of
the local rangers, medical professionals, and the Cámara de Comercio—aligned
to generate a multipronged discourse about Madsen as a site of growing criminality, disease, and social disorder.[3] Ultimately, the superintendent of Parque
Nacional Los Glaciares (PNLG), Carlos Corvalán, closed Madsen. Indeed, the
closing was part of a wider project to stage locality in ways that appealed to the
tourist gaze, eliminating the village's rough edges to more closely align with upper-
middle-class taste. Though accepted as part of the frontieresque, bohemian char-
acter of El Chaltén for a time, Madsen increasingly became a thorn in the side of
the political and economic elite and a threat to its hegemonic vision for ecotourism based on upgrading the alpine landscape to cater to a well-heeled clientele.
The state-capital alliance at work in El Chaltén became visible in the joint action
to evict the golondrinas in the name of conservation and public health, the rami-
fications of which included compelling workers to pay more of their wages to
landlords.

THE DISCOURSE OF FRONTIER OPPORTUNITY

Quitting their jobs during the summer of 2009, Anita Pari and Servando Bulgakov sold their furniture, packed their minibus, and drove to Patagonia. There was
a kind of starry-eyed romanticism to their journey, as they began a new life in a
village neither of them had ever visited before. Anita found work at a travel
agency. Servando started out working in construction, but he burned out after a
couple weeks. With his excellent English, he soon landed a position at a bed-
and-breakfast, working at the front desk.

The couple imagined El Chaltén as a space of opportunity to advance their
social position. Servando remarked: "Patagonia has fewer professionals than in
the north, and so less saturation in the job markets, which is good for us. Anita
has a communications degree and I've worked in business management for a
while. Also, the pay is better down here, and so it's really a question of being okay

with the climate and how isolated the place is. But after living in cities, we're more than happy to be somewhere incredible like this, away from all the pollution and craziness of the city. We love the mountains, nature, and wildlife. No, this is perfect for us." Servando reflects some of the key beliefs that define the discourse of frontier opportunity. First, Patagonia is a region that pays higher wages than other parts of Argentina for comparable jobs. Second, there is a lack of workers in the region and an assumption that the job market is expanding. Third, Patagonia is a remote space of nature removed from the rigors of metropolitan life. Many golondrinas go to El Chaltén to escape the ills associated with city life: pollution, crime, noise, congestion, and the lack of opportunity. Fourth, new workers who establish residency get land grants. "We realized there was no way that we could ever own a house in La Plata. That's part of the attraction of Chaltén," Servando noted. "I know it's only been a few weeks," Anita continued, "but our plan is to gain residency and apply for a land grant." These popular beliefs about Patagonia facilitate the recruitment of new golondrinas each year. They reflect the history of the ecotourism boom under President Kirchner and the expansion of job opportunities.

The discourse of frontier opportunity intersects with the ideal of formalized, propertied, middle-class citizenship in El Chaltén. Golondrinas are keenly aware that many business owners began as seasonal laborers in the tourism industry and worked their way up the social ladder. For residents, the middle class refers to business owners and professionals like teachers and park rangers. The formal status of members of the middle class derives from their having legal, registered businesses or being members of public-sector unions. For the aspiring golondrina, achieving the dream of upward mobility begins with establishing permanent residency. After two years, a resident may apply to the Consejo Agrario Provincial (CAP; Provincial Agrarian Council of Santa Cruz) for a land grant to build a home or business. Among residents, the distribution of land grants is a hotly contested process that has occasionally led to public protests and land occupations. The desire for land is tied to the struggle for social recognition. For Chaltenenses, the issue of who deserves land is closely connected to the time, sweat, and dedication one has given to the building of *la comuna* (the collective or community). No matter how many years one has lived in town, one does not have a claim to full citizenship—sociopolitical standing in la comuna—without being a property owner. Even some middle-class residents do not yet have land, implying their exclusion from full recognition. In this fashion, Chaltenenses appropriate the categories of labor-based citizenship and rework them in new ways. To become formalized, one must not only have regularized employment status but also become a landowner. Within a few weeks of arriving in town, Servando and Anita had set their sights on gaining land.

The service class has more and less privileged fractions. "Skilled labor" refers to positions—such as head guides, receptionists, and managers—that require foreign-language fluency, technical training, or the ability to supervise other workers. "Unskilled labor" refers to jobs where these competencies are neither required nor remunerated. The skilled-unskilled division often maps onto the distinction between "front region" and "back region" work (Goffman 1990, 107, 112). In a tourism economy, front-region employees interact directly with tourists, which means that the employees must have a facility with foreign languages like English, while the back region refers to spaces apart from tourist interaction. There is also a divide between the guiding sector and the urban sector. The former includes the hundreds of professional guides, assistant guides, and porters who work for commercial guiding companies. The latter includes hundreds of jobs in the village, held by people who provide direct and indirect services to tourists. Finally, there is a marked gendering of work spaces in El Chaltén. The guiding sector is dominated by males, while the urban sector includes both genders. This is significant because the guiding sector includes the highest paid jobs in the tourism economy. The key divisions between skilled and unskilled employment, front and back regions, the guiding and urban sectors, and work spaces dominated or not by one gender give rise to more and less privileged class fractions.

Anita and Servando found skilled labor positions as receptionists, though under different legal conditions. As English speakers, they worked directly with tourists. Anita booked passages for clients at a travel agency. Working formally with a legal contract, she earned wages and benefits reported to the state. Servando worked closely with tourists at Hostería Nunatak Viedma, the business owned by Claudia Soto. Claudia employed workers informally (without a contract), a practice common in many businesses. She had a reputation for being an overbearing boss, and Servando very quickly soured on the situation. Despite facing different legal conditions, the couple had skilled labor positions that paid higher wages relative to the domestic workers who cleaned the hostería and travel agency every day—receiving "poverty wages," as Servando put it.

The high cost of living erodes the dream of frontier opportunity. According to workers, El Chaltén does pay higher wages on average than other parts of the nation for comparable jobs. However, the high cost of living undercuts the purchasing power of workers. There are some goods and services—such as bread, bus tickets, and time at internet cafés—that are sold at reduced "local prices" to residents. But most goods and services are sold to everyone at prices set for affluent tourists. With high inflation during the Fernández administration, workers in El Chaltén faced a situation of devaluation each year, since their wages were fixed at the beginning of each season. Coupled with the elimination of free camping at Madsen, golondrinas experienced a growing sense of downward mobility as their capacity to save was eroded.

The social hierarchy within the service class became apparent to some as the taproot of opportunity began to wither. Raquel Ibañez remarked:

> Chaltén has its diverse groups. You have the powerful: the business owners and those who have their small businesses here. Then you have the people who supposedly aren't interested in money, because they love the mountains and have a discourse of complete freedom—which, for me, is a bit untruthful because they hold onto their power—and they make up a very select and closed-off group. And then you have the very hardworking laborers, among them the *gente humilde* [humble folk] who are the construction workers, or the housekeepers, or the hotel maids. . . . And they pass by like a *fantasma social* [social ghost]. They don't go out and don't spend money, and their wages aren't that high, so you don't really get to know them.

Raquel identifies the entrepreneurial class as the most powerful, while placing the professional guides below them. She associates this most privileged fraction of the service class with a "discourse of complete freedom" that includes contempt for mere moneymaking. Raquel also identifies the gente humilde as the least privileged fraction, those with the lowest wages who are far less likely to go out at night to socialize with other workers. The term "gente humilde" refers to poor people who are often racialized as distinct from the white majority. In El Chaltén, the gente humilde includes workers from Paraguay and northern Argentina of indigenous descent. Raquel notes that the gente humilde are invisible to the privileged workers, ultimately reduced to the status of the fantasma social—specters who represent the exploitation of labor within the green capitalist economy. While members of the skilled class can afford to socialize at night at the microbrewery, discotheques, restaurants, and bars, the unprivileged fraction of golondrinas is rendered invisible.

The growing scarcity of land presents a significant barrier to frontier opportunity. Anita and Servando faced the spatial constraints of an ecotourism village. There is an upper limit on the plots of land that the state can grant to residents, since El Chaltén is circumscribed by the PNLG to the north, south, and west, and by the De las Vueltas River and a privately owned ranch to the east. During the 1990s, the CAP gave out large plots of land, seeking to attract new residents to the border zone. As more people arrived, the CAP shrank the lot sizes to create a greater urban density. By the late 2000s, the hundreds of applications for land exceeded the number of remaining plots. The CAP sought to give priority to applicants with five years of residency, especially families with school-age children, and individuals seeking to open businesses. Despite their hopes for the future, Anita and Servando began to recognize the structural barriers to achieving local citizenship, such as the high cost of living, eviction from Madsen, rising inflation, and land scarcity. These barriers reduced opportunities for golondrinas and reinforced middle-class power. Despite the 2007 election of Cristina Fernández de Kirchner, who promised to expand the progressive Peronist agenda initiated by her husband, the growing experience of risk exposure for golondrinas led to less optimism for the future. There were very real limits on the capacity of a post-neoliberal government to expand labor-based citizenship in El Chaltén and move rising numbers of golondrinas into the middle class.

LABORING *EN NEGRO* AND *EN BLANCO*

From 2008 to 2010, Raquel Ibañez worked at Poincenot Travel—a popular internet café and travel agency—as the head receptionist and manager. A woman in her early thirties who had come from Salta, Raquel straddled two domains in the service class. As a skilled laborer dealing with tourists, she was part of the privileged fraction, earning wages high enough to go out to bars and restaurants most evenings. As a woman of Incan heritage, however, she had an identity that was in tension with white racial hegemony in Argentina. During our frequent conversations, Raquel voiced deep-seated anger at the casual prejudice and micro-aggressions she experienced at the hands of other workers, residents, and tourists. Raquel had experiences similar to the racialized workers from northern Argentina and Paraguay who were paid as unskilled laborers.

Chaltenenses use the national categories of being *en negro* (in the dark) and *en blanco* (in the light) to describe their employment status. Residents rhetorically use "negro" and "blanco" as a binary opposition to differentiate between informal and formal statuses, respectively, or to establish a spectrum of different degrees of labor exploitation. Rather than a clear dualism, this spectrum accepts various shades of lighter and darker gray. Residents can thus use these two categories in absolute or relative senses. As a waitress, Raquel worked informally for her boss, Manolo Artigas. However, her promotion to the head receptionist position came with a formal contract. Raquel understood her new status as blanco but still exploitive: "The people who work at Poincenot Travel have contracts, but it's precarious. I'm contracted month by month. The first of the month I'm hired, and at the end of the month I'm let go. And again at the first of the month I'm rehired. Every month I have to sign a contract, and what this does is eliminate any seniority for the time you've worked. I've worked for four years with Poincenot Travel, but I have working seniority of one month, because they always hire me on the first and let me go at the end of the month." Raquel's statement mirrors wider discussions among service workers about "garbage" or "trash" contracts and the tricks that bosses use to curtail rights (Whitson 2007a; Lazar 2012). Her boss uses an accounting trick to compel workers to sign away their seniority rights. Despite working en blanco, Raquel perceives her situation to involve an exploitive patron-client relationship that keeps her compliant from month to month. In her terms, it's not purely blanco. Instead, it's a "blanco that hides much."

Most workers are informal and identify their status as "negro." In Argentina, the informal economy extends to both the public and private sectors. Marisol Tellez remarked:

> I worked en negro for eight years for the government. What working en negro means is that you have never worked. Those eight years of my life I essentially did nothing. You don't have anything except the small amount of money provided by your wages. Being en negro means you don't have rights to anything. They don't have to pay you for extra hours or even by the hour, but rather a daily wage. A day worked equals a day's wage. It's not legal, but it's normal. It's an absurdity! I worked in the Casa de Gobierno [Provincial Government Palace] for eight years where supposedly that shouldn't happen, but it's very common in Argentina. An economy that grows 8–10 percent per year—this is only what's going on en blanco. I'd say that half of the population of Argentina lives en negro and makes a minimum wage that doesn't [allow people to] afford a good home or a good education in general.

Marisol draws attention to the large number of people laboring en negro in Kirchnerist Argentina, who earn low wages, cannot "afford a good home," and are barred from upward mobility. For employers, formalized workers are expensive because the state requires the payment of payroll taxes to fund pension and health insurance programs. Marisol "never worked" in the sense that her labor remained invisible to the social security system. Moreover, she did not have access to the social health insurance system known as Obra Social, instead relying on the underfunded public system.[4] In El Chaltén, the entrepreneurial middle class has kept many workers in the shadows, stripped of the social rights associated with labor-based citizenship. Higher rates of capital accumulation in El Chaltén turn not only on the extraction of surplus value (Marx 1990), but also on imposing the disciplining conditions of informal work.[5]

Tourism businesses generate dual identities based on publicly accounted revenues and hidden cash flows. Andreiña Zamora, a government worker, explained how some businesses operate in El Chaltén: "A hotel or a guiding agency, for example, might have a handful of legal workers, en blanco, who supposedly do all the work that is accounted for on the books. But actually, the amount of money they get paid is divided up among the handful of workers they [business owners] employ legally and the many dozens more they employ under the table, in cash, en negro. So on the books it looks like everything is legitimate, but most people are actually working illicitly." Lax government oversight and the drive to maximize profit have led to a disregard for labor laws. However, Andreiña notes that many tourism businesses are neither entirely en blanco nor en negro, but a combination of the two. As legal entities, businesses use formal workers to establish a semblance of propriety in the eyes of the state. However, this licit identity enables businesses to hide the illicit cash flows that owners use to pay en negro employees, who work off the books.

Workers struggle for higher wages and better benefits, but they frequently negotiate this one-on-one with their boss. In the absence of unionized bargaining (apart from a nascent union for guides), the boss—seen as a charismatic patron—flourishes in El Chaltén. As Nancy Scheper-Hughes has described this dynamic among Brazilian domestic workers, the "bad boss" becomes a "scapegoat" who is subject to "ridicule" because he or she "is said to have violated the trust between patron and client," whereas the "good boss" is someone who "helps to smooth over, conceal, and sometimes resolve the contradictions inherent in the perverse relations of power and dominance" (1992, 125–126). In El Chaltén, there are a number of well-known "bad bosses" who are said to treat their workers poorly, pay low wages, and shame employees who do not perform well. Though scorned by workers, the bad boss helps reinforce the image of the good boss. Indeed, the good boss in El Chaltén is a charismatic patron who takes care of his or her workers. In addition to providing slightly higher wages, the good boss makes unexpected gifts such as money, goods, or vacation time that confirm a relationship of intimate, personalized care.

Informality also draws upon what Barbara Sutton has called the "racial coding of class" relations in Argentina (2008, 108). The terms "negro" and "blanco" literally mean "black" and "white." Sutton argues that hegemonic whiteness is based upon a celebration of European identity that attempts to marginalize the significance of *mestizaje*—a "mixed" racial heritage of European, indigenous American, and African ancestors—in the population. In part, this racial ideology enables Argentina to envision itself as distinct from other Latin American countries. Indeed, elites have long referred scornfully to the proletariat, the poor, prostitutes, and peasants with the term "negro" (James 2001, 31). Racial blackness has become indicative of membership in a class of social undesirables. In El Chaltén, residents often use the term "negro" playfully and humorously in conversations. However, it also has a pejorative meaning, since it is associated with the urban poor who live in shantytowns, whom members of the respectable middle class might call *negros sucios* (dirty blacks) or *negros de mierda* (black shit). To be working en negro, then, carries very powerful cultural meanings in Argentina that are linked to racial hierarchy and class subordination. For some golondrinas, their negro status was a stigma, since it communicated their relegation to second-tier citizenship in El Chaltén in particular and Argentina in general. For others, en negro status was a normal condition of their being in the world, given how widespread informality was under both neoliberal and post-neoliberal governments. What mattered most to this latter group—which included people like El Morocho, Rosita, Jorge, and Grisela, who lived at Hostel Lago Viedma— were the wages they earned, rather than their legal standing. They had long ago given up hope of ever rising into the formalized middle class.

The service class faces conditions of negro and blanco employment that draw attention to their social marginalization. Many workers have been stripped of the social rights historically associated with labor-based citizenship in Argentina, while also experiencing a process of racialization linked to national prejudices concerning social undesirables. Employers fragment service class cohesion by negotiating on an individualized basis with workers, while the charismatic paternalism of the "good boss" helps diffuse tensions between capital and labor. In the process, members of the service class come to understand their subordination as second-tier citizens.

SPACES OF PLAY

The closure of Camp Madsen eliminated the social center of the service class. During the 2008–2009 season, workers dispersed across El Chaltén into private campgrounds, apartments, and hostels. In the wake of this spatial fragmentation, members of the service class increasingly turned toward play—understood as expressions of aesthetic freedom—as the organizing thread of youth culture. Though long a central dimension of social life for golondrinas, play acquired a new significance that was tied to growing social marginalization.

Aesthetic freedom in the workplace involves the marking, display, enjoyment, and skilling of the body. Golondrinas display a variety of subcultural (Haenfler 2013) identities in the working environment. Some jobs have strict dress codes, but many bosses allow golondrinas a fair amount of latitude, permitting them to dress in casual clothing, dye their hair or wear it in dreadlocks, and display piercings and tattoos. Many entrepreneurs also dress informally, reflecting the sartorial code of mountain casual in El Chaltén that emphasizes outdoor gear and clothing made of natural fibers. The dominant subcultural identity among golondrinas is the *escalador(a)* (climber), an identity that appropriates the mountain casual style and pairs it with an interest or expertise in climbing. Golondrinas also draw upon subcultural identities and genres such as the hippie, the Rasta, and the punk. Golondrinas submit to the work demands of their bosses, but the visual marking of their bodies communicates their aesthetic freedom. In certain occupations, workers enjoy a degree of autonomy that lets them set their work schedule and engage in activities that are unproductive from the point of view of capital formation, such as slowdowns, interruptions, and the taking of personal time. Workers with "good bosses" point toward these more casual environments— which could include tacit approval of drug use—as fringe benefits that compensate for the drudgery of repetitive tasks. Also, certain occupations permit more aesthetic freedom than others. Guides, assistant guides, and porters are most likely to view their jobs as a form of play. During an ice-climbing tour, the head guide and instructor remarked: "It's a pretty good job, no, getting paid to do this?" The conceit of "getting paid to play" is a dominant narrative among workers in the commercial guiding sector, including the porters who get paid the least and carry heavy loads for clients on excursions. Rather than spending the entire season confined to a particular shop, hotel, or restaurant, porters have the opportunity to access the wilderness, experiencing something on a daily basis for which affluent tourists pay dearly.

Play typically occurs within leisure contexts. Leisure activities—having communal meals and barbeques, frequenting bars and discotheques, climbing, and hiking—provide a vital source of intraclass socialization related to pleasure seeking, the giving and receiving of buena onda, and expressing countercultural values. Rock climbing is the most salient expression of leisure play among the service class. The climbing identity of workers is visible not only in the extremely casual and often deteriorating clothing that they wear, but also in their bodies: they have callused hands, toned muscles, and bulging veins. Escaladores with local jobs are the residents who are most connected socially to mountaineers. Escaladores often host parties for alpinists, interact with them at bars, and climb alongside them at the indoor gym and on the canyon walls surrounding the village. Some escaladores are members of the mountaineering community. Faced with shrinking opportunities, a few local mountaineers have focused on becoming super-elite alpinists. In doing so, however, they run into the center-periphery relations of power implicit in the sponsorship world of the Euro-American outdoor industry.

Escaladores appropriate the urban margins of El Chaltén for rock climbing. "Bouldering" involves climbing rock walls and boulders that are low to the ground, often less than five meters tall. To begin bouldering, one needs only a pair of climbing shoes, which greatly lowers the cost of entry. Indeed, the vast majority of workers begin on bouldering routes. The more costly option is "sport climbing." On the canyon walls surrounding El Chaltén, escaladores have constructed routes of varying heights and levels of difficulty. These routes are protected by bolts and anchors that climbers have drilled into rock faces to achieve higher levels of safety for teams. It costs much more to start sport climbing than to start bouldering because the former activity requires ropes, harnesses, helmets, and carabiners. On boulders and sport routes, climbers move laterally or vertically on rock faces, respectively, gaining physical strength, muscle tone, and gymnastic balance. At popular bouldering sites on the outskirts of town, women and men listen to music, smoke marijuana, and drink maté. Escaladores laugh, tell stories, make fun of each other, and debate the merits of different techniques, but they also take seriously the building of competencies while creating a space of play. Veronica Rosales, who works in a retail shop, said: "You get away from your job, annoying boss, difficult tourists—you know. Here I have my friends; we can listen to music, maybe smoke a joint. But most important, it's just you and this rock. There's a great peace in focusing on movements, gripping the holds, using your energy efficiently, keeping your balance evenly distributed.

It's hard work, for sure, but also the most calming thing you can do." Veronica comments on the sensory and spiritual freedom she identifies with rock climbing. In forested grottos and on canyon walls, escaladores appropriate spaces— beyond work, bosses, and tourists—to practice an art of the skilled body focused on movement, tactility, and balance.

The ability to engage in leisure play is conditional on the ability to not work. Leisure opportunities are much more constrained for urban-sector workers, who typically have fixed contracts with one day (often assigned by the boss) off per week (see Figure 4.1). In contrast, most guiding-sector workers have free contracts. Free employees contract on a daily basis with any of the tour companies in town. The members of this male-dominated sector enjoy the privilege of being able to set their own schedules, exercising the freedom to go rock climbing when the weather permits. Juan Frías, an assistant guide, remarked: "If they [guides and porters] were motivated by cash, then they could make a lot of money. But I don't think they are motivated by cash. The majority are motivated by the location, so many assistants [and] guides, if it's a sunny day, they take the day off, and they go up into the mountains. So they're maybe working four days a week, depending on work availability and motivations. So from that perspective, no, they probably aren't living as comfortably as they could, but if they worked the same hours and the same amount of days as people here on fixed employment, then they would bring in some serious cash." Rather than being motivated by "cash," guides are motivated by "location" or climbing venues: boulders, canyon walls, and mountains. As opposed to worshiping income generation above all else, guides attempt to strike a balance between the need for wages and the priority of play, in the process forgoing "serious cash." Juan's narrative points to the laboring inequalities that exist between the two sectors. The male-dominated guiding sector enjoys a privileged position relative to the urban sector, which has a higher proportion of women. Not only do guides make the highest wages in the service class, but they also have more free time to spend on leisure activities. In the face of growing barriers that constrain upward mobility, golondrinas have increasingly embraced the value of play in work and leisure spaces.

To be at play, however, is a privilege that segregates the more publicly visible, white, skilled fraction of workers from the more exploited, racialized segment of unskilled golondrinas. Rodrigo Valverde, a Guaraní man from Asunción, talked about leaving Paraguay for Argentina in the early 1990s to search for work, and his settling in La Plata. Reflecting on his reason for being in El Chaltén, he noted: "In La Plata I worked in construction and made enough for my family, but I heard that the wages here in Chaltén were much higher, so I borrowed money from my brother back in Paraguay to buy a plane ticket and came here to work on the bus terminal they are finishing." Unfortunately, Rodrigo found that his wages—though higher in El Chaltén than La Plata—did not improve his overall

FIGURE 4.1. Two fixed-contract service workers enjoying a rare day off (photo by author)

situation once he factored in the cost of local housing and food. Although he had originally hoped to remain for the entire season, Rodrigo stayed for only a couple of months until his crew finished the terminal, by which point he had saved enough money to repay the debt to his brother. In the evenings he stayed in, eating dinner, watching television, and socializing with other hostel visitors, rather than going out to expensive bars and restaurants. Indeed, he became close to Jorge and Griselda, the mother and son who eked out a living tending the hostel. Rather than having the luxury to be at play, the three of them saved what little money they could, watching dancing or variety or sports programs and preparing for the next day's work.

In addition to his position in the informal working class, Rodrigo exemplified the structural exclusion of indigenous populations within the Patagonian green economy. The green economy has been built upon a history of military violence, territorial exclusion, and political subjugation of indigenous populations. In the Southern Patagonian Andes, only a few pockets of extant indigenous communities remain in a region once populated by the Kaweshkar, the Aonikenk, the Yaghan, and Selk'nam (Briones and Lantana 2002). To survive, many of the descendants of these peoples intermarried with European, Chilean, and Argentine settler-colonists and entered a labor force in which they were expected to subordinate all traces of their indigeneity. This history is quite distinct from that of the Northern Patagonian Andes, where the Mapuche people endure in the face of enormous adversity and political repression (Mallon 2005; Richards 2010; Klubock

2014; Bacigalupo 2016). Rather than a place within the Aonikenk lifeworld, El Chaltén has become a site of migration and productive laboring for indigenous and other subaltern populations from across the Southern Cone, who are regarded as different from the white middle class and the more privileged fraction of golondrinas. These racialized and ethnicized others labor within the informal lower ranks of the ecotourism industry, preparing beds, cooking meals, building houses, and selling consumer goods—some of which celebrate the supposedly vanished native society of the Aonikenk.

THE INFORMAL WORKFORCE

Patagonian golondrinas are part of the large national population of informal workers that has persisted under the Kirchner and Fernández administrations and the tiered system of citizenship that in El Chaltén divides the formalized middle class from the largely informalized service working class. The existence of the golondrina population points to another contradiction that exists within Argentine post-neoliberal politics: despite the progressive rhetoric of the social state and popular inclusion, the green economy demonstrates that accelerated capital accumulation has come at the expense of the very labor force that Kirchnerismo aspires to protect. The growth of the social power of capital has led to the marginalization of the service working class and constrained opportunities for advancement into the propertied, middle-class citizenry. Workers have faced eviction from Camp Madsen, a rising cost of living, high inflation, land scarcity, and widespread conditions of informality. The socioeconomic risks of marginalization and precarity have become evident to golondrinas, whose subaltern position emerges in opposition to entrepreneurial capital and the conservation state. Many golondrinas continue to labor at the social margins of the green economy, framing youth culture around pursuing the freedoms of play. Green productivism has worked to expand capital accumulation and job creation, but the latter has been achieved through arrangements outside the normative parameters of labor-based citizenship that is tied to formalized employment.

The Patagonian green capitalist economy has facilitated a risk society based on differentiated subject positions. Collaborating with the conservation state, business owners have created urban- and park-based services that work to commodify the alpine landscape, extract revenue from the growing numbers of tourists, and elaborate the meanings of the El Chaltén place brand. Visiting the zone, trekkers and alpinists interact in a mutually reinforcing fashion to generate the distinct risk subjectivities that comprise the theater of alpine adventure. Entrepreneurs have fostered consumption by using the high-risk imagery of mountaineers to sell backcountry glacier tours to trekkers, employing service workers to staff these excursions and secure tourist bodies. Entrepreneurial capital has continued to perpetuate informal employment conditions among the service class, which depress wages, eliminate benefits, and protect employers' profits. While facing their own set of investment hazards related to los Kirchners and the emergence of an upper class, comerciantes have shifted investment risk downward onto workers. The golondrina population includes more and less privileged class fractions based on divisions between skilled and unskilled labor, park and urban sectors, and the front- and back-regions' workforces in terms of gender. Within this capitalist ecology of risk, each subject position engages with and values different types of risk that derive from this interactional world. Subjects perceive and thematize their positionality through lived experiences of risk exposure. However, this ecology of risk supports and reproduces hierarchies related to class, race, gender, and nationality.

The green productivist agenda has facilitated ecotourism-led development based on tourism consumption, capital investment, and service worker employment. Expanding flows of tourists have created the consumer demand to power the capitalist economy and establish the social power of capital over its largely seasonal labor force. The social and economic changes deriving from green productivism have facilitated political cultural responses to Kirchnerismo and its national ideology of labor-based citizenship, the social state, and greater inclusion for the lower classes in the wealth of the nation. Residents have articulated positional understandings of labor-based citizenship and ambiguous governance by the double state—Kirchnerismo as doubly defined by a legitimate neo-developmentalist agenda and the illegitimate, personalized use of state power. The political culture of Kirchnerismo becomes all the more important when examining the politics of the conservation state, as the park service seeks to involve local residents in a participatory development agenda for sustainability.

PART 3 THE SPHERE OF THE CONSERVATION STATE

5 · COMMUNITY-BASED CONSERVATION

Land Managers and State–Civil Society Collaborations

The National Parks Administration of Argentina (Administración de Parques Nacionales, or APN) has four distinct levels of bureaucracy: the executive council of the central office in Buenos Aires, which includes political appointees; technical delegations of land managers that have authority over entire regions and their protected areas; superintendent offices at each protected area; and *seccionales* (individual ranger stations). In El Chaltén, the personnel of the Seccional Lago Viedma (SLV) ranger station are authorized to engage in conservation policing. SLV rangers implement the scientific sustainability framework created by land managers working for the Delegación Técnica Regional de Patagonia (DTP; the Patagonian Regional Technical Delegation).

Scientific sustainability is an expert discourse based on ecological science, bureaucratic review, and public engagement. The DTP has custody over Parque Nacional Los Glaciares (PNLG) and the other protected areas in the region. Staffed with natural and social scientists—such as biologists, ecologists, botanists, and anthropologists—the delegation creates and updates park management plans, conducts scientific research to determine baseline levels of biological diversity, and spearheads environmental impact assessments. The DTP has established a good working relationship with the SLV ranger corps in El Chaltén through past efforts to create a robust park management plan and ongoing efforts to facilitate research concerning mountain ecology and endangered native species such as the Andean *huemul* deer (*Hippocamelus bisulcus*). In addition to working within a framework of ecological science, DTP land managers also engage in the bureaucratic review of actions taken by rangers. If rangers want to redesign, modify, or expand the trail system, they need the approval of the DTP, whose managers will weigh the benefits of increased tourism against the costs of greater environmental impacts. Moreover, the DTP reviews any conservation proposals submitted by domestic or foreign NGOs that would alter park infrastructure or ecosystems. Lastly, the DTP carries out its mission through public engagement. For land management policies to be viable, the DTP recognizes the need for it to engage with the different social groups that make up the communities abutting or living inside parks in creating sustainability guidelines. However, this means that communities can lodge objections and delay the implementation of sustainability plans desired by land managers. As a consequence, scientific sustainability is not an expert discourse generated exclusively by land managers. Instead, it emerges through complex interactions between scientists, park rangers, NGOs, and community residents, with the DTP having the final say. As a strategy of political rule, scientific sustainability draws upon an approach more commonly known as community-based conservation (CBC).

CBC is the final pillar of green productivism, alongside the alpine sublime and ecotourism. The APN has direct and sole control over its parks and exercises its ability to extract ground rents in the form of user fees charged to tourists and members of the commercial guiding sector. The APN has worked with local chambers of commerce to brand ecotourism destinations and improve the landscape in ways that mirror the expectations of the desired consumer group. These public-private collaborations have helped create a semiotic estate based on the capacity to monopolize territorial access to parks and the symbolic repertoires that have become associated with Patagonian nature. The APN has used this revenue to upgrade formerly agrarian landscapes and create more perfect images of alpine wilderness. Moreover, the APN has encouraged members of civil society—market and civic actors—to invest time, labor, and money in this collaborative project. CBC is the political approach taken by land managers, superintendents, and rangers to situate civil society action within the legal framework of scientific sustainability. Rather than acting as an autocratic bureaucracy, the APN seeks to incorporate local opinions, perspectives, and criticisms into building a regime of sustainability that is based on popular consent. For land managers or rangers to push too hard to implement stricter forms of sustainability is to risk losing local support.

Land management provides the first of two vantage points within a conservation state that focuses on thematizing risk through the politics of nature. Previous chapters have examined the green economy and risk society by paying attention to tourist consumption and service production. The conservation state works to integrate these disparate subject positions into a collective social charter related to risk exposure. As an expert discourse, scientific sustainability generates a public conservation subject position that includes community residents and NGOs as participants with conservation state actors such as park rangers and land managers. The scientific sustainability discourse attempts to define the interaction between the conservation state and civil society through shared

CBC values such as decentralization and grassroots democracy that structure local development. As actors engage in practices as varied as trekking tourism, professional guiding, hotel administration, and real estate investment, participants collectively work toward the goals of park conservation and the fostering of sustainable development. Public conservation is a subject position that land managers can expand or contract to include or exclude, respectively, any actors it deems beneficial or threatening to protected areas and ecotourism. The flexibility of this subject position is precisely what makes it so useful to land managers working to win public consent for park management plans. As these plans are revised and strengthened, boundary making plays a major role in framing sustainability. Land managers work to depict certain subjects as ecologically harmful and thus excluded from the public conservation subject position. As a result, the public conservation subject is premised on the mobilization of ecological risk to achieve the goal of creating a hegemonic front (Laclau 2007; Laclau and Mouffe 2014) of support for scientific sustainability. Land managers are not the only people who work to create public conservation subjects. NGOs and park rangers also labor to extend the hegemonic front that supports scientific sustainability through conservation practices.

THE NATIONAL POLITICS OF CBC

The pursuit of scientific sustainability by the conservation state first emerged during the 1990s. According to the APN:

> In 1996, with the creation of the Regional Technical Delegations, the National Parks Administration (APN) initiated a healthy process of decentralization. . . . And it contributed to the creation of spaces of cooperation with settlers, neighboring localities, provinces and conservationist NGOs, such as comanagement with the Mapuche communities in Lanin National Park or the Yungas Ecological Corridor. The current APN leadership seeks to strengthen these guidelines. Especially the integration of its park units with local, regional and national society through consensus-driven management, models of sustainable development that respect existing cultural diversity and the active participation of social actors, which guarantees as much its commitment to conservation of the natural and cultural patrimony as community control in decision making. (Administración de Parques Nacionales 2012, 16–17)

During the early 1990s, the APN embraced scientific sustainability by creating the regional technical delegations. In doing so, the APN sought to "professionalize" its administration of conservation—as one land manager put it—by employing scientists to oversee and systematize the execution of environmental governance across disparate ranger stations and parks. The APN also sought to decentralize power on two key fronts. First, the regional technical delegations represented the devolution of power away from the APN executive body in Buenos Aires. Second, the new model of sustainability required land managers to engage in a "consensus-driven" type of park management that created "spaces of coopera-tion" and the "active participation" of local partners. This form of community-based politics represented yet another level of decentralization that sought to incorporate local actors into a framework for integrating conservation and development.

The national embrace of scientific sustainability based on community partici-pation mirrored wider trends in global conservation (Walley 2004; Honey 2008; Brockington, Duffy, and Igoe 2010). As Arun Agrawal notes, the shift within global environmental governance from state-centric to community-based mod-els has been linked to "neoliberal politics" (2010, 200).[1] Agrawal's point is that CBC shifts the responsibility for environmental governance from the state to nonstate actors such as local communities, for-profit companies, and environmen-tal NGOs, which mirrored neoliberal aims to downsize the state and decentralize power, thereby eliminating obstacles to better democracy, good governance, and more robust market growth. Though often associated with neoliberal politics, CBC is—I contend—a pliable political strategy that regimes of diverse ideologi-cal stances can implement. CBC is one of the contingent strategies of political rule that the administrations of Presidents Néstor Kirchner and Cristina Fernán-dez de Kirchner have adopted and employed across the federal bureaucracy to achieve the broader goals of neo-developmentalism, build electoral coalitions, and promote the legitimacy of their version of post-neoliberal politics.[2] Argen-tine post-neoliberal conservation thus involves a combination of elements—ecotourism, CBC, and the alpine sublime—that are operationalized under the flag of Kirchnerismo.

The APN's embrace of CBC has intersected with an institutional commit-ment to democracy in the postauthoritarian period.[3] The APN underwent a process of democratization following the end of Argentina's last military dicta-torship (1976–1983) that sought to transcend past associations with centralized, autocratic rule. APN officials note: "With the return of democracy, the reigning ultra-protectionism gave way to a more integral vision. Under this influence, conservation units stopped being perceived as mere refuges for threatened species or opportunities to come into contact with nature. Rising to the top was their condition as genetic banks, guarantees of essential processes for quality of life and economic development, fruitful fields for scientific investigation and labora-tories for productive sustainable models. In this way, the parks became reacquainted with the hungers and desires of their human environment" (Administración de Parques Nacionales 2012, 16). Rejecting "ultra-protectionism," the APN has empha-sized democratic forms of sustainable development grounded in the "human" context of its protected areas, recognizing the need to link parks to economic development and quality-of-life measures for surrounding communities. This democratization ideology has constructed an APN past tied to authoritarian values and a present grounded in openness, dialogue, and socioeconomic improvement. Though nourished by the decentralizing ideology of global neoliberalism during the 1990s, CBC has provided Kirchner and Fernández with a form of ecopolitical rule identified globally with democratic accountability and good governance.[4] The APN has embraced the opening of parks to communities to promote jobs and economic growth, recasting itself as a progressive state agency devoted to social justice that is consistent with environmental care. However, it is important to examine the divergence between CBC ideology and practice. To what extent have El Chaltén's residents gained political and economic access to park resources? How far has the APN gone in devolving power to communities?

LAND MANAGERS AND THE 1997 PNLG MANAGEMENT PLAN

Rather than relying on park superintendents and staff members at individual ranger stations to craft a patchwork of idiosyncratic regulations, during the 1990s the newly created DTP took the lead in standardizing conservation efforts. The DTP began the task of creating a scientific management plan for each protected area in Patagonia, with each plan outlining: the existing knowledge of natural and cultural resources; problems facing conservation efforts; and opportunities that existed for public use by tourists, entrepreneurs, and nearby communities. In 1997, land managers published the *Plan Preliminar de Manejo, Parque Nacional Los Glaciares* (PMLG; Preliminary Management Plan for Glaciers National Park). Though infrequently visiting El Chaltén and the SLV ranger station, land managers played a significant role in establishing the social and legal order that shaped the green economy. The PMLG recast many of the existing social uses of the park into the authorizing language of science, while also working to eliminate a segment of practices identified with serious ecological harm. Soliciting input from elected officials, town leaders, entrepreneurs, and rangers from El Calafate and El Chaltén during the 1990s, the DTP used the planning process to build public consent for a specific kind of conservation framework. This form of environmental governance used the democratic approval of a majority of key economic and political actors to isolate and condemn a minority devoted to a type of livelihood viewed as antiquated. The PMLG linked scientific investigation and ecological knowledge to the spatial reorganization of the park in support of the nascent green economy.

　　As a scientific text, the PMLG catalogues existing academic knowledge related to the park and establishes a baseline or catalogue of existing ecological damage. The authors survey the geology, climate, flora, and fauna of the park, paying special attention to endangered species such as the condor, rhea, torrent duck, and the huemul deer. The plan then identifies past land use as the key source of ecological harm to be rectified. With respect to the northern zone of the park, the authors note: "The area exposed to the impacts of livestock, which at first glance might be considered relatively limited within the total exposure, represents in reality a highly elevated percentage of the protected area capable of being used for this end. Discounting the areas corresponding to the continental ice field, glaciers, lakes, and high semideserts, the area under pasturage is significantly large. Within the most strongly impacted zone one finds sectors with steppe and ecotonal [the transition zone between the steppe and Andean forest] character-istics, which are the most apt [ecologically appropriate] for this type of use" (Administración de Parques Nacionales 1997, 24).

The PMLG frames livestock farming as the principal factor generating severe erosion within the El Chaltén area. Beginning in the early twentieth century, settler-colonists had opened up the hills and mountain valleys for pasture by burning the forests, mirroring a widespread practice within Andean Patagonia on both sides of the border (Aagesen 2000; Klubock 2014). Equally problematic was the overuse of the fragile belts of vegetation existing in the steppe. The APN had passed a resolution in 1983 to exclude livestock entirely from the northern sector, but this rule had been unevenly enforced (Administración de Parques Nacionales 2004, 19). However, the SLV rangers had made some progress, so that by the time of the plan's publication in 1997, they had largely removed cattle from the touristic zone of the trail system, though herding continued in more marginal areas. Recognizing this enforcement failure, the plan envisions a future in which park authorities have remedied the massive erosion associated with estancieros and their herds. Treating livestock farming as an irrational prac-tice of the past, the plan advocates for sustainable tourism as a way to ensure the future integrity of the park. The interplay of ecological risk and security is central to the genre of park management plans as scientific texts.

The PMLG posits zoning as the key to ensuring that tourism is sustainable. Against the backdrop of livestock farming, the plan defines sustainable develop-ment as "new economic activities or forms of production tending to minimize negative environmental effects" while ensuring the "betterment of the quality of life of the population" (Administración de Parques Nacionales 1997, 48). High-lighting tourism as a sustainable economic activity, land managers recognize that improving the quality of life of communities like El Chaltén will generate the public legitimacy needed for the new types of policing and regulation. To improve the community's quality of life while defending the environment, man-agers advance the spatial zoning of the PNLG for different uses. The authors divide the park into four principal categories of use: "intangible zones," where only scientific research is permitted; "extensive public use zones," where tourists, trails, and campgrounds are permitted; "intensive public use zones," where hotels, restaurants, and other types of infrastructure can be created; and "natural resource exploitation zones," where livestock farming in a way that "guarantees the sustainable use of natural resources, [and] the protection of genetic material" is permitted (44–45). The zoning map presented in the plan provides one small site for sustainable livestock farming and a large intangible zone to protect the endangered huemul deer. The map also maximizes extensive use zones and concentrates intensive use within El Chaltén. Implicit in the proportion between extensive use and intensive use zones is a preservationist aesthetic supported by land managers, rangers, and residents (see chapter 7). Many residents sought to limit development of any kind inside the park, instead locating any infrastructure within the village. Rather than finding hostels or restaurants along the trail system as in Chile's Torres del Paine National Park, the aesthetic of the PNLG promoted the ideal of the park as a pristine wilderness untouched by humans. The plan helped codify the preservationist aesthetic with its zoning map, banning the future creation of hotels, highways, or kiosks in a space devoted to adventure trekking. Of course, national politicians had the power to override, change, or neglect the legal boundaries of the green economy.

A sustainable future for El Chaltén and the PNLG based on tourism emerges against the backdrop of long-standing political efforts to constitute livestock farming as a threat. Since the park's creation in 1937, conservation state authorities had advanced the goal of supplanting livestock pasture with an alpine landscape geared to appeal to international tourists. However, the political work of tying ecological risk to farming avoids or minimizes a number of key harms associated with tourism. El Chaltén is a village governed by provincial law that is outside the jurisdiction of the APN. As an ecotourism hub, the pueblo continues to struggle with pollution resulting from inadequate waste and water treatment facilities, as well as electricity generation. Urbanization continues, but its environmental effects undermine the conceit of scientific sustainability presented by the PMLG. Indeed, the plan fails to consider how massifying tourism would lead to more forest fires, greater disruption to ecosystems, and increased water contamination inside the park, and additional greenhouse gas emissions stemming from air travel.

Moreover, this scientific discourse works to construct a public conservation subject based on inclusion or exclusion from the new green economy. The PMLG remains quite vague about who belongs to the sustainable tourism industry. However, the plan is very specific about which social actors do not belong: the estancieros and paisanos associated with massive deforestation, soil erosion, the overgrazing of livestock, and ongoing desertification of the fragile steppe. Having defined those who are excluded, the plan implies who does belong: the rangers, service workers, entrepreneurs, trekkers, mountaineers, and others working to create El Chaltén as an ecotourism destination. Simply put, sustainability science advances culturally specific notions of risk and security that construct the social and legal parameters of the green economy, defining who belongs and who does not, which threats are most pressing, and which can be ignored.

LAND MANAGERS AND THE 2004 EL CHALTÉN *AUDITORÍA*

Claudio Chehébar invited me into his office at the DTP in the northern Patagonian city of Bariloche. Months earlier I had met him, the president of the DTP, at the ranger station in El Chaltén, where he was checking in with the Sustainable Trails Project NGO (STP), which had been authorized to begin repair work on a severely eroded path to Monte Fitz Roy. I had recently worked with the NGO and discussed with Claudio some of the progress the STP had made. Having spent much of his career at the DTP, Claudio had led field research in El Chaltén during the late 1990s and early 2000s to create the second management plan for the zone. The *Auditoría Ambiental* (environmental audit) was published in 2004. Building on the framework of the PMLG, the *Auditoría* added much needed substance about scientific sustainability, while attempting to enlist residents in new ways of relating to the environment.

The *Auditoría* identified El Chaltén and the PNLG as having arrived at a crossroads in the development of the green economy:

> We believe that we find ourselves at a genuine point of inflection given that we are in the middle of a very important growth in the magnitude of use, and at the same time—even while there are significant and grave environmental damages in some sectors and points—there is still time to avoid the worsening and expansion of these environmental impacts until they become irreversible. Like at every point of inflection, one can foresee two possible future trajectories: if one does not act rapidly and decisively the area—and in particular its spectacular attractions—could pass into a state of grave deterioration, more generalized and difficult to reverse; but if one takes some key rapid and decisive measures for the management of the area one can manage it sustainably. (Administración de Parques Nacionales 2004, 80)

The authors presciently anticipated the ecotourism boom that had begun under President Kirchner. Much like the PMLG, the *Auditoría* established a set of possible futures for park and pueblo contingent upon the preventive actions taken by land managers, rangers, and residents. Having demonstrated the pressing need for radical action to avoid an unsustainable future, the authors then documented the existing baseline of ecological harm: the expansion of unauthorized campgrounds and trails, the lack of effective policing and regulation of the commercial sector, the degradation of the trail system by horses, the accelerating growth in the numbers of tourists, and limited funding to hire more rangers. Advancing a discourse of ecological risk associated with specific aspects of the tourism industry and the conservation state, the *Auditoría* established a new set of rules and regulatory expectations to ensure the park's scientific sustainability. The *Auditoría* recognized that the green economy had given birth to its own set of threats.

The *Auditoría* advanced a particular understanding of state–civil society relationships based on CBC. In Argentina, CBC has resulted in different types of institutional relationships. In some parks, like Lanin and Nahuel Huapi, the APN has instituted a comanagement system that grants political authority and formal voting power to indigenous Mapuche communities (Martín and Chehébar 2001; Miniconi and Guyot 2010). In other parks, the APN has declined to grant residents the power to vote on land management decisions. In general, however, the APN has emphasized an ideological commitment to becoming an open institution that transcended the "ultra-protectionism" of the past. When we met in his office in Bariloche, Claudio remarked: "The first management plans were created with little participation. There was a different tradition among the technical teams, but also there was little interest among civil society in participating. Parks consulted very little, but also the involved sectors often were not interested. Today, though, it is obligatory for there to be participation in the management plans of new spaces because there is much more interest within civil society in participating." According to him, the strengthening of Argentine civil society has acted as a political check on the development of management plans. Opening up the planning process to the participation of the community alters the top-down bureaucratic style that many land managers initially used and requires direct engagement with civil-society actors to build the political consent needed to make key changes. Though this participatory impulse was rather weak during the 1990s, the DTP—and other regional technical delegations—soon shifted to a horizontal, inclusive model based on dialogue and a public forum for critique and revision. Under the Kirchner-Fernández administrations, the APN deepened its commitments to this participatory democratic approach. Despite accusations of authoritarianism and unilateralism in the media and from opposition political parties, the Kirchnerist administrations—at least through the governance style taken by the conservation state—have displayed their sensitivity to majority consent, public engagement, and grassroots democracy.

Prior to the publication of the *Auditoría*, land managers spent much of their time building a political coalition of civil-society actors to back the new set of regulations. Given that some rules negatively affected certain actors, the strategy was to build a majority coalition that legitimized the regulations in spite of minority dissent. Claudio discussed the fieldwork that he and his team had conducted before finalizing the *Auditoría*. One example he gave was the rule to eliminate the use of horses:

> I think we did three campaigns in the area, each between one week and ten days [long]. We walked all the trails except for the *Vuelta de Hielo* [icecap traverse].... But together with the rangers in the area we walked all the other trails, and we had many meetings with the personnel of the national park service ... hours and hours and hours of maté. And also with the guides. I'm not sure if with all the guides, but with many, and a lot of time with the *prestadores* [owners of commercial guiding companies], with the businesses. And all the ones that manage the horses, with Don Rodolfo [Asturias] and the others. We made rough drafts over two or three years. We began to gather information. We circulated the drafts to the personnel of the national park service.... They discussed the drafts among themselves, and finally we had a final draft.... [We also had] a workshop with the guides and prestadores, because they are the main actors. This workshop was to discuss the *Auditoría* and generate agreement. Everyone was there: Patagonia Salvaje, Cerro Torre Expediciones, the guides. They talked for two hours, and we were almost all in agreement to eliminate horseback riding and cargo transport.... [Then we] opened it up for public comments for thirty days. It was advertised in Chaltén and sent to all the businesses in town, saying that anyone who wanted to read, criticize, and give feedback could. We received responses largely from guides and prestadores. In general the opinions were positive in the sense that they agreed with what we were doing, and this was a relief for us. It was a radical change to take out the horses, and so it emerged that we were all in agreement. After the public criticism we sent it [the *Auditoría*] to Buenos Aires for approval.

Creating the *Auditoría* involved an enormous amount of face-to-face politicking, which for Claudio required input from rangers, guides, guiding company owners, cargo transport businesses, the Cámara de Comercio, and residents at large. These interactions were the context for the creation of a public conservation subject position that bound state and nonstate actors together based on a shared commitment to a new, stricter vision of the green economy. The rule to ban horses because of their erosive impact on the trail system affected the horseback riding companies, which had long transported visitors into the park. The rule also hit guiding companies, which relied on horses to transport visitors, gear, and food to the three commercial tourist camps located in the park. Implementing this ban forced horseback riding companies to develop tours outside the park, while guiding firms hired human porters and used the less-damaging alpaca to transport cargo. Opening up the draft of the *Auditoría* to the public at large, land managers targeted the main actors whose approval they needed: the guides and guiding company owners. Though representatives of the horseback riding businesses voiced significant dissent, they represented only a minority position. Here, the state-capital alliance controlling the semiotic estate comes into view. Without the backing of the guiding sector, the APN risked undermining the public-private alliance upon which the ecotourism industry depended. Claudio and other land managers spent a great deal of time convincing entrepreneurs that it was in their long-term interest to support stricter conservation efforts, particularly since this would attract higher-income tourists. Moreover, land managers helped bring into being a social charter that shifted diverse risk subject positions toward a shared understanding of sustainability and a collective sense of ecological risk and security.

Claudio's reflections on the process of building consent for the *Auditoría* also reveal the limits of CBC. Rather than a system of comanagement that incorporated community representatives into the conservation state as permanent voting members in the bureaucracy, the *Auditoría* granted Chaltenenses a consultative role in resource management. Because of Claudio's commitment to the spirit of CBC, residents exercised a rather robust veto over any proposed regulations but did not have any formal authority to push new regulations or roll back older rules. Under a new DTP president, however, things might be different. Though residents were granted no formal voting power in the bureaucracy, it is important to recognize the significant shift from a top-down command-and-control model to a consent-based model of governance that began during the neoliberal years of the administration of President Carlos Menem and was consolidated under the post-neoliberal regimes of Kirchner and Fernández. At least in the realm of conservation, both the center-right and the center-left wings of the Partido Justicialista embraced the shift toward decentralized, federalized power that valorized the growing importance of civil-society forces. In El Chaltén, this process of face-to-face politicking led by Claudio became for many residents a prime example of the Argentine state at its best: soliciting the public for input to create democratic legitimacy for new forms of regulation. Rather than the ambiguous governance later associated with the Instituto Nacional de Estadística y Censos (INDEC; the National Census and Statistics Institution of Argentina) and the manipulation of national statistics, the *Auditoría* offered a model of good governance based on the clear delineation of new rules, a public forum for voicing criticisms, and a long-term process of consultation to generate a hegemonic front for stricter sustainability. Though most residents reacted positively to the writing of the *Auditoría* in the early 2000s, the situation was quite different by the late 2000s following the Great Recession, when SLV rangers faced a lack of public confidence (see chapter 6). Residents then experienced the growing strength of the conservation state as a potential threat to their livelihoods and as an abrogation of the collective agreement forged by Claudio in the early 2000s.

CIVIL-SOCIETY PARTICIPATION
AND THE SUSTAINABLE TRAILS PROJECT

Civil-society actors in El Chaltén have the opportunity to promote scientific sustainability as defined by the 1997 PMLG and improved upon in the 2004 *Auditoría*. Land managers and rangers encourage residents to respect the zoning policies and regulations of the park, which prohibit hunting, fuel extraction, the use of horses, and any types of commercial activity not authorized by the APN. Residents are individually entreated to become environmentally conscious subjects and participants in public conservation, along with rangers and managers. Beyond this, the APN encourages residents to join NGOs, volunteering time, effort, and labor not just to promote El Chaltén as a tourist destination but also to protect the environment. Some of these NGO actions might occur outside the park, in the form of recycling campaigns, political efforts to challenge development projects like hydroelectric dams, or educational initiatives to raise consciousness about endangered species. Other NGO actions could take place inside the park, including activities related to park maintenance and biodiversity protection to ensure scientific sustainability. If NGOs seek to work inside the park on public conservation initiatives that alter the landscape or affect ecosystems, their plans have to pass bureaucratic review by the DTP.

Created and led by Rolando Garibotti, the STP was the one international NGO that operated in El Chaltén from 2008 to 2010. At the time, there were various civil-society organizations—such as a bird conservation group, the Club Andino mountaineering association, and the Cámara de Comercio—whose members were local residents. The STP was unique insofar as it brought to El Chaltén a small group of Americans who worked for the U.S. Park Service on trail crews. These Americans worked collaboratively with a volunteer group of Argentine climbers. Created to help restore a section of the severely-eroded trail leading to Laguna de los Tres at the base of Monte Fitz Roy, the STP emerged through the connections that Rolando had to U.S. climbers, alpinist organizations, and outdoor corporations. During the 1990s, Rolando had left Argentina and moved to the United States to work as a professional guide. He became friends with Yvon Chouinard, the founder of Patagonia, Inc. Rolando pitched the idea of the STP to Chouinard, who had long taken an interest in conservation work in Andean Patagonia and agreed to fund the project (Chouinard 2006). The American Alpine Club became the primary legal entity that distributed the funding and administered the project.

The STP then had to gain the APN's approval and the imprimatur of scientific sustainability. Any modifications made to the trail system in El Chaltén had to pass muster with the DTP. To gain the APN's approval, Rolando first hired a U.S. trail expert to prepare a scientific assessment of the erosion issue as a way to frame the remediation plan. After receiving the expert's report, Rolando created a master plan for repairing the Laguna de los Tres trail, which was submitted to the DTP for approval. Expanding upon language in the *Auditoría*, the STP identified the Laguna de los Tres trail as an unsustainable path likely to lead to more ecological harm. Rolando then used his contacts at Grand Teton National Park to attract volunteers, especially crew leaders. In addition to paying their travel and living expenses, he guaranteed that they would periodically have time off to go climbing, a condition that Chouinard made when he promised funding.

The volunteer work of the STP was concentrated primarily into two six-week intervals of intense trailwork—one period in late 2008 and the other in late 2009. Rolando had hoped that the SLV ranger station would supply additional workers, but this initially happened only on a very inconsistent basis. During the first work period, a core group of a dozen volunteers redesigned sections of the path to Laguna de los Tres. This included building raised pathways, constructing bridges, moving boulders, and gathering raw materials to engineer a trail that would be protected from the harsh weather. During the second and final period, team members picked up where they had left off the previous year and sought to complete the restoration of this key trekking artery that doubled as a pathway for alpinists to access the routes on Fitz Roy and adjacent peaks.

Rolando conceived of the STP as an international climber-led initiative that demonstrated the conservationist bona fides of the mountaineering community. He hoped that the project would inspire not just local climbers, but residents more broadly to contribute volunteer time and effort to the park, expanding the scope of civil-society involvement. In this capacity, the STP worked to incorporate residents into a public conservation subject position that advanced scientific sustainability. In the final year of the project, however, Rolando expressed disappointment at the lack of interest among local climbers and guides, many of whom he considered friends or acquaintances. Though their livelihoods relied on functional trails, guides had failed to recognize their duty—Rolando argued—to give back to the park as a public resource shared by the entire community.

Though framed as a "gift" (Mauss 1967; Godbout and Caillé 2000) of goodwill from climbers to the APN, the conservation work by the STP had a political motivation. As the unofficial leader of the Patagonian mountaineering community, Rolando had spent years working as an activist to challenge any park regulations that threatened climbers' access to the mountains. He had long cultivated allies within the APN, especially among local rangers and the DTP in Bariloche. Rolando understood that the APN had the legal authority to eliminate the access of mountaineers to any climbing zones in Argentina, implement a bevy of new restrictions, or charge user fees. Years earlier, he had successfully challenged a decision made by the DTP to implement climbing fees in El Chaltén to pay for costly rescue services in the backcountry.[5] Though not ideologically opposed to paying fees, Rolando argued that this move inadvertently made the national park service liable for performing rescues, exposing the agency to potential lawsuits down the road. Instead, he argued that the service should retain the current approach of considering trips into the backcountry as being "at your own risk" and using a largely volunteer search-and-rescue team. He enlisted the support of mountaineering clubs to fight a rule that ultimately was never enforced. Clearly understanding the power that the APN had over alpinists, Rolando initiated the STP as a way to build political goodwill with the national park service.

The STP's conservation initiative advanced the APN's hegemonic vision for scientific sustainability and CBC. The STP represented a visible contribution by a community group—climbers—to advance the vision outlined in APN management plans by tapping into foreign funding and international connections. Claudio jokingly referred to Rolando as "Saint Garibotti" in acknowledgment of his efforts to help the APN with the problem of trail degradation that pertained to parks across the region, not just the PNLG. Indeed, regional and local actors within the APN—Claudio, Carlos Corvalán (then superintendent of the PNLG), and rangers in El Chaltén—recognized the value of the gift offered by Rolando on behalf of the climbing community. How and when, if ever, this goodwill might be matched by a counter-gift from the APN remained to be seen. Most immediately, however, the STP became a model for civil-society participation and drew political attention to the unsustainable conditions of the trail system in the trekking capital of Argentina. Despite the relatively short life of its conservation work in the PNLG, the STP had a number of key implications for the ongoing development of the APN. In addition to modeling civil-society participation within CBC, the STP identified the important ecological harm that unsustainable trails could cause, which prompted institutional action by the APN through the efforts of one ranger, Ernesto De Angelis, the maintenance chief of the SLV ranger station.

RANGER PARTICIPATION AND THE *BRIGADA DE SENDEROS*

Ernesto De Angelis stood outside the U.S. Embassy in Buenos Aires. There was a long line of well-dressed Argentines who were waiting to apply for tourist visas. Ernesto wore his ranger uniform and carried an envelope with a letter of invitation from the U.S. Park Service. He had stopped by the central administrative office in Buenos Aires to meet with the APN president and finalize his leave to go to the United States. Ernesto's interview at the embassy to get a visa went smoothly, though it began with a hiccup when someone inadvertently walked off with his envelope when Ernesto was going through a security checkpoint. He was soon on his way to Gringolandia, as residents of El Chaltén refer to the United States. Ernesto flew to Salt Lake City, drove up to Jackson Hole, and began a two-month residency at Grand Teton National Park, where he worked alongside some of the Americans who had participated in the STP. During this time, Ernesto learned how to design and maintain trails, bridges, and causeways suited

FIGURE 5.1. Trail restoration by SLV park rangers (photo by author)

to particular environmental conditions. The course anchored these tactics within a land management approach dedicated to minimizing ecological impacts, using local materials, and designing structures to aesthetically harmonize with the surrounding landscape. Following this period of study, Ernesto returned to El Chaltén for the beginning of the 2009–2010 season.

The STP had inspired Ernesto to go to the United States. As maintenance chief of the SLV ranger station, Ernesto had duties that ranged from being an auto mechanic to repairing trails. The 1997 and 2004 park management plans had successfully established a spatial zoning system, including a master plan for primary and secondary trails. However, rangers' attempts to implement this plan always ran up against the limited funds for hiring more personnel. Ernesto had a handful of *brigadistas* (seasonal rangers) at his disposal to help out with trail repair (see Figure 5.1), but the lion's share of the labor power came from volunteers. Each season, more than a dozen people—mostly Argentines, with some foreigners—signed up to volunteer for a month in El Chaltén. Like permanent and seasonal rangers, volunteers rotated through a list of jobs that included patrolling and giving environmental education talks at the visitors' center, but they spent one-third to one-half of the month on trail repair. Recognizing the limitations of his knowledge about trail work, Ernesto took the opportunity presented by the STP to begin to acquire expertise. Noting Ernesto's growing interest, Adam Gillespie (one of the American volunteers) offered to host him at Grand Teton and get him a letter of invitation to come train in the United States. However, Ernesto had to convince the APN leadership—all the way up the chain of command—to allow him to take time off. He was skeptical about his chances, particularly as Argentina slid into a recession.

Park rangers participate in the discourse of scientific sustainability and the formation of the public conservation subject position along with land managers, NGOs, and community residents. Rangers enforce the sustainability guidelines in park management plans, while engaging tourists and residents as participants in conservation. For land managers like Claudio, rangers are another political constituency whose members must agree to any new management plan and the ongoing refinement of these "living documents"—to appropriate a phrase from constitutional jurisprudence. A management plan continues to evolve as a superintendent issues new decrees and rangers allocate their funding, labor power, and time to prioritize certain goals over others. Moreover, rangers can use the discourse of scientific sustainability to scale up a claim about ecological harm beyond the level of the ranger station or the park superintendent to the attention of land managers or even APN executives.

Ernesto recognized that the trail system in El Chaltén was plagued by a set of conditions that caused it to be unsustainable and had the capacity to disincentivize tourist visitation. Reflecting on his years of experience as the SLV maintenance chief, Ernesto said:

> There's a trail system inside the park, and this trail system has trails forming a main branch, as it's called, [and] a secondary branch, and the backcountry.... Both of the principal trails, [to Monte] Fitz Roy and [Cerro] Torre, have involved tons of work over five or six years. It's not enough, because of the type of soil we have and the number of visitors that come. The work isn't sufficient for the trails to have a controlled or sustainable life over time. Year after year you note the erosion of the trails—trails that five years ago had a width of 35–40 centimeters and a depth of 5 centimeters now have a width of 1.0–1.5 meters and a depth of some 20 centimeters. In only four years. The forecast is that people will not only continue coming, but [that] more of them [will come] each year. But the quantity of people coming isn't proportional to the quantity of work that occurs with respect to trails.... For us, operationally, within the national park service it's not complex work we're doing because there are so many necessities. Massive amounts of work are generated, and you do good work—but when you see all the work that's left, it's demotivating. You don't see a grand evolution, but only small things in a place that's collapsing in on itself. And I think if this place continues to grow without certain measures, it's counterproductive because the people who come to visit and camp for one night and don't have a good quality of visit—this person will not incentivize more people to visit this place, and that undermines the economic activities of this place. Thinking about the maintenance of this place is thinking about the sustainability of the investments that people make, and in the place itself. It's thinking about it all, but today there does not exist the necessary

amount of resources, and there aren't enough effective measures to appropriately control this place.

Ernesto's statement draws attention to the interconnected problems of soil type, climate, erosion, and the growing tourist traffic generated by green productivism. He highlights the work that rangers need to perform to maintain the ecological and infrastructural conditions necessary for capital accumulation to occur, for either tourism entrepreneurs or the park service. This is not happening, however, in a park "that's collapsing in on itself." Though verging on hyperbole, his statement reveals the deep sense of frustration felt by rangers who see tourists' numbers multiplying every year and public investment growing but still struggling to keep up. Public investment in the trail system thus becomes a key way to move beyond a reactionary situation for rangers toward a "grand evolution" that secures the park environment in a way that facilitates green economic growth.

Employing this narrative, Ernesto sought to bring the ecological and economic harms of unsustainable trails in El Chaltén to the attention of his superiors. The series of arguments that he made to the SLV station director, the PNLG superintendent, the DTP president, and the APN president took the form of emphasizing the integral role of a sound trail system in park and community development. According to Ernesto, a failure to address the mounting problems of trail erosion—quite visible in major parks throughout Andean Patagonia—placed an upper limit on the capacity of the APN to encourage more tourists to visit. As a rentier state institution, the APN sought to capture increasing rents to fund greater public investment in key tourism parks, as well as to subsidize the operations of those protected areas in the federal system that received few visitors. As a state agency, the APN had experienced significant growth in previous years, but to maintain or expand existing levels of development, it needed to invest in a pilot project that he, Ernesto, would direct. Ernesto requested funds to pay for his travel expenses for two summers, as well as to create a small *brigada de senderos* (trail crew) in El Chaltén. Ernesto would gain trail work expertise in the United States and then train a group of brigadistas who would specialize entirely in trail maintenance. The eventual goal was to build a national trail brigade that could operate in key trekking parks. It greatly helped his argument that the STP had had a successful first year of operation, which had attracted interest from national APN officials. The proposed pilot project struck a chord with the leadership, which granted approval for Ernesto to train in Grand Teton and implement the pilot in El Chaltén.

As the STP ended its two-year effort to restore the Laguna de los Tres trail, Ernesto took control of the newly formed brigada de senderos. Though his efforts to inspire civil-society actors to become conservation volunteers had been limited, Rolando's major success was in building the transnational network that enabled Ernesto to create the brigada, thereby institutionalizing his vision within the conservation state. Ernesto returned to Grand Teton in 2010 to complete his training and visit ŞTP friends at Zion and Grand Canyon National Parks. Following his course work, he hired a small group of Chaltenenses to become the founding class of the brigada. Rather than relying on untrained volunteers, Ernesto began to develop a highly skilled crew devoted entirely to trail conservation.

SCIENTIFIC SUSTAINABILITY

Scientific sustainability emerges across the interactional space that links land managers, park rangers, NGOs, and residents together as subjects acting to promote public conservation and fashioning a social charter attentive to their collective risk exposure. Backed by APN institutional authority, DTP land managers occupy a central role in defining sustainable development in the PNLG through scientific investigation, the production and revision of management documents, the bureaucratic review of projects that affect park ecosystems, and the public engagement of local communities. Land managers work to win consent for management plans that define the social and legal parameters of the green economy, putting together a hegemonic front to counter the resistance or objections of social groups engaging in economic activities that are defined as ecologically harmful. DTP scientists then work with rangers and civil-society actors—residents, civic groups, and even international NGOs—to promote conservation projects like trail restoration that advance the goal of sustainable ecotourism. In the process, the conservation state validates specific discourses of ecological risk and security to promote these projects or plans. While entrepreneurial capital has consolidated power over the tourism industry inside the confines of the pueblo, scientists and rangers control the politics of nature through an encompassing environmental protection framework that governs the pueblo-park relationship. Through the formulation of park management plans and public conservation work, land managers and rangers collaborate with entrepreneurial capital to maintain the public-private alliance over the semiotic estate. Moreover, the APN has worked to invest public resources—and support private investment by NGOs and foreign corporations—in park infrastructure that helps foster growing ecotourism. These state–civil society alliances contribute to the growing power of the conservation state.

Green productivism has utilized CBC as a strategy of political rule to generate legitimacy for ecotourism-led development. Anchored in center-left populism, the Kirchner-Fernández regimes communicated their support for decentralized governance, grassroots democracy, civil society inclusion, and participatory development through CBC. Through the actions of land managers, CBC works to construct a division between ecologically beneficial and harmful practices.

This fashions a public conservation majority through the condemnation of a minority. As the discourse of scientific sustainability changes over the years, the APN expands (or contracts) the boundaries of inclusion (or exclusion) with respect to the popular majority (or minority) position. However, sustainability politics rarely invites open antagonism toward those in the minority position, who are seen as promoting ecologically harmful practices. Through building a hegemonic front of consent, the APN works to construct a sense of political power originating with the populace, rather than emanating autocratically in a top-down fashion from Buenos Aires. Instead, midlevel scientists in the state bureaucracy become the public's key interlocutors.

CBC works to legitimate a procapitalist agenda based on the expanding strength of both the conservation state and entrepreneurial capital. This political strategy works not to diffuse or diminish risk within the community, but rather to amplify particular understandings of risk and security. The winning of consent occurs through expert discourses of risk and security that fashion a social charter conducive to the political aims of the conservation state. With respect to the Kirchners, in the realm of the green economy post-neoliberal political rule has involved the construction of popular environmental fronts that facilitate the green productivist agenda. In villages like El Chaltén, these popular environmental fronts have taken root as the binational Andean Patagonian region has tilted sharply toward green development (Mendoza et al. 2017). In large cities like Bariloche, these fronts have had far less impact on entire populations, involving instead only a set of key actors: local politicians, NGOs, the tourism industry, and the conservation state. Whether in villages or cities, though, popular fronts endeavor to build consensus for modes of scientific sustainability that facilitate expanding capital accumulation to benefit industry and the state.

6 · CONSERVATION POLICING
Education and Environmental Impacts

The Seccional Lago Viedma (SLV) ranger station has authority over the forests, glaciers, visitors, and commercial activity in the northern section of Parque Nacional Los Glaciares (PNLG). Roughly two dozen rangers work in El Chaltén during the tourism season, a number that shrinks by more than half during the winter. The station is staffed by full rangers, assistant rangers, brigadistas, and administrative staff members.[1] Supplemented by volunteers who sign up for one-month stints during the summer, the ranger corps implements park management plans like the *Auditoría Ambiental* (Administración de Parques Nacionales 2004) and works to create public conservation subjects. Prior to the 1990s, the SLV station had just two rangers. With the growth of ecotourism, the PNLG superintendent has increased the public financing of the station to hire more personnel, buy equipment, and invest in park infrastructure. Rangers engage in conservation policing: educational, punitive, and security-making practices to enforce environmental regulations and sustainable development protocols. To do so, rangers repair trails, lead search and rescue operations, fight forest fires, patrol the trail system, regulate tours, and educate tourists. With formal employment status as part of the unionized public sector, rangers are considered members of the local middle class. Many rangers have applied for land grants to build homes and become formally recognized citizens of El Chaltén. For golondrinas, the National Parks Administration of Argentina (Administración de Parques Nacionales, or APN) offers another route—beyond becoming an entrepreneur—to secure formal laboring status, though only a few positions open up every year.

The 2008–2010 tourism seasons represented a nadir in the park-pueblo relationship. Not only did Chaltenenses begin to realize that the ecotourism boom was over, but a climate of public mistrust regarding the ranger corps prevailed in many quarters. Over the previous decade, rangers had steadily tightened park regulations and denied the public access to resources, such as pastures for cattle and firewood, and the commercial use of horses. The SLV director had implemented a system of permits to monitor the commercial guiding sector more closely.

With the onset of the global financial crisis, Chaltenenses became fearful of what new measures the APN might introduce. Rumors began to circulate about the impending closure of private commercial campgrounds inside the park. Such a move would destroy the livelihoods and investments of many people. The very success of green productivism in El Chaltén had affected not only the eco-tourism industry, but also the conservation state. Able to capture greater sources of revenue, the conservation state had increased its institutional power and capacity to regulate the national park more strictly. This generated public criticism about the APN, which was viewed as crypto-authoritarian.

Rangers provide the second point of entry into understanding the conservation state and the politics of nature, adding to the above discussion of land management. Ranger subjectivity arises through the attempt to implement sustainability plans inside the park and police visitors, the commercial guiding sector, and pueblo residents. Rangers thematize their risk positionality through the attempt to mitigate the environmental impacts generated by tourists, the tour industry, and residents in general. In the face of these hazards, rangers have developed the ideology of educational policing. Shaped by community-based conservation (CBC) values, educational policing has privileged the educating of tourists and the public, while attempting to minimize the use of coercive force. Educational policing is a way for rangers to embrace the democratizing reforms made by the APN to move beyond its legacy of militaristic values and association with the armed forces. Though focused on community partnership, SLV rangers have implemented educational policing in ways that prioritize the tourist population rather than local residents. After I discuss the political culture of the conservation state, I examine ranger risk subjectivity and educational policing through interactions with tourists, guiding companies, and Chaltenenses.

THE POLITICAL CULTURE OF THE CONSERVATION STATE

Presidents Néstor Kirchner and Cristina Fernández de Kirchner have personified an Argentine double state defined by both a legitimate program of progressive reform and the illegitimate use of governmental power for personal gain. For Chaltenenses, corruption was not entirely a bad thing since they stood to benefit from the public works projects initiated by the Kirchners. "That's something that happens under every president," remarked Ernesto De Angelis. "It was the same under [President Carlos] Menem." Indeed, many residents spoke glowingly about sizable federal investments in completing the highway between El Calafate and El Chaltén, which greatly reduced the travel time for buses and cars. Nevertheless, the corruption of presidential power—according to residents—could equally hurt El Chaltén. Presidents could exert their power to create new towns that might compete with it, or they could act—through the APN—to curtail the access of residents to park resources. As difficulties mounted in the wake of the Great Recession, some entrepreneurs and workers began to voice concern about the corruption of the conservation state, which was linked to the ambiguous governance of los Kirchners. Residents strained to distinguish the legitimate practices from the illegitimate ones initiated by park rangers.

SLV rangers shared many of the residents' assumptions about the political culture of Kirchnerismo. Some rangers had voted for the Kirchners but viewed their administrations as much too focused on the economic development of park tourism and less concerned with conservation. The concession grab by Patagonia Salvaje (see chapter 3) greatly affected how rangers related to the APN as a whole. SLV rangers had nothing but praise for the land managers of the Delegación Técnica Regional de Patagonia (DTP; the Patagonian Regional Technical Delegation). However, many rangers expressed skepticism about Carlos Corvalán, the PNLG superintendent who was considered "very friendly" with los Kirchners.[2] At times, rangers regarded the APN leadership with extreme scorn. During the concession grab by Patagonia Salvaje, both SLV rangers and DTP land managers criticized the illegal action. However, APN officials overruled their opposition. The rangers never forgave the politically appointed leaders, viewing them as complicit in and symptomatic of the wider corruption associated with the Argentine state (Faulk 2013; Muir 2016). Rangers struggled to legitimately enact state power in spite of the perception of illegitimacy that plagued the APN.

Rangers strongly identified with the wave of democratic reform that affected the APN following the end of the military dictatorship.[3] Members of the national ranger corps had long been trained to use firearms and enforce conservation regulations in a militaristic fashion. In the 1990s and 2000s, ranger training instead emphasized a self-consciously lighter deployment of state power that viewed parks as biodiversity sanctuaries and economic resources for the surrounding communities. Marcela Barros, a retired SLV ranger, noted that whereas previous generations of rangers had viewed tourists as destructive agents, the more contemporary perspective recognized their positive dimensions. In Argentina, attracting domestic tourists became a political project that allowed the APN to build mass support for the national park system.

Along with democratization, the APN increasingly became a rentier state agency. Since the creation of the APN in 1934, its leaders have promoted international tourism (Bustillo 1999). The leaders' positive view of tourism has often clashed with the negative view of the rank-and-file rangers charged with policing parks. The shift toward a more positive perspective on tourism by the ranger corps that occurred during the 1990s facilitated the transformation of the APN into a state capitalist agency that increasingly welcomed tourists and extracted revenues from key parks in the federal system. Green productivism has accelerated this turn toward rent capture within the "green estate" of public protected areas.[4] As an autarkic entity, the APN keeps the revenues it extracts. Key parks like the PNLG are the vital drivers of capital accumulation in a system of graduated redistribution that subsidizes parks that have a high biodiversity value but are of less interest to tourists. In the PNLG, the southern zone of El Calafate is the sole site for collecting rents. A portion of this income is sent to El Chaltén to fund the operation of the SLV station. Indeed, access to the northern sector of the PNLG is free to the public, unlike access to the heavily commercialized southern portion. This rental income has allowed the SLV station to invest funds in hiring more rangers and improving park infrastructure. Rangers have made the landscape more suitable for trekking, thereby contributing to the place branding of El Chaltén. The growth of the Patagonian green economy thus has not only facilitated capital accumulation by tourism entrepreneurs but has also greatly strengthened the conservation state through the capturing of ground rents tied to the place value of ecotourism destinations.

CREATING ECOTOURISTS

Claudio Messi hears the first bus pull into the driveway outside the SLV ranger station. "They're here," he calls out to Veronica Auyero, who is checking the U.S. National Oceanic and Atmospheric Administration's weather report on the internet.[5] Claudio and Veronica set up the welcome sign at the entrance to the visitors' center and greet tourists as they enter, directing them to the appropriate rooms for the *charla* (informal talk) in English or Spanish. They pass out pocket-size pamphlets that contain essential information about the northern section of the PNLG: a map of the zone, a list of key destinations, the elevation gain and distance for specific hikes, and the rules of conservation.

Two dozen visitors file into the English-language room for a charla about park conservation and trekking options. As they wait for the talk to begin, tourists look at the exhibits that adorn the walls. One display discusses the history of exploration in the region by scientists and pioneers, while the second—and more prominent—depicts the history of alpinism. There are professional photographs of the major peaks, their significant routes, and the names of first ascenders. Next to these images is a dummy dressed in a helmet, crampons, and other climbing gear. In the corner is a television set where—particularly on rainy days—rangers play mountaineering videos for visitors that document landmark expeditions. The exhibits signal the centrality of alpinism in the local history of exploration, while positioning tourists within the symbolic space of outdoor adventure. In the adjacent room, there are displays that emphasize the history of environmental harm associated with wildfire and tourist disregard for nature, as well as the conservation norms developed by the park service to ensure sustainable interactions between visitors and wildlife. Images of native deer, mountain lions, condors, and foxes show tourists what fauna they might encounter.

Environmental education is an integral component of ranger conservation. In addition to the displays that adorn the walls of the visitors' center, the charla is the primary vehicle that rangers use to communicate environmental norms and construct visitors as ecotourists. Claudio and Veronica remain at the entrance, handing out more pamphlets as the second and third buses arrive and visitors file in. Claudio takes the English-language room and counts the number of visitors, later entering this figure in the logbook. Dressed in the signature tan and green uniform of the ranger corps, he makes his way to the front of the room and stands beside a large map of the trail system that is reproduced in the pamphlets each visitor now possesses. Greeting the tourists, who have just arrived from El Calafate, he launches into the standard twenty-minute talk that rangers—permanent, seasonal, and volunteer—are expected to give.

The first half of the charla orients visitors to the area and discusses the key aesthetic objects of the tourist gaze. Rangers face the significant challenge of having to manage a part of the park that is zoned as "open access," which means that as long as visitors fill out a permit and have the requisite competencies, they can hike anywhere they want, venturing off trails into forests and taking game paths. However, if visitors were to fan out evenly across the park, this would generate significant environmental impacts and raise public security issues for rangers. The charla works to circumscribe the possible trekking options that exist in the park, creating a list of must-see destinations that accord with information in popular guidebooks. After discussing where El Chaltén is located in Patagonia, Claudio says: "There are two major hiking trails and destinations in the park: the trail that goes up to Laguna Torre and the trail that goes up to Laguna de los Tres. At Laguna Torre, you will be able to see this [he points to Cerro Torre] and at Laguna de los Tres, you will have this amazing view [he points to Monte Fitz Roy]." Tourists nod eagerly in approval and whisper to their traveling companions. Claudio invites the trekkers to explore the alpine landscape and its sublime destinations while being cognizant of hazards such as dehydration, storms, exposure, injuries, and getting lost.

The second half of the charla forges environmental consciousness. Rangers recognize that many visitors have trekking backgrounds but are concerned about the growing number of tourists who have no experience. After highlighting the most aesthetically valuable destinations, rangers discuss the no deje rastro (leave no trace) rules of park conduct. These norms—including packing out trash, not lighting fires, and staying on the trails—provide explicit guidance for visitors who are framed narratively in the charla as the primary source of harm. "Do you see this photo?" Claudio asks as he points to the image of a charred forest. "This forest fire was caused by a careless hiker who tried to burn toilet paper after using it. Be careful! Please! Remember that fires are not allowed." Claudio goes down the list of prohibited activities to create an ideal, ecologically minded tourist who acts conscientiously in light of such knowledge, protecting the park—which became a UNESCO World Heritage Site in 1981.

The charla is a governance technique that attempts to create political subjects who abide by the no deje rastro rules. Marcela Barros, the retired ranger, remarked: "The charla . . . generates prior awareness about entering a protected area. And they [tourists] leave behind their crap. Because if you go into the park and find someone starting a fire or dropping garbage, you get angry because you know what you're not supposed to do. It's awareness. The charla signifies for this place the possibility of sustaining these resources, keeping this place clean and tidy. There's a very small set of people who don't follow the rules, which are not rules of repression but of coexistence, [especially] when you explain them to people beforehand." The charla aims to create ecotourists who regulate their conduct according to conservation norms that promote "coexistence" rather than "repression." The no deje rastro rules derive from the management practices for the global conservation of protected areas. The validity of conservation governance by SLV rangers, then, emerges in part from the broader field of ecological science (Ogden 2011; Martínez-Reyes 2016) that casts rangers as promoting sustainability in ways that mirror what happens in national park systems in North America and Europe. By framing park rules as in alignment with the best practices of global conservation, rangers work to legitimize their exercise of power.

The charla is a key marker of a ranger institutional culture devoted to public-private alliances. With the ongoing growth of tourism, rangers attribute their success to the charla, while recognizing that reliance upon this practice exposes them to the whims of tour bus companies. Rangers have spent years convincing bus company owners of the value and necessity of having their drivers stop at the visitors' center every time they come into town. Owners could decide to eliminate the stop, which often adds more than a half an hour to the trip, but rangers have enlisted the support of business leaders to apply pressure. Rangers view their efforts to create goodwill, rapport, and trust among drivers and owners as a tenuous state of affairs. Indeed, this type of public-private alliance building is integral to the promotion of sustainable ecotourism. The dominant arrangements surrounding ecotourism arise through the tedious, everyday efforts of the ranger corps to maintain the support of entrepreneurs for environmental education.

The charla also signifies a type of vocational work that engages tourists as positive agents of conservation. In an era of soaring visitation, rangers have poured enormous resources—the working hours of personnel and funds for the renovation of the station—into an educational project that views tourists as conservation advocates. Visitors act as potential political agents after returning home, advancing the mission of the APN to promote conservation values. "They spread the word about the value of the national park service in Argentina," noted Ernesto De Angelis. This perspective casts rangers as evangelists who help tourists connect spiritually with wilderness. Moreover, rangers work tirelessly to promote this message, often even on their days off and after hours. Indeed, most see their work as a vocation. Rangers thus construct the ecotourist as both a source of environmental impact and a participant in public conservation who helps promote sustainability.

After finishing his talk, Claudio fielded questions from a few visitors, while the rest left the station and boarded their buses. The drivers started their engines and beeped their horns to signal the last call for any stragglers. A couple of minutes later the station was empty of tourists and conspicuously quiet. Veronica, Claudio, and I shared a maté as we waited for the next wave of buses to arrive.

PATROLLING THE TRAILS

Ernesto dropped Elena Colorado and me off at the start of the trail to the Fitz Roy Valley. Every day, the SLV station sends at least one or two rangers out on patrol into the park. Rangers pack in first aid kits, handheld radios, and a stack of the pamphlets given out to tourists at the visitors' center. Rangers conceive of conservation policing as inhabiting a continuum between education and coercion, in which they attempt to maximize education and use force only as a last resort. The charla is a purely educational practice that seeks to construct the ecotourist through attunement to the no deje rastro rules. The *recorrida* (patrol) is an attempt to enforce the conservation norms outlined during the charla. With limited personnel, the rangers often police only one trail on any given day, relying on representatives of the commercial guiding sector and tourists to extend the reach of state regulations through self-policing.

Elena checked her backpack and tested the radio before we headed up the trail. Unlike hiking as a tourist, a recorrida involves walking slowly through the park, talking to visitors, checking the permits of guides, removing debris from the trail, monitoring radio communications for any accidents, and surveillance. The majority of the recorrida involves chatting with tourists—the intentional extension of the charla to the trail system. Rangers view the patrol as primarily a way of continuing to educate visitors about conservation norms, as well as ensuring public safety. On the first leg of our hike to Laguna Capri, Elena stopped and talked with five groups of hikers, asking them how they were faring on such a sunny day, if they had any problems, and whether or not they had the park pamphlets. The tourists responded cordially to Elena, telling her that everything was going well. We met a couple of Argentine tourists who had arrived in cars and had not stopped at the station. Elena gave them an abbreviated charla on the spot, focusing mostly on the principles of no deje rastro. At Laguna Capri, Elena checked the papers of a guide who had arrived with a large party of hikers. We then headed to Camp Poincenot, the main campground in the Fitz Roy Valley.

Rangers evaluate the presentation of the tourist self to gauge who does and does not belong in a particular part of the park. Rangers recognize that there is a growing risk of injury the deeper a visitor heads into the frontcountry. There is also an increasing difficulty associated with rescuing a victim in more remote areas. As a result, rangers evaluate each trekking group they pass on patrol, identifying whether the trekkers look experienced, confident, and knowledgeable. "If I see a lady wearing dress shoes or a man wearing a collared shirt, for example, I immediately know that they have absolutely no business being deep inside the park, so I politely send them back to town or direct them somewhere safe and populated," noted Ernesto. As we hiked toward our destination at the edge of the frontcountry, Elena discerned who did and did not belong, using gait, poise, clothing, and gear as signs of trekking expertise. She told a few inexperienced hikers that the way up to Laguna de los Tres was "long and difficult," hoping to convince them to return to town.

Patrolling also involves regulatory enforcement. At Camp Poincenot, Elena toured the tent camp, reminded visitors of the need to pack out waste, and broke apart the windbreaks that a few people had constructed out of downed branches and stones. Leaving the camp, we encountered two Argentine campers washing their dishes in a stream. Elena walked up to them, identified herself as a ranger, and said: "I just want to remind you that we ask campers to clean their dishes at least fifty steps away from any water source, so we don't contaminate it. We hope everyone respects nature and [understands that] if everyone washed dishes in the river, it would be polluted. This water comes from glaciers up above and is pristine. And we want hikers to be able to drink right from these rivers if they want. So would you mind washing up somewhere else?" The Argentines apologized and moved off the riverbank, as Elena smiled. While the two had listened to the charla, they had forgotten this particular rule. Elena's response to this infraction demonstrates the educational basis of patrolling. Rather than framing their action as rule breaking, Elena highlights the environmental impact they were creating. She makes primary the tourist-environment relationship, rather than the ranger-tourist relationship (the relationship of police and policing subject). She invites the tourists to consider that they are creating an impact that pollutes the pristine water. After the interaction, Elena continued hiking up to Laguna de los Tres, considering the matter closed.

Educational policing arises in opposition to the authoritarian past of the Argentine ranger corps and park administration. During an interview after our hike, Elena remarked: "At the beginning, rangers had military training focused on control. Now it's not nearly as focused on that, instead performing more of an educational function. . . . [At] this point, the old ranger who never adapted to these changes is almost out of the system. . . . Until about twenty years ago, or fifteen years ago, rangers had a directive to focus on control: no one could enter the park, and no one could hunt. This [emphasis on] control meant that parks practically weren't open to the public. This is something that I think happened in all the protected areas around the world." Though Elena overstates the degree to which parks were closed off to the public in Argentina, her statement points to an important distinction between education and control that frames her notion of open and closed parks. In the aftermath of the state violence perpetrated against citizens during the military dictatorship (Feitlowitz 1999), a new conservation state emerged that sought to transcend the past associations of the Argentine ranger corps with the armed forces. At a national level, the APN moved from fortress conservation toward the more democratic, participatory CBC. Educational policing is a localized cultural response to this legacy—a meaningfully lighter deployment of state power in a way that recognizes tourists as threats to the environment, but also as political allies. Elena distinguishes between the "old ranger" who is "almost out of the system" and the younger generations of rangers trained in the new approach.

The coercive force of the state is the last resort for rangers. During recorridas, rangers use education and the rhetoric of environmental impact to prevent and rectify infractions. When rangers identify serious offenses—such as lighting campfires—they start with instruction and gauge the reaction. If the interaction goes poorly, then rangers may resort to giving the visitor a ticket. Rangers use the threat of physical expulsion from the park only as the last line of policing power. Expulsion requires the rangers to radio the station to request the assistance of the border police to compel the visitor to leave.

Elena continued past the mountaineering camp at Río Blanco and up the severely eroded section of switchbacks being worked on by the Sustainable Trails Project (see chapter 5). At Laguna de los Tres, she walked around the area, looking for any trash, checking the permits of the guides she encountered, and conversing with tourists. We lingered there for over an hour, eating lunch and enjoying the scenery. Monte Fitz Roy was entirely visible, and a few tourists took the opportunity to sunbathe. The wind whistled past us as we studied the North Pillar on Fitz Roy, looking for alpinists but seeing none. Elena had recently begun building a home in El Chaltén, after acquiring a small plot of land and—like most rangers who had a handful of years of residency—joining the formalized property-owning citizenry. She was eager to return home to continue working, so we packed up, radioed the station, and began the slow walk back to town. She was pleased with the outcome of the recorrida. There had been no infractions by guides and no belligerent tourists. Ernesto picked us up in the truck and drove through town. Ernesto and Elena waved at friends and acquaintances, occasionally shouting a greeting. Despite the tensions between residents and the APN, individual rangers inhabited different social roles outside of work—as friends, next-door neighbors, and homeowners—which helped diffuse conflict on a case-by-case basis.

MANAGING THE COMMUNITY

Mateo Lopez walked through Camp Confluencia with his checklist in December 2008, the last remaining public campground near El Chaltén. The importance of campground management had declined considerably since the previous season, when rangers had to administer Camp Madsen and its large population of service workers and tourists. Mateo applauded the park superintendent's closing of Madsen (see chapter 4), reflecting the opinion of the majority of rangers. Campground management was one aspect of the community relations work done by SLV rangers in addition to patrolling the park and giving environmental education talks.

Mateo checked Confluencia for unregistered occupants and those who had overstayed the two-week limit on camping. The regulations governing the public use of Confluencia reflected the history of problems that rangers associated with the now-shuttered Madsen. Rangers had devoted considerable time to dealing with waste management, noise complaints, and petty crime. Though many regarded Madsen as socially, culturally, and economically beneficial to the scores of service workers who stayed there for free, rangers also believed that it was the duty of El Chaltén's local government—rather than the park service—to deal with the crisis of affordable housing that plagued the village. To stop Confluencia from becoming a new Madsen, rangers stipulated that any users—seasonal workers or tourists—could stay there for only two weeks per season. All campers had to register at the visitors' center, getting a permit and a numbered stake. The duty of the campground manager was thus to check names and tents against the assigned permits, expelling anyone who attempted to camp without being registered or who had overstayed their welcome. The Confluencia regulations had the desired social effect: seasonal residents largely avoided staying at the campground, and trekkers and mountaineers were the principal users.

Mateo and I found a couple dozen tents but few campers in Confluencia. Mateo went down his checklist of permits as I picked up food scraps, beer bottles, and other litter. In a corner behind some trees, Mateo found evidence of a campfire. "Look at this bullshit," Mateo remarked as we studied the charred remains of tree branches. "We will need to send someone back here later tonight to see if we can catch the person," he continued. Apart from a few small forest fires, the last decade had been kind to the ranger corps, despite a significant expansion of tourist numbers. Across the border in Chile, Torres del Paine National Park had endured enormous blazes in 2005 and 2011—both started by backpackers. Mateo eventually found some campers hanging out in their tents and prodded them for information about the campfire.

The Confluencia regulations are part of a longer history of environmental governance that has circumscribed the community's use rights in the park, which runs counter to the participatory, socially inclusive values of CBC as a political strategy of rule. The strengthening of the ranger corps over the past two decades has facilitated a narrower definition of the park as strictly for tourism, restricting previous uses that involved livestock pasturing and firewood gathering. Though the Argentine park service has embraced CBC since the 1990s, the "community" is a flexible signifier whose meaning can change greatly depending on the political circumstances. In El Chaltén, the "community" authorized to use the resources of the national park includes the owners and workers in the commercial guiding sector. Though guiding companies participate in the economic life of the park, the rangers view residents as posing key threats to the corps. Rangers distinguish between the largely ecologically conscientious tourists who visit the park and village residents who are perceived to lack a conservationist ethic. Moreover, rangers recognize tourists as posing few threats politically to their ability to regulate the park, whereas residents constitute a significant risk insofar as they are backed by the power of the local government and the business community. Wealthy empresarios who own multiple businesses represent the most serious threats, since they are thought to have connections to national politicians that enable them to circumvent SLV authority.

Confluencia became a sign to many Chaltenenses of growing unilateral action by the park service to erode the use rights of residents in favor of tourists. Though entrepreneurs and the Cámara de Comercio had supported the closure of Madsen, seasonal workers had opposed it. The restrictions imposed on Confluencia to limit use rights only confirmed the widespread belief that the APN was displaying an increasingly authoritarian streak. Rumors abounded that the APN would close Confluencia entirely at the end of the 2008–2009 season. Many residents identified rangers not just with promoting the interests of entrepreneurs, but also with a legacy of corruption tied to the concession grab by Patagonia Salvaje. In a wider context of state corruption associated with the Kirchner-Fernández administrations, the APN became a federal agency that workers and other residents could use to interpret how national forces of corruption permeated the village.

Rangers acknowledged that many residents associated the APN with the illegitimate exercise of political power. A veteran ranger, Jorge Piazzolla remarked: "The problem is that people here really have no idea what the national park service is or how it runs. And [they think that] because it's an agency of the state, and the politicians who run the state are corrupt, then the national park service must be corrupt. There's no sense that one part of the state might actually run well." Jorge acknowledges the residents' perspective on general state corruption, while dismissing its applicability to all federal agencies. His commentary draws attention to the complexity and disunity of political power within any state (Abrams 1988; Mitchell 1991). Indeed, the notion of ambiguous governance is implicit in his message, as residents and rangers differ in where they draw the line between legitimacy and illegitimacy within the Kirchernist state. As a result,

FIGURE 6.1. Public celebration of the National Day of Argentine Parks
(photo by author)

rangers face two very different political subjects in their work. Tourists largely
view rangers as legitimate enforcers of park authority, while many residents
regard them as tainted by the illegitimacy pervading Kirchnerist institutions.

Educational outreach is one avenue pursued by rangers to build consent for
their approach to environmental governance. "You need to reach the children,"
remarked Juliana Marquez, who specialized in outreach. In addition to her duties
as an administrator, Juliana had developed curricula for educating children in
primary and secondary schools about the mission of the APN, the value of conservation to Argentina, and how students could get involved in park initiatives.
The yearlong schedule culminated in the National Day of Argentine Parks, on
November 6 (see Figure 6.1).[6] There is a strategic focus on the children of El
Chaltén by the rangers, which is coupled to the belief that adult residents are
unable to fully embrace the value of conservation. This belief is tied to urban
ecology problems in El Chaltén: the lack of a building code that has resulted in a
mélange of aesthetic styles, the pollution of rivers, the presence of trash in the
streets, and a petrol-powered electricity generator. For rangers, the inability of
residents to create an urban ecology that minimizes pollution is a testament to the
lack of a public conservation ethic. Thus, Juliana has devoted extensive time to
building support for rangers among the youngest generation. This political strategy is another domain in which educational policing has gained meaning, as
rangers target specific social groups to include in their consent-building project
through CBC.

Mateo finished up his surveying of Camp Confluencia. We returned to the ranger station to help out with the crush of tourists milling about. Mateo manned the registration desk for mountaineering expeditions, taking down names, nationalities, insurance information, and emergency contacts for a pair of climbers hoping to ascend Aguja de la S, a minor peak in the Fitz Roy Range. As a seasoned rock climber, Mateo had extensive information to communicate to the newly arrived alpinists. After registering a couple of expeditions, Mateo and I retreated upstairs to eat lunch. We discussed the rumors of the impending closure of Confluencia, and I wondered how residents would react to the news of the elimination of yet another public resource.

REGULATING THE COMMERCIAL GUIDING SECTOR

Enrique Contrera is the most senior employee at the SLV station, a ranger who was trained during a different institutional era for the park service. Voluble and charismatic, Enrique nearly runs up the trail as he and I begin our recorrida. Enrique notes that the ranger corps has recently had trouble with litter in campgrounds. His goal is to reestablish compliance with the conservation rule of packing out garbage. Unlike younger rangers who take an educational approach to conservation policing, Enrique has a more authoritative presence. He stops every visitor we meet on the trail, asking each of them a series of questions that includes whether they have been camping. If the hiker replies "yes," Enrique demands to see his or her garbage. Eventually, he catches a trio of Israeli hikers who do not have their trash. Rather than explaining how their actions create an environmental impact, as Elena does, Enrique immediately embraces the more punitive option. He angrily denounces their actions, marches them back to their camp, watches them gather their garbage, and then ejects them from the park. The backpackers initially comply, but they become increasingly agitated by Enrique's running commentary. "What do you mean, *you people*?" one of the hikers asks, having picked up on the fact that Enrique's rhetoric has shifted from criticizing the trio's actions to a generalizing national and ethnic discourse on criminality. Later, Enrique tells me that their behavior is symptomatic of the "Israeli problem" in the park, which he associates with the supposedly higher rates of deviance among Israelis when compared to European or North American tourists.

Rangers have established a relationship with the commercial guiding sector that defends the jobs of guides and extends the conservation policing power of the SLV corps. Considered "old school" by other SLV rangers, Enrique takes a much more aggressive and punitive approach to conservation policing that shows up not only in how he deals with tourists—especially Israelis—but also members of the guiding sector. As a long-term resident of El Chaltén, Enrique has established friendships with the many guides who return year after year. Though distrustful of tour company owners, whom he sees as simply interested in making money, Enrique demonstrates concern for the jobs of the hundreds of head guides, assistant guides, and porters who come to the zone. During our recorrida, Enrique encounters a large group of elderly Dutch backpackers. "Who's your guide?" He asks. A few uncomfortable minutes ensue before a younger woman admits to being the tour leader. Enrique berates her for not having hired a local guide, as required by park regulations. The tour leader eventually admits culpability as her clients look on in disbelief, having paid a tidy sum of money for their package tour through southern Patagonia. Enrique radios news of the infraction to the station, alerting the director, and then ejects the group from the park. As the group heads off into the rain, Enrique says to me: "You know, there's no one who will be waiting down at the trailhead to write them a ticket. I told the tour leader to stop by the station, but it's more likely that she will skip town. We just don't have the numbers needed to enforce things correctly." By regulating the labor market, Enrique and other rangers help the local guiding sector flourish. In turn, he explained, guides help extend the disciplinary system of conservation. Guides multiply the nodes of surveillance at work within the park, using their radios to communicate information about accidents, fires, and other concerns. Moreover, guides implement the directives of the SLV corps by educating clients about the no deje rastro rules. There is a mutually beneficial relationship that has emerged to defend a form of sustainability based on jobs for local workers and APN park norms. Ranger policing works to create a local market that maintains the collective monopoly that guiding companies have over park destinations and the symbolic capital of place.

However, rangers have also viewed commercial guiding as a threat to park authority. Though they depend on guides to extend the reach of state power, rangers have implemented a system of permits to more tightly regulate an industry seen as flouting park rules and engaging in unruly and illicit commerce. Elena Colorado remarked:

Three years ago [in the 2005–2006 season], there was not much information about the permits that each business had here in the park: what their cargo capacity was, what they were and were not authorized to do. And so these last few years the idea has been to organize this [information], because increasingly there are more demands, especially commercial demands, on the park. To organize this, control is the action we take in the field. Control is realized through the ordering of services, which are the vouchers. Vouchers are the only way we can control whether or not a business is doing what they are supposed to be doing—that they have the right number of people, for example. The voucher is the tangible element of control.

Elena comments on the past prevalence of illicit business inside the park. Though they defend the employment rights of guides, rangers have also worked to create a formal market that requires the political technique of "control." They have embraced interdiction as a way to reestablish the legitimate authority of the ranger corps in the face of perceived regulatory weakness. Elena, Enrique, and others stop every commercial party encountered inside the park. The ranger first asks for the identification of the guide, which is a card indicating that the guide has passed the PNLG exam and received the appropriate technical credentialing. The ranger then asks for the voucher, which is the paper record of the number of tourists that a guide is authorized to have when traveling to a particular destination. Though the checking of a guide's papers is often outwardly friendly, the exchange is ultimately a matter of commanding and obeying. If a guide fails to provide papers on demand, then the situation escalates from regulation to ticketing. This policing of professional guides and tour companies is bound up with the wider move to create a formalized ecotourism market. Though many guides and porters may have informal employment status, the SLV ranger corps ensures that the professional tour at least has a formalized status in relation to the conservation state. Rather than checking the employment status of workers at their companies, rangers scrutinize the licensing credentials and permits for guides and businesses to operate inside the park.

The commercial guiding sector has developed strong working relationships with the ranger corps while bristling at the latter's apparent overreach. Not surprisingly, guides raised objections to the implementation of the permitting system during the 2008–2009 season, particularly since the regulatory practice suggested that rangers fundamentally distrusted them. The daily checking of papers confirmed the sense of many guides that rangers were, in fact, police officers. However, guides believed strongly in the mission of park conservation and respected the attempt by rangers to enforce the rule that required the hiring of local guides. Guiding company owners interacted with the SLV director and the PNLG superintendent to maintain relationships that (ideally) facilitated a conflict-free business climate. Nevertheless, there were a number of infractions flagged by rangers each week that demanded the attention of owners. Many rangers viewed company owners as weasels and whiners often able to get out of paying their tickets by complaining to the PNLG superintendent.

Despite friction, rangers and guiding company owners (and the tourism business community more broadly) collaboratively promote conservation. At the beginning of each season, there is a two-day seminar hosted by the park service on the collective duties and practices of rangers and the community to ensure the long-term conservation of the park. Rangers take turns discussing the history of the APN, its bureaucratic organization, the no deje rastro rules pertaining to the PNLG, mountain ecology, invasive species, and biodiversity protection. Many businesses in town send a representative to the conference to gather information and then disseminate it among their respective workforces.

However, guides and company owners identified their risk exposure to new park service initiatives. Looking back over the 1990s and 2000s, owners and guides recognized that the conservation state had expanded and grown stronger, which enabled rangers to regulate the park more strictly. Using the discourse of sustainability, rangers—acting in concert with the PNLG superintendent—moved to curtail various forms of public use that were seen as generating significant environmental impacts. Rumors began to circulate that rangers might close Camp Prestadores, the private campground that companies ran inside the park to house visitors on multiday trekking excursions. There were other rumors about the move to make Grande Glacier, another site for ice-trekking and ice-climbing tours, into a monopoly concession like Viedma Glacier. Rather than multiple businesses being able to sell tours to Grande Glacier, only one would be able to do so under a concessionary model. One of the most extreme rumors was that the rangers might convert the entire tour industry into a monopoly concession, giving the park use rights to just one business. These rumors proliferated among owners and guides, adding to the negative impression that many residents had of the APN.

EDUCATIONAL POLICING

"It's done," Mateo Lopez remarked one evening as we cooked dinner. "What is?" I said. "Confluencia is shut down at the end of this season," he said. "The word came down from Charly [Corvalán]." "People are going to be really angry," I replied. "They know," Mateo said, referring to the superintendent's office. Mateo then talked about the lack of resources, labor power, and time demands that prevented the corps from maintaining Madsen and now Confluencia. Months later, I interviewed Marcela Barros, who had been a ranger at the SLV station in the 1990s and early 2000s. She said:

> The decision that seems even worse is to shut Confluencia. Madsen I wasn't in favor of, but to shut Confluencia seems like going backward. There are plenty of people who come here expecting to be able to camp and don't know that you can't camp down here [in El Chaltén]. So they arrive here with their backpacks and ask where they can sleep. You have the [private] campgrounds in the pueblo with services, but they aren't enough for the numbers—in addition to which they are expensive and not very good. . . . And a few years before, the *seccional* [the SLV station] decided that it wasn't viable long term to keep it [Madsen] open, and it was decided to close it. That was more or less the same policy adopted by the superintendent regarding the [Perito] Moreno Glacier. Places where there were conflicts, they just shut down. They didn't look for a way to resolve the issue.

Marcela viewed Confluencia—with its two-week limit on free camping—as a good way to resolve some of issues raised by the Camp Madsen closure. By eliminating Confluencia, however, the PNLG superintendent's office suggested the existence of a troubling pattern of action. Whenever there were social conflicts regarding access to public campgrounds, the administration simply took the easy path of eliminating the resource. Each time, this reduced the public services provided by the park to residents and tourists. The problem with such a political approach was that it undermined the long-term work by land managers and rangers to build public conservation subjects and a hegemonic front supporting scientific sustainability. As a consequence, residents perceived the APN as an increasingly crypto-authoritarian agency that talked in the language of democratic inclusion but actively sought to limit the public's use of park resources. But rather than having their faith in sustainability undermined, residents began to reject the legitimacy of the conservation state in general and the SLV station in particular. This generated concerns within the community as to what public resource might next be affected.

Ranger risk subjectivity emerges through the attempt to mitigate the environmental impacts generated by tourists, the guiding industry, and Chaltenenses. Rangers address these risks from their privileged position as agents of the conservation state, formulating an educational policing approach that attempts to lighten the exercise of state power, particularly in the wake of postauthoritarian democratization in Argentina. Amid local and national perceptions of state corruption, rangers have attempted to create a legitimate enactment of state authority by emphasizing education over coercive force. In the process, ecotourists have become the primary subjects of educational policing, rather than the guiding sector or pueblo residents—both of which are perceived as having the potential to undermine ranger authority.

The conservation state has worked together with entrepreneurial capital to control the territorial and place-branding dimensions of the semiotic estate. Despite their differences and mutual mistrust, the ranger corps and tourism company owners have engaged in public-private alliances to extend the reach of ranger surveillance, enforce conservation rules, and promote sustainable development. El Chaltén is just one instance of a broader pattern in which, despite friction and conflict, national park and tourism industry actors find common ground in Patagonia to promote ecotourism and conservation. In El Chaltén, this state-capital alliance has been formed across multiple domains of collaboration: the authoring of park management plans and incorporation of industry concerns; seminars to train tourism employees about park norms; meetings between rangers and the Cámara de Comercio; and ongoing efforts between land managers, rangers, and representatives of the tourism industry to keep the park open to commercial activity. Though rumor and recrimination exist on both sides of the table, this state-capital alliance has served as the foundation of the green capitalist economy.

Green productivism has facilitated the growth of the conservation state as a rentier agency, extracting revenue and investing in institutional development and park infrastructure. To generate support for rentier capitalism, the APN has embraced CBC as a political strategy of rule. Land managers and rangers have sought to draw civil-society actors into the collaborative project of public conservation to promote scientific sustainability. This long-term work to establish a popular environmental front has intersected with the partial delegitimization of the APN as part of the Kirchnerist state. Though residents have supported sustainability, they have increasingly viewed the ranger corps and the APN as potentially corrupt and increasingly setting aside popular concerns in favor of consolidating power. The success of green productivism in expanding conservation state power has led to the growth of popular environmental support but also hierarchical control, which pull in two different directions. Residents have increasingly recognized the asymmetry of power in the park-pueblo relationship: the pueblo is fundamentally dependent on the APN, since it controls the collective resource base upon which tourism depends, but the APN is not dependent on the pueblo. This has resulted in the tarnishing of the credibility of CBC, particularly as rangers bear the brunt of the public's anger.

With its direct monopoly control over parkland, the APN has developed an increasingly stronger bureaucratic apparatus. To attract more affluent tourists, park superintendents and ranger stations have worked to tighten the regulatory and disciplinary forces of the green economy. Rather than the retreat of state-based environmental governance, Argentina has seen the opposite. The Argentine conservation state has embraced the CBC politics of decentralization and community consent, but within a rentier framework of expanding state institutional development.

PART 4 THE POLITICS OF THE GREEN ECONOMY

7 · DEFENDING POPULAR SUSTAINABILITY IN *LA COMUNA*

Residents and visitors walked across the last field of undeveloped land remaining inside El Chaltén. In the distance was a gathering of enormous boulders, each the size of a small house. The sounds of music and people talking and laughing began to grow louder. Arriving at the edge of a grotto, nestled between a boulder and a forested hill, one could see the crowd of people that had gathered for the final celebration of the Bouldering Festival. Much of *la comuna* (the collective or community)—families, park rangers, guides, restaurant and hostel owners, porters, and domestic workers—had turned out for an evening of merriment.

The end of the climbing season had arrived, and many mountaineers were heading home to various parts of Argentina, Europe, and North America. The annual Bouldering Festival celebrated alpinist accomplishments in the Chaltén Massif, as well as the history of climbing in the region. The focal point of the festival was a bouldering competition that drew visitors from across Argentina. The contestants tackled bouldering problems suited to different levels of skill. On the final night, the festival organizers gave out various prizes for the bouldering winners, as well as the Piolín de Oro (Golden Cord) award to celebrate the best mountaineer of the season. The night was raucous as residents cheered the honorees, ate food, and drank Fernet, an Italian amaro liqueur, with Coke. Bands played music, and children played tag. Climbers showed off their moves on an artificial climbing wall that had been erected to entertain the audience.

El Chaltén hosts various celebrations throughout the season, much like other ecotourism destinations across Patagonia. In October, the pueblo commemorates the anniversary of its founding with athletic competitions that include long-distance races (half and full marathons), as well as a town-hall meeting attended by the governor. In February and March, there are the Bouldering Festival and the National Trekking Festival, the latter drawing the most sizable crowds to town, again to participate in athletic events such as cross-country trail running through Parque Nacional Los Glaciares (PNLG). Festivals are a key way to construct El Chaltén as an imagined community (Anderson 2000), calling into being meaningful aspects of cultural identity and difference.[1] The three festivals (bouldering, trekking, and anniversary) publicly display and render materially concrete the values thought integral to the place's identity: the aesthetic splendor of nature; the uniqueness of the alpine landscape; and the centrality of sport, athleticism, competition, and outdoor expertise to social life. Throughout this book, I have taken apart the notion of a unified community, emphasizing the distinct risk subject positions—produced and stabilized by the green capitalist economy—that exist in tension with one another. This chapter explores how la comuna is imagined and brought into being as a collective subject. It also highlights the limits of la comuna as a subject that engages different scales and types of risk exposure.

There are two key axes of imagination that fashion El Chaltén as a collective subject. The first defines la comuna in terms of the place-branding logic that represents El Chaltén as the national trekking capital. This is a form of translocal imagination that formulates El Chaltén as an elite destination desirable to particular types of global consumers. As I discussed above, the conservation state and entrepreneurial capital work to produce space in ways conducive to the tourist gaze that reinforce their control over the territorial and symbolic dimensions of the semiotic estate. The second axis of imagination is the politics of security: the envisioning of how collective security might be maintained in the face of threats that challenge ecotourism-led development and the protection of the park environment as a collective resource. In some cases, the social division of labor specifies how dangers should be contained, remedied, or managed. For example, park rangers take the lead on educating tourists to be environmental stewards of the park, thereby minimizing the risks of water pollution, forest fires, and injuries. However, many threats are not effectively managed by the local division of expertise. These collective threats to la comuna require the mobilization of various actors, sometimes through civil-society institutions but often on an informal basis. The specification and mitigation of these collective dangers are key domains where the collective subject of El Chaltén is made visible. These two axes of imagination—the politics of security and place branding—are fundamentally connected. By dealing with collective security issues, residents work to maintain the social solidarity, economic opportunities, and political autonomy that ensure the long-term viability of the ecotourism market.

Sustainable development does not involve only ecological science, conservation policing, and regulated ecotourism. It also includes the broader processes surrounding public security that defend the naturalized categories, boundaries, and rules brought into being through scientific sustainability. I distinguish between the scientific sustainability associated with the conservation state and the broader domain of popular sustainability that involves multisectoral coalitions of residents that mobilize against threats perceived to be internal and external to the community. Chaltenenses bring into being la comuna as a collective subject through grassroots mobilization to engage dangers with the potential to upset the existing contours of scientific sustainability formalized in park management plans. I examine popular sustainability through concrete mobilizations: political fights against privatization and protests against los Kirchners. These cases of collective action show how the Patagonian risk society is enmeshed in provincial and national dynamics that both threaten and provide political opportunities to buttress local authority and understandings of the proper relationship between the park and pueblo. I also highlight the limits of popular sustainability by addressing the accelerating threat of climate change. The exposure of El Chaltén to global climatic shifts raises the issue of the long-term viability of the green economy.

POPULAR SUSTAINABILITY

El Chaltén was founded in 1985. In addition to a pair of park rangers, the first residents were public employees such as border guards, police officers, and teachers. Beginning in the early 1990s, entrepreneurs began to open hostels, cafés, restaurants, and grocery stores. Prior to the 1997 PNLG management plan and the 2004 *Auditoría Ambiental* (Administración de Parques Nacionales 1997 and 2004), there was no legal framework that specifically defined the contours of sustainability in the PNLG. Instead, park rangers worked together with residents to establish a set of expectations to guide the newly emerging tourism industry. These ongoing discussions led to the creation of a popular sensibility about how the park should be developed. This local perspective crystallized around a preservationist aesthetic. Not just an intellectual creed, this preservationist sensibility involved judgments of taste—thus, my use of the term "aesthetic." Chaltenenses voiced support for rewilding a park long used for cattle ranching and for concentrating as much tourism infrastructure as possible inside the limits of the newly formed settlement. In the process, la comuna separated itself from an agrarian society involving estancieros and paisanos.

Marcela Barros, who was a park ranger during this period, reflected on the preservationist aesthetic that reigned in El Chaltén:

> The policy of this place has always been to impede the development of infrastructure [inside the park].... You start with a small *refugio* [chalet or hut], with latrines, and in a short amount of time the refugio is too small for all the people going there. And then you need to put in water, because the people who are going there are not enjoying using a latrine. So you pipe in water and put the bathroom inside. In Argentina, putting in infrastructure has always resulted in growth.... [But]

our policy is to maintain the primitive state of these places. . . . And once the pueblo came into being, we started to use this as a counterargument. If you have a village only two hours away, and you put in a refugio, it is going to compete directly with the pueblo. We already had the infrastructure here. Why would we want more in there [in the park], when it will change the space? And so we've advocated the most minimal course in this place.

Marcela uses the metaphor of a commercial refugio to highlight the slippery slope problem of exponential development. She notes that residents have advocated the use of the most minimal infrastructure possible inside the park, such as the trail system, that is consistent with the ability to recruit growing numbers of tourists. The idea is to concentrate services inside the pueblo. Implicit in her statement is the view that a preservationist aesthetic has shaped popular notions of sustainable development. This aesthetic views the park as a wilderness that should be as free of visible human impacts and infrastructure as possible. It also expresses notions of taste, of what is a tasteful form of ecotourism. For Chaltenenses, Chile's national trekking park, Torres del Paine, has been developed in a tasteless way, with hotels, restaurants, and refugios located inside the park and adjacent to the main trekking circuit. In contrast, the PNLG is thought to be uniquely tasteful by minimizing visual pollution and locating structures inside the village limits. This aesthetic has been central to the place-branding strategy of El Chaltén by the conservation state and entrepreneurial capital, a strategy that seeks to gain a market advantage over Torres del Paine by appealing to adventure enthusiasts who want to feel immersed in wilderness.

Scientific sustainability has built upon this popular sensibility. The preservationist perspective factored into the formulation of the 1997 and 2004 management plans, which legally codified this aesthetic through the spatial zoning of the park. The pueblo was zoned as an intensive use space for hotels, restaurants, and other types of tourism-related businesses, while the surrounding parkland was zoned as an extensive use space in which tourism infrastructure was banned (Administración de Parques Nacionales 1997). Through the efforts of land managers, the conservation state sought to create a hegemonic front to support management plans that reflected popular beliefs and values. As discussed above, the community-based conservation (CBC) strategy was founded on constructing a public conservation subject position based on collective notions of ecological risk. The 1997 plan identified livestock farming as the key ecological danger, which labeled estancieros and paisanos as the primary culprits. The 2004 plan focused on threats emerging from within the ecotourism industry, while denouncing specific practices—such as the use of horses for cargo and transportation—as ecologically damaging. These ecotourism-related threats implicated a variety of actors, including those in the commercial guiding sector. Land managers worked to create buy in especially from people in the tourism industry to recognize the threats it posed to long-term sustainability. The 1997 and 2004 plans worked to build popular support for a set of spatial zoning principles and park regulations that legally established the preservationist aesthetic. Moreover, scientific sustainability created a social charter for dealing with collective risk exposure. Not only did land managers work to define, elevate, and amplify understandings of collective risk exposure, but they also fashioned a set of policies and practices to ensure security. Over the years, this process built popular support for stricter sustainability and led to the naturalization of its categories, precepts, and values as part of what is "taken for granted" and constitutive of the "true shape of social being" (John Comaroff and Comaroff 1992, 28). It was particularly astute of land managers to construct a sustainability framework that recognized and built upon existing local perspectives, albeit ones that were very recent creations.

Popular sustainability refers to the evolving public support for an existing sustainability framework. Scientific sustainability depends upon this popular support to legitimize the ongoing practices of conservation state actors such as rangers, scientists, and superintendents. Following the Great Recession, the rangers endured a crisis of legitimacy in El Chaltén, as some residents began to view the National Parks Administration of Argentina (Administración de Parques Nacionales, or APN) as a threat to their livelihoods. Rather than questioning the broad sustainability guidelines, residents instead focused on park rangers and the superintendent as individuals with dubious motives. Through the difficult times of recession, residents continued to place their faith in the social charter of sustainability as part of the everyday common sense of a pueblo structured around ecotourism. In addition to serving as the sociopolitical bedrock for park management plans, popular sustainability is central to the politics of security. Residents have engaged in grassroots action to challenge collective hazards beyond those considered by land managers and to defend or even expand the social and legal parameters of the green economy. An expression widely used in El Chaltén, "la comuna" means different things to different actors. Within an event of collective action, la comuna operates as a "floating signifier" (Laclau 2007, 31) or master image around which various actors—rangers, entrepreneurs, workers, climbers, and others—mobilize to create a popular front of support. Precisely because it is semantically open to a diversity of meanings, la comuna becomes a central rallying point for and theme of the channeling of multisectoral energies. In the process, Chaltenenses configure the risk society in relation to particular threats.

THE POLITICS OF THE NATURE-SOCIETY DIVISION

The formation of Chaltenenses into la comuna has involved various events of collective action to remedy economic threats that challenge everyday assumptions about the division between nature and society, as well as discourses of fair market competition and opportunity. Since the creation of El Chaltén in 1985, residents have struggled with the severe climate, barebones infrastructure, rudimentary services, and isolation that afflict many Patagonian settlements. Since El Chaltén officially had fewer than a thousand residents until the late 2000s, the village did not qualify for municipal status, which entitles a town to elected officials. Residents could not always count on a local government—the Comisión de Fomento (Development Commission)—that was ruled by appointees of the governor to invest in local priorities for development. Chaltenenses thus organized themselves into the Asociación de Vecinos (Association of Neighbors)—a civil-society body that included service workers, entrepreneurs, and state employees like teachers and park rangers—to advocate for their collective interests. In contrast, the Cámara de Comercio focused on promoting the tourism market and protecting the interests of entrepreneurs. Though both organizations worked to pressure the provincial government to invest in public infrastructure (such as the creation of a health clinic, schools, and a natural gas distribution network), they also mobilized to deal with threats arising from within la comuna. The controversy surrounding the 182 Bis land dispute is one example of how Chaltenenses have organized to deal with collective security issues and defend the beliefs and values operative within popular sustainability.

182 Bis is a plot of land owned by the province that includes the northernmost section of the Chaltén Massif. To access this northern portion of the massif, trekkers and mountaineers set out from the Eléctrico River valley and climb up a steep set of switchbacks to reach an advanced base camp. Above this camp, visitors continue climbing toward a mountain pass, Paso del Cuadrado, from which climbers can access the Fitz Roy Range or rappel down into the Torre Valley to access the Torre Range. Long used by mountaineers, Paso del Cuadrado is now also visited by a small but growing number of expert trekkers who seek out the more remote areas of the park to escape the tourist masses. Though a geomorphic part of the Chaltén Massif, 182 Bis is not legally included in the PNLG.

In 1999, two businessmen, Francisco de la Vega and Alfredo Sánchez, approached Rolando Garibotti about their plan to privatize and commercialize Paso del Cuadrado. At the time, 182 Bis had the legal designation of *tierra fiscal* (public land managed by the Consejo Agrario Provincial [CAP; the Provincial Agrarian Council]), and was available for sale to private owners. Throughout the province, the CAP had sought to convert tierra fiscal into private property to expand the landholding citizenry, encourage development, and solidify Argentine territorial sovereignty over the contested borderland. Though residents had assumed that this area was actually part of the park, de la Vega and Sánchez discovered that 182 Bis was available for sale. They applied to the CAP for a temporary use permit, with the goal of installing refugios in Paso del Cuadrado to sell lodging and food. The partners could eventually apply to buy the land after making improvements on it. Rolando remarked:

> Francisco told me about it. We were at [Hostel] La Rimaya, and Francisco pulls me aside and shows me a map. And in that map he marks the piece of land and he tells me that "we have it," in essence. And he wanted to ask me because I had lived in the United States and knew about the Access Fund, and what he wanted to do was keep the front part, the eastern side, private.... But the back part he wanted to make it into an Access Fund type of thing where everyone could have access.... But I was a fucking asshole and played along, so he... shows me the structures.

Rolando did not immediately reveal his anger and instead gathered intelligence. The metallic refugios were just waiting to be transported up to the mountain pass by helicopter. The Access Fund he referred to is an organization run by U.S. climbers that advocates for climbers' rights. The businessmen wanted to designate the western portion of 182 Bis—which is part of the Fitz Roy Range—a common area open to mountaineers. In doing so, they hoped to preempt any backlash from the Patagonian mountaineering community to their plans to buy the land.

Francisco and Alfredo were respected businessmen in El Chaltén. Alfredo had bought land on the north side of the park, where he opened Hostel La Rimaya—which very quickly became a bustling establishment. Francisco was a renowned Argentine mountaineer who had spent years in El Chaltén and pioneered the creation of the commercial guiding sector. In the late 1990s, Francisco was still a comerciante who had not yet made the jump to becoming a powerful empresario. By the late 2000s, however, he had acquired partnership stakes in the Torre Expediciones and Patagonia Salvaje firms, the latter of which held the (illegally acquired) concession for Lake Viedma and Viedma Glacier (see chapter 3). The conflict surrounding 182 Bis transformed Francisco from a celebrated local mountaineer into a devil vilified for his secretive efforts to monopolize and commoditize a highly desirable destination.

Rather than a mere plot of land, 182 Bis was part of the collective patrimony of nature through which Chaltenenses constructed a global identity. Once Rolando returned to town, word quickly spread about Francisco and Alfredo's plan. Rolando and Eduardo Rivadavia, the leader of the Asociación de Vecinos, contacted *La Opinión Austral*—the chief provincial newspaper, which is published in the capital of Río Gallegos on the Atlantic coast. They spoke with a reporter, and the paper published an article the following morning (*La Opinion Austral* 1999), resulting in a flurry of activity in El Chaltén as residents identified the project as a threat to la comuna. Although 182 Bis was actually not part of the

PNLG, residents had long perceived this space as part of protected wilderness and treated it accordingly. They categorized the entire chain of mountains comprising the Chaltén Massif as national parkland, and thus not available for private ownership and commercialization benefiting only the holders of permits or titles. Nevertheless, Francisco and Alfredo sought to claim a property that included the glaciers and mountains on the northern flank of the massif, including the north and west faces of Monte Fitz Roy.[2] Residents were outraged by the notion that two investors could own not just sections of the park's namesake glaciers, but also the very mountain for which the town had been named: Monte Fitz Roy's secondary name was "Chaltén," the name given by the Aonikenk Tehuelche people. For the Aonikenk, Chaltén was a sacred site, the place where a divine hero, Elal, had descended to earth, eventually creating humans and teaching them how to hunt and protect themselves by using fire (Alonso 2004, 54; see also Pero 2002). Residents of El Chaltén were very familiar with the mythic value ascribed to Monte Fitz Roy, or Cerro Chaltén. They recognized the iconic and sacred status it had in their region.

Residents organized a letter-writing campaign to prevent the privatization of 182 Bis, enlisting members of the Asociación de Vecinos and the Cámara de Comercio. After the newspaper story was published, Francisco and Alfredo denied the accusations made in it and dismissed Rolando's account of what had happened. The Vecinos convened to determine the best course of action, directing residents to write letters to Governor Kirchner denouncing the move to privatize Monte Fitz Roy and excoriating the CAP for approving the permit. Moreover, the Vecinos called for Kirchner and the provincial government to declare 182 Bis a provincial natural monument. Such a legal designation would have made this land subject to environmental protections and precluded its commercialization. The Cámara also backed the campaign and circulated the following statement:

> The Chamber ... proclaims that the delivery of part of this natural resource into private hands acts against the harmonious development of the area and puts in private hands an esteemed provincial symbol (it adorns our flag), which has an incommensurable tourist value as one of the most recognized mountains in the world, and on which rests the tourism activity of Chaltén. We believe ... that putting a lot that is an integral part of this resource in private hands puts at risk the tourism activity of the rest of the operators in the area, creating a disequilibrium that should not be fomented by the state.... [The] status of protected area offers all the operators the possibility of using it equally; and to the entire community, the security that the natural resource on which their economy is based will continue to be undamaged by attempts to use it for [private individuals'] benefit.

The Cámara identified a symbolic issue thought to resonate with Governor Kirchner: Monte Fitz Roy was the key image on the provincial state flag. The possible privatization of this provincial icon contravened popular understandings of Kirchner as a strong supporter of public land, national parks, and territorial sovereignty. The privatization of 182 Bis also put at risk a key feature of the ecotourism market: the equality of access to public resources by entrepreneurs. By granting a permit to Francisco and Alfredo, the provincial state created a fundamental inequality within the business community, undermining the local ideal of a level playing field within the market.

Chaltenenses drew upon their transnational connections to create a much wider sphere of civic action. Residents defined the privatization of 182 Bis as a threat not only to the village, but also to the mountaineering community and its long-standing access to the Chaltén Massif along the northern slopes above Paso del Cuadrado. Rolando published letters in the key climbing magazines of Europe, North America, and South America, publicizing the issue and seeking to enlist support. Individual climbers, the British Mountaineering Council, the U.S. Access Fund, and Yvon Chouinard (founder of Patagonia, Inc.) sent letters to Governor Kirchner. Residents suggested in their letters that they might contact UNESCO if the necessary steps were not taken to protect the zone, since the PNLG was a World Heritage Site. In April 2000, the provincial government issued a new law that designated the contested land as a provincial natural monument, thereby ensuring that it would never be sold as private property.

In sum, residents mobilized to deal with what was perceived to be an internal threat to the community deriving from the secretive actions of Francisco and Alfredo. Implicit in their action was the popular understanding of the division between nature and society that was mapped onto the distinction between the national park and provincial land. Apart from the actual legal designation of 182 Bis, residents had long viewed the northern section of the Fitz Roy Range and its surrounding glaciers and lands as part of national park nature. The outpouring of popular support for the transformation of 182 Bis into a provincial natural monument sought to align the legal status of the land with hegemonic notions about the proper division between nature and society. Involving these assumptions about nature and society, the 182 Bis land dispute included expressions of the views of an antiprivatization popular front that were given slightly different ideological forms: by climbers concerned about access; by entrepreneurs worried about an uneven playing field; and by residents scandalized by the idea of individuals owning part of Monte Fitz Roy, the sacred symbol of the province and locality. In the process, residents engaged in a form of public conservation advocacy that extended the social and legal parameters of the green economy laid out in the 1997 PNLG management plan, creating a new provincial protected area abutting the national park.

The 182 Bis controversy is one instance of collective action and intrasectoral coalition building within the Patagonian risk society to address a perceived threat to the long-term viability of this ecotourism destination. Residents drew upon the hegemonic assumptions of the nature-society division that informed popular notions of sustainability. In the process, residents enacted la comuna as a collective subject that was organized to combat internal threats.

DEFENDING LOCAL AUTONOMY FROM LOS KIRCHNERS

I walked across the partially finished bridge (see Figure 7.1). Underneath me, the De las Vueltas River rushed by on its way to Lake Viedma. El Chaltén and the PNLG were behind me on the west side of the river. On the east side was a privately owned estancia that contained a wall of impressive cliffs where climbers practiced. Previously, climbers or residents had accessed the estancia by using a tirolesa. Climbers hooked their harnesses to the cable using carabiners and pulled themselves across while hanging supine. Reaching the far bank, I stopped to take some pictures of the structure and then saw a cyclist approaching. Alejandro Castillo introduced himself, and we started chatting about the bridge. Like most local residents, Alejandro was extremely contemptuous of it. He summed up his opinion in the following way: "Someone should bomb it! Blow it up! It's a disgrace!"

Most residents regarded the bridge as threatening to local autonomy. One day, a construction crew had shown up in town and begun to work on the bridge. Though residents and civil-society organizations like the Asociación de Vecinos and the Cámara de Comercio had long sought greater investment by the provincial and national governments in local infrastructure, Chaltenenses had also sought to maintain control over what projects received funding. Alongside local notions of the nature-society division, the popular vision of sustainability also included la comuna's authority to determine what types of development were consistent with the preservationist aesthetic. The problem with the bridge was that it served no identifiable public good, apart from facilitating easier access to climbing routes. One resident noted: "I don't know much, but it seems to be a form of trampling all over the community because no one can tell us why they created the bridge. And no one can tell us what is the rationale for [building] the bridge with the resources of the state." There was no road on the other side of bridge on the estancia, just a set of dirt trails that climbers had created. What, then, was the bridge's purpose? This was the nub of the issue: the fundamentally obscure reason for building what some residents referred to as the "bridge to nowhere." Neither construction workers nor local authorities—such as the park service representatives—could make sense of the bridge. In the absence of a stabilized set of meanings, residents drew upon particular cultural frames that saw the hand of the Kirchners behind the project. The bridge thus became another instance of public investment by the Kirchner-Fernández administrations in the province to boost the tourism industry, much like the paving of the highway that went from El Calafate to El Chaltén or the building of a bus terminal. Neverthe-

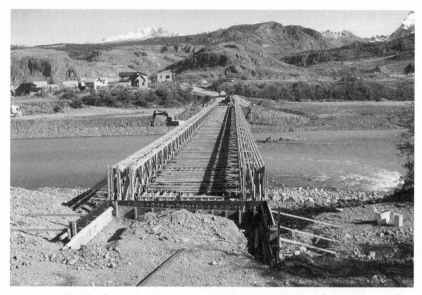

FIGURE 7.1. The "bridge to nowhere" across the De las Vueltas River (photo by author)

less, residents saw the bridge as a potential threat to their collective security. The bridge became a sign of the spectral power of los Kirchners to control local development and the extraction of wealth.

Why residents interpreted a small bridge as a collective security issue speaks to the political exposure of the Patagonian risk society to Kirchnerist power. In El Chaltén, there is a history of protesting plans made by the Kirchners to develop the Chaltén area. One instance occurred in the mid-2000s, when rumors began to circulate that the Kirchners intended to build a highway to Viedma Glacier on the rugged shoreline of Lake Viedma. Years earlier, the APN had worked with the provincial government to build a paved road from El Calafate out to Perito Moreno Glacier. This project helped supercharge the commercialization of the southern zone of the PNLG, which became the most visited tourist attraction in all of Patagonia. Chaltenenses interpreted the rumored highway project in light of the road to Perito Moreno Glacier, predicting the future creation of an observation deck next to Viedma Glacier as well as various shops, restaurants, and hotels. Chaltenenses also viewed the highway as a Trojan horse designed to allow the Kirchners to gain control over a major development opportunity in the zone. As real estate investors in El Calafate and El Chaltén, the Kirchner family already owned a number of businesses. Though officially labeled as public works, projects such as the bridge and the rumored highway were interpreted by the residents chiefly as ways for the Kirchners to gain control over strategic assets in El Chaltén. In this respect, the highway project was perceived as enmeshed in the shadowy field of personalized, corrupted power associated with los

Kirchners. The double state of Kirchnerismo—as both a legitimate agenda of progressive politics and the illegitimate, personalized exercise of state power— came into view. The highway signified both a legitimate public project (if unwanted) to advance tourism and the personalized use of state power by President Kirchner to advance the economic interests of his family. Residents organized to resist the project.

Kirchner was scheduled to visit El Chaltén with APN President Héctor Espina to commemorate the anniversary of the founding of the village. Marcela Barros, the retired park ranger, was married to Eduardo Rivadavia, who was the leader of the Vecinos for many years. She reflected on how the protest unfolded:

> People started to get together who were against the highway and decided that something had to be done. . . . So one month before [the commemoration] it was decided to put a red band on your arm, and to put red signs on the way to [Lake] Viedma and in the gym, where the event would take place. And at this time, the *comisionado* of Chaltén [the politically appointed leader of the local government] was a man from Piedras Buenas, and it occurred to him to bring soldiers for a parade. So there were signs saying "No" on the way to Viedma and a ton of people with red armbands, and when they were parading, two guys from the pueblo unfurled a banner that said "No to the Road to Viedma." They stood beside the parade [of soldiers], and people went crazy.

This collective act embarrassed the Kirchners, particularly since the media had shown up to cover the event. Also embarrassed was Espina, since park rangers such as Marcela played a key role in helping organize this act of resistance.

The Kirchners and Espina very quickly did an about-face. Espina called an impromptu hearing on the topic, since the APN had to approve any plan to build a new highway into the park—a process that at the very least required an environmental impact assessment and a public hearing on its findings. Residents had interpreted Espina's presence with the Kirchners in El Chaltén as meaning that the APN leadership looked favorably on the plan. Marcela said: "Espina then held a hearing. . . . And he had to say, no, well, the road in fact was just a proposal, and that the people had overreacted—that the project was not that well developed and it might happen in the future, but that they had to do all the assessments related to it." With the media publicizing local opposition, the plan was quickly shelved, though it had by no means been entirely defeated.

This collective act helped forge solidarity among diverse social groups such as seasonal workers, park rangers, and business owners. The imagined community emerged through a makeshift political alliance to confront a threat to la comuna's collective security. Like the 182 Bis controversy, the Viedma highway protest reaffirmed the acceptable division between nature and society that was at the foundation of popular sustainability. As they sought to prevent the intrusion of

Kirchnerist power into the zone, residents defended the assumed boundaries between a preserved nature with minimal infrastructure and the provincial space of the village, where development ought to be concentrated. Given this history of Kirchnerist attempts to commercialize Lake Viedma, residents assumed there was a shadowy Kirchnerist presence behind plans to build the bridge across the De las Vueltas River in 2009, after the Kirchners had been wielding presidential power for six years.

Many residents linked the bridge to rumored plans for a new village to be created on the opposite side of the river, a proposal that the Kirchners had mentioned during previous visits. Residents feared that any such new village might become an enclave for the wealthy elite rather than the residents who had applied for land grants to build homes and open businesses. Antonio Jimenez, a young resident and climber, interpreted the significance of the "bridge to nowhere" as presaging the creation of an elite enclave: "I'm not very informed, but it seems to me, from what I've heard, that it [the bridge] was built by the province or the state, and that it will function as a way to expand the village into other sectors. But keeping in mind that the land is private, what I think is that they are going to divide it up into lots in *estilo country* ["country club style," with gated communities]." Antonio's point was that the bridge would open up the privately owned estancia on the east side of the river, allowing the owner to sell off a chunk of land to developers to build private neighborhoods for the wealthy. Having grown up in Buenos Aires, Antonio was familiar with the private enclaves that dotted the beach resorts on the Atlantic coast.

Antonio then reflected on the opportunities for corruption presented by a new village, especially in light of the economic difficulties facing entrepreneurs with the continued fallout from the Great Recession. The Kirchners figured centrally in his comments:

> In our country, we live within a crisis where there are highs and lows and fashions quickly change. Right now [the province of] Santa Cruz ... is in fashion, and perhaps in a few years it won't be. They are heavily commercializing this place, but perhaps there will be a decline in tourists, and I'm not sure that it's going to be profitable. But all these hotels, perhaps they are not being built to be profitable, but for another reason much more *negro* [illicit]. There are many people that need to *blanquear* [launder] money, and many times hotels are good ways to blanquear the money, but I don't know. . . . A president, like any other person with political access, has many more advantages than someone with money who doesn't have political access. In Santa Cruz, they [the Kirchners] have many businesses, and the reality is that right now businesses generate substantial [amounts of] money. For example, if I had the money to put up a hotel, and this hotel generates a lot of money, I'll put up another hotel, and this hotel will double my money. What is most probable is that I'm going to continue putting up hotels and

that I will continue making loads of money. . . . If they do or don't use the presidency, or used the governorship as was the case earlier, to help them with these businesses, I don't know. But that they have hotels and that these hotels generate money and that they are likely to continue putting up hotels is obvious, whether they are doing so politically or not. They can do it both ways. They could do it with money from the state or perhaps not, because it's not as if they don't have wealth. They have their wealth, and perhaps they are doing it cleanly. Perhaps not.

Antonio elaborated a number of points regarding the investment possibilities presented by a new village. This imagined village could offer investors opportunities to licitly or illicitly build hotels in a private enclave with a great view of the Chaltén Massif. Rather than seeking profit, these investments could actually be ways to launder money from other sources. Indeed, the blanco-negro distinction discussed above regarding formal versus informal workers also applies to investments. Antonio identified the double status of los Kirchners as both private citizens who were invested in the green economy and the most powerful political couple in Latin America, with control over the presidency. The blanco-negro distinction played out again here, as Antonio expressed uncertainty about whether or not the Kirchners had used their political power to benefit themselves economically. He noted that everyone in town was aware that the Kirchners had a few legitimate businesses (en blanco). His statement, though, hinted at another domain of speculation: the prospect that Kirchner capital was spread further than the public knew. Indeed, many residents expressed opinions about the businesses in which the Kirchners were rumored to have a hidden (negro) partnership stake. Residents identified different hotels, bus companies, and travel agencies as businesses in which the Kirchners were supposedly silent investors who were using these firms to launder their money. These cases pointed to the spectral hand of the Kirchners perceived to be at work behind the scenes of everyday life.

In sum, the bridge to nowhere became a collective security issue. The problem was how to organize a protest against something about which no one had any definitive knowledge. In the absence of a stabilized set of meanings for the new bridge, residents reasoned analogically from past experiences, such as the Viedma highway controversy, to make sense of this opaque action by the provincial state; and they saw the hand of los Kirchners in this public works project. The Viedma highway controversy, however, had become a key site of collective protest that had forced the Kirchners and Espina to back down from their plan to build a highway to Viedma Glacier. Residents understood the bridge and the highway projects in terms of the naturalized "common sense" underlying popular sustainability, which privileged the defense of local political autonomy. The key difference between the highway and bridge projects was that the former led residents to confront the Kirchners, Espina, and the media, gathering as la comuna. The latter case became an instance of uncoordinated opposition and the vocalization of individualized dissent, such as the angry words of Alejandro, who suggested that the bridge deserved to be bombed. This remark made sense only in the context of popular fear of external forces threatening to usurp local power and undermine the viability of ecotourism as conceived of by residents. Ultimately, however, the bridge to nowhere was finished. What it signified about the future remained an open question.

CLIMATE, GLACIERS, AND GLOBAL ECOLOGICAL TRANSFORMATION

The ranger station was packed with residents—guides, teachers, and other concerned citizens—eager to hear a public lecture by Ricardo Villalba, the well-known director for many years of the Argentine Institute for Snow, Glacier and Environmental Sciences (Instituto Argentino de Nivología, Glaciología y Ciencias Ambientales, or IANIGLA). For years Villalba had brought teams of researchers to El Chaltén to study glacier, forest, and climate dynamics. He had been a member of the Intergovernmental Panel on Climate Change that was awarded the 2007 Nobel Peace Prize in conjunction with Al Gore. Villalba's message to pueblo residents was direct and troubling: climate change was not an issue of the distant future but rather a clear and present danger that would affect Argentina as a nation and Patagonia as a region. Villalba presented the different scenarios facing the region, depending on whether or not the global community acted swiftly to curb greenhouse gas emissions and transition to a postcarbon economy or pursued a business-as-usual approach with minimal effort devoted to the mitigation of climate change. He situated these scenarios in the global history of fossil fuel consumption and the carbon debt owed by Europe and the United States to developing nations. Though seemingly hopeful during the talk, Villalba expressed skepticism about the likelihood of concerted global action during an interview I conducted with him months later at IANIGLA. Rather than promoting mitigation, he argued that the Argentine government should invest resources in adapting to climate change and scaling up alternative energy sources such as wind and solar power.

Villalba's lecture intersected with broader scientific narratives about regional climate change and glacial degradation. Scientific research concerning the glacial dynamics of the Southern and Northern Patagonian Ice Fields has long been hamstrung by limited data, few weather stations, and the remoteness of glaciers, pushing scholars to use remote sensing technologies and satellite imaging analysis. Studies have identified an increase in regional surface temperatures of 0.4–2.0 degrees centigrade during the twentieth century and a loss of 24.4 ± 1.4 gigatons (a gigaton is one billion metric tons) of ice per year from the two ice fields, causing the sea level to rise an estimated 0.067 ± 0.004 millimeters per year

(Willis et al. 2012). Scientists have confirmed that Patagonian glaciers are in the midst of an accelerating degradation, though this should not be viewed as implying that the ice fields will soon disappear. The real worries are not the dozens of massive glaciers that comprise the ice fields, but the hundreds of small mountain glaciers. Embedding his public lecture within the context of scientific research, Villalba positioned the local ecology—glaciers, forests, and wildlife—as highly vulnerable to climate change. Without a political consensus to drive the radical reduction of emissions, El Chaltén's mountain glaciers were especially susceptible to accelerating thinning and retreat. As an ecotourism destination based upon the selling of the alpine sublime, El Chaltén faced a situation of global ecological risk that had the potential to undermine its consumer image as an exceptional locale for glacier trekking.

Chaltenenses have increasingly articulated discourses of ecological insecurity tied to climate change. In particular, residents have foregrounded glaciers as symbols of this growing danger. The media, public figures, and environmental NGOs have played a role in citing changes in glaciers as early warning signs of a looming ecological disaster. Indeed, the dramatic retreat of Upsala Glacier in the southern part of the PNLG has been well publicized by Greenpeace and Al Gore. Moreover, residents' observations of glacier degradation over the past twenty years have also identified ecological change. These observations have inspired a sense of loss in many people. As we were hiking through the park together, one resident commented on the glacier across the valley: "Look at Piedras Blancas. The lower part keeps getting smaller every year. . . . Do you see that rocky outcrop, there [pointing to the finger of rock sticking out the middle of the glacier]? You couldn't see that in 2003. Think of how much the glacier must have thinned over the last six years to do that. . . . It's such a travesty to think about the future of these glaciers with global warming. I'm glad I'm here now to see this before it's all gone." Glaciers are cultural symbols that allow residents to articulate a communal identity linked to nature, wildness, and spaces of aesthetic consumption. Formally recognized by the very name of the national park, the Andean glaciated landscape is the key environment in which the comuna of El Chaltén is situated. Because glaciers foster collective identity, their degradation has created a field of vulnerability that crosses lines of class, gender, race, and age within the pueblo. This suggests that climate change is both an observable process of ecological change and a collective feeling of exposure in which the emotional ties that bind members of la comuna together are expressed in a set of symbols. Indeed, the resident who pointed out the thinning and retreat of Piedras Blancas Glacier did so with a marked tone of sadness. Being able to "see this before it's all gone" was a refrain not only for residents, but also for some tourists who wanted to visit Patagonia while its glaciers were still largely intact.

In the face of this global ecological threat, Chaltenenses have failed to create a united front of collective action. The perceived planetary scale of the problem has precluded local action. Many residents have echoed Villalba's view of the carbon debt owed by the global north to the global south, thereby shifting responsibility to actors outside Latin America. Conceiving of Argentina as underdeveloped, many residents have thought it best to focus on more pressing and immediate matters, such as poverty, unemployment, and economic growth. The national park service has had little to say on the issue of climate change, though it threatens the basis of scientific sustainability. An APN official reflected on what the agency has done to address climate change: "Very little, very little, and almost nothing. . . . It's obviously a problem that we're doing very little about. . . . There are problems to resolve before we can begin to work on issues related to climate change. I'm not saying [we can do] 'nothing,' but there are some things that are more pressing. There are some reports, but in terms of a specific policy, there's really nothing." This official recognized that while climate change will have devastating impacts on regional ecosystems over the long term, there are more pressing concerns to address—such as the need: to implement stronger conservation measures inside parks; to develop a biodiversity monitoring system; and to mobilize people to resist the pressures of urbanization and the expansion of mining and commercial forestry. This official's argument, then, turns on perceiving the Argentine conservation state as still in a state of underdevelopment and relative weakness compared to the socioeconomic forces bearing down on it. Much like their response in the case of the bridge to nowhere, Chaltenenses have related to the climate change threat in ways that fail to give material political form to la comuna as a collective subject.

Despite the risk of ecological transformation, El Chaltén's green economy has an ace in the hole. At the local level, climate change is believed to increase the chance of drought, wildfire, and precipitation shifts. With rising regional temperatures, some mountaineers have begun to note that specific climbing routes are increasingly dangerous to ascend during the late summer. With the weakening of ice bonds in the mountains, rockfalls are more common. Though its mountain glaciers might be at risk, El Chaltén is still situated alongside the Southern Patagonian Ice Field, an icecap so massive that many scientists believe there is little to no chance of its degrading completely during the twenty-first century. In other words, El Chaltén is well positioned to take advantage of the accelerating impacts of climate change on alpine landscapes around the world. Given its location adjacent to the ice field, El Chaltén has a significant long-term comparative advantage over other alpine tourism destinations in Peru, Bolivia, the European Alps, and the Canadian Rockies. Despite residents' sadness at the ongoing degradation of its mountain glaciers, El Chalten's green economy is uniquely situated to benefit from accumulation through climatic transformation.

Accumulation through climatic transformation is a concept that refers to the capacity to benefit economically from the uneven national, regional, and local outcomes of global climate change and ecological destabilization. Andean Patagonian communities may well capitalize on the uneven geography of changing climate.

DEFENDING LA COMUNA

Chaltenenses have engaged in collective action to defend a popular vision for sustainable development against internal and external threats to the imagined community. Reinforced by the social and legal structures governing the green economy, popular sustainability reaches beyond ecological science and APN land management to contend with contingent hazards that threaten ecotourism and the existing distribution of market opportunities, the collective patrimony of nature, the global identity of El Chaltén that associates it with iconic landforms, the nature-society division, and local political autonomy based on a preservationist aesthetic. Popular sustainability generates and amplifies discourses of collective risk and security that provide the basis for grassroots mobilization across social divisions in the pueblo. During these instances of public action, la comuna comes into being as a collective subject invested with different types of positional meanings. As an open subject position, la comuna has flexible boundaries that residents can expand or contract to fit the situation. In the case of the 182 Bis land dispute, la comuna presented a hegemonic front opposed to two local businessmen who were viewed as internal threats. Though they were residents of El Chaltén, these two men were temporarily excluded from the imagined community, their actions galvanizing the pueblo to work toward the creation of a new provincial protected area with the approval of Governor Kirchner. During the Viedma highway controversy, la comuna drew entrepreneurs, workers, rangers, and other residents together to create a unified front of opposition to the Kirchners and the APN leadership as external threats. However, the De las Vueltas bridge issue proved more difficult, given that its public rationale remained opaque. As a result, residents were unable to articulate an integrated expression of collective opposition and to define the boundaries of la comuna against the threat. In addition, climate change represented an insurmountable political problem for residents and was a global threat against which collective action was never taken. Though potentially undermining sustainable development, climate change also offered the long-term possibility that El Chaltén might be able to capitalize on the degradation of alpine environments around the world.

The defense of popular sustainability provides the first point of entry into the politics of the green economy. As demonstrated by this chapter, ecotourism destinations seek to create connections with and anticipate interventions by local and national forces. Like other areas in Argentina, El Chaltén is fundamentally exposed to the opportunities and perils deriving from the provincial and national conditions of Kirchnerist power. Scientific sustainability provides an institutionalized framing of collective risk and security related primarily to local actors and their relationship to the park environment. Popular sustainability opens up a broader, contingent framing of collective risk and security. The Patagonian risk society emerges through its efforts to secure legitimate and desired public investments and laws from the Kirchner-Fernández administrations (such as the provincial protected area), while limiting the illegitimate imputed power of los Kirchners over la comuna (as in the cases of the bridge and highway infrastructure projects). Chaltenenses seek to differentiate the licit from the illicit contents of the Kirchnerist double state to fashion a social charter for collective life based on sustainable ecotourism.

8 · KIRCHNERISMO AND THE POLITICS OF THE GREEN ECONOMY

Kirchnerist green productivism has fostered state-capital alliances in Patagonian ecotourism destinations. The conservation state has acted in concert with entrepreneurial capital to monopolize park destinations and collaborate in place-branding activities. As it has recruited growing numbers of people, the green capitalist economy has given rise to a variety of risk subject positions across the spheres of tourism consumption, service production, and the conservation state. Subjects have worked—either together or at cross-purposes—to gain access to valuable consumer experiences, safeguard and expand their capital investments, advance socioeconomically in communities, and mitigate the environmental impacts of ecotourism on protected areas. State-capital hegemony has worked to refashion previously agrarian spaces into alpine landscapes, excluding various actors from social power. The conservation state has played a coordinating role in generating popular environmental fronts—in El Chaltén and elsewhere—that support scientific sustainability and mobilize to confront internal and external threats to communities.

Grounded in dynamic visions of sustainability within ecotourism locales, green productivism also communicates key values of Kirchnerismo as a political ideology. This chapter examines Néstor Kirchner and Cristina Fernández de Kirchner first as provincial politicians resisting the neoliberal regime of President Carlos Menem and then as presidents implementing a post-neoliberal vision for national development. I have thus far explored the Kirchnerist green agenda in terms of ecotourism, community-based conservation, and the alpine landscape sublime. Here, I consider the broader political context in which the Kirchners have engaged with the green economy to enact key values defining Kirchnerismo: the defense of territorial sovereignty; economic development through resource exploitation; and the assertion of stronger state control over natural resources to generate public revenue streams that fund investment in development and social welfare. Nevertheless, the agenda has contributed to growing tension between the green economy and extractive industries, spawning social movements of resistance in various quarters. I begin with an examination of the provincial politics of territorial sovereignty and resource exploitation, and then I consider the national politics of the rentier state and conflict between the green and extractive sectors.

DEFENDING TERRITORIAL SOVEREIGNTY

The Kirchner-Fernández administrations have supported the green economy as part of a political effort to defend territorial sovereignty. Scholars have pointed to the Islas Malvinas (also known as the Falkland Islands) as the most significant domain of geopolitical struggle where the Kirchners have sought to advance Argentine national claims and enlist the support of other Latin American countries to counter British settler colonialism (Benwell and Dodds 2011; Dodds 2012). Far less attention has been paid to Argentina's contested border with Chile. The Kirchners' promotion of the green economy has intersected with long-standing geopolitical efforts by the Argentine state to use protected areas and international tourism to build settlements, establish a greater population base, secure territorial sovereignty, and aestheticize the so-called Andean desert. In the 1990s, the Kirchners gained national recognition through their defense of the El Chaltén zone during the controversies related to Lake del Desierto and the Southern Patagonian Ice Field.

In 1965, the Argentine military received a distress call from Ricardo Arbilla, an estanciero who reported that a small contingent of Chilean soldiers had moved into the Lake del Desierto valley and taken up a defensive position on his land. For over a century, tension had waxed and waned between the Argentine and Chilean governments over the locations of the borders of Patagonia in general and the El Chaltén zone in particular (Navarro Floria 1999; Bandieri 2005). The soldiers offered to grant Arbilla tax-exempt status if he publicly declared his land to be part of Chile, but he declined—and was later recognized as an Argentine patriot. Following diplomatic talks, the Chilean government agreed to withdraw its forces from the area, but Argentine reconnaissance confirmed that this had not been done according to the specified schedule. In Operation Desert, Argentine soldiers moved into this extremely rugged part of the El Chaltén zone and surrounded the Chilean outpost (Rojas 1975). In the ensuing firefight, the Argentine military killed one Chilean soldier and captured three more, with the remaining soldiers fleeing across the border. Despite the battle, neither state declared war on the other. In response, the Argentine government moved to establish a state presence in the El Chaltén zone, creating a military outpost to defend it against Chilean incursions and the Seccional Lago Viedma ranger station to police Parque Nacional Los Glaciares (PNLG).

Twenty-six years later, in 1991, Cristina Fernández de Kirchner, a future president of Argentina, stood on the shore of the Eléctrico River with a contingent of provincial lawmakers from Santa Cruz. In the middle of the austral winter, the politicians had left the capital city of Río Gallegos on the Atlantic coast and traveled hundreds of kilometers across the province to the Chaltén Massif, passing through the hamlet of El Chaltén—which had been founded only in 1985. Back in Río Gallegos, Néstor Kirchner (who was mayor of the city in 1987–1991) was running for governor. Close to the 1965 battlefield, provincial representatives began a special meeting of the Chamber of Deputies and passed Resolution 83, which affirmed Argentine sovereignty over Lake del Desierto. This highly symbolic event began to position the Kirchners—members of the center-left wing of the Partido Justicialista (the Peronist party)—as defenders of territorial sovereignty over the contested borderlands.

The Eléctrico River resolution highlighted one site of political dissent emerging with respect to the center-right presidency of Menem, then leader of the ideologically diverse party. Menem had begun to pursue an agenda that initially focused on reining in the hyperinflation of the 1980s, but that soon morphed into a more radical program of neoliberal reform to privatize state companies, deregulate the economy, promote free trade, flexibilize labor, and supercharge foreign capital investment (Féliz 2012, 107). In an age that glorified the notion of a borderless global market, Menem sought to eliminate the long-standing border conflicts with Chile that forestalled his efforts to promote market integration between Argentina and its neighbor. During the early 1990s, the Menem administration worked with that of Chile's President Patricio Aylwin to resolve twenty-two disputes through a bilateral commission (Allan 2007, 747). Menem submitted the Lake del Desierto case to the Organization of American States (OAS) for arbitration, an action that was criticized by Patagonian politicians since it legally exposed Argentina to the possibility of losing this territory. Indeed, Argentina had lost the Beagle Channel arbitration case to Chile in 1977. In 1994, however, the OAS vindicated Menem, ruling in favor of Argentina.[1] Lake del Desierto remained part of the El Chaltén zone.

The western border of the El Chaltén zone soon became another site of geopolitical conflict. At issue was the boundary between Argentina's PNLG and Chile's Bernardo O'Higgins National Park—in particular, a section running from Monte Fitz Roy down to Cerro Daudet within the Southern Patagonian Ice Field (see Map I.1). This conflict became a golden opportunity for the Kirchners to celebrate Argentine nationalism and the defense of territorial integrity in contrast to Menem's vision of neoliberal globalization. In late 1991, Néstor Kirchner was elected governor of Santa Cruz, where he served until becoming president. Cristina Fernández de Kirchner was elected to various political offices, such as provincial deputy (1989–1995), national senator (1995–1997), and national deputy (1997–2001). During her time as a national senator, she worked within and beyond the Peronist party to cobble together a broad front opposing the bilateral treaty with Chile negotiated by the Menem administration.

This political coalition that included factions within the Peronist party and the Unión Cívica Radical (Radical Party) raised a number of points against the proposed treaty (Sopeña 2008). First, it would unnecessarily cede huge amounts of land and natural resources to Chile. Second, it would give away the glacial headwaters of the Santa Cruz River, which flowed down to the Atlantic Ocean. Indeed, the fight over the ice fields involved the region's principal source of fresh water and potential hydropower. For Patagonians, the ice cap represented a crucial future source of renewable energy, once national oil and gas reserves had been depleted (Melgarejo 1999, 47–48). Third, many Patagonian politicians were offended by the way that Menem referred to the ice fields as just some bits of glacier, as if they were largely worthless. Menem's lack of sensitivity to regional identity and the importance of territorial sovereignty worked to the advantage of the Kirchners.

Senator Fernández framed the debate as one in which Menem sought to give away an inalienable part of the national patrimony merely to promote economic integration with Chile. Though economic treaties could be approved or discontinued, she argued, territorial decisions were irreversible (Sopeña 2008, 204–206). During this period, the Kirchners became a thorn in Menem's side as they vocally denounced the treaty and the trade-off between market integration and the national patrimony. Pressed on the issue of whether she felt marginalized within the Peronist party, Fernández replied: "On the contrary, I feel more like a Justicialista than ever. In this very complex but significant issue for the people of Santa Cruz, I will be consistent with the ideas that I have always defended. . . . I am doing the Peronism of the good, the Peronism of General Perón" (*La Nacion* 1996). Fernández's point was that Menem had strayed from implementing the "good" work of the Peronist party that drew upon the political positions staked out by the founder of the party, Juan Perón. Though incurring the ire of the Menemist bloc, Fernández sought comfort in embodying and representing the original tenets of Peronism based on national territorial sovereignty.

As a political movement, Kirchnerismo emerged as an anti-Menemist political front through the defense of territorial sovereignty over the El Chaltén zone, the PNLG, the ice fields, and the Patagonian borderlands. In the process, the Kirchners established national profiles for themselves and articulated a foundational principle of Kirchnerismo: the global market integration of Argentina should not occur at the expense of diminishing the national patrimony. The Kirchnerist desire to promote the green economy is historically situated in the defense of territorial sovereignty, protected environments, and national nature. To accelerate ecotourism-led development was to build populations in geopolitically sensitive zones like El Chaltén to ensure their Argentine identity. Though the boundary line that includes Monte Fitz Roy has never been finalized, Chaltenenses

communicate—through the place brand of the "national trekking capital"—
their integration into the Argentine body politic.

ECONOMIC DEVELOPMENT THROUGH
RESOURCE EXPLOITATION

The Kirchners' support for the green economy has been part of a broader emphasis on economic development through resource exploitation that emerged during
their time as provincial politicians. The Kirchners embraced a "light green" politics that promoted conservation and environmental stewardship primarily within
the Andean region, while also advancing extractive industries in different parts
of the province. This light green politics depended on the spatial compartmen-
talization of resource domains, not because of any master zoning plan but rather
because of the historical legacy of industries developing in relation to the geo-
logical depositing of resources. The Kirchners crafted differentiated messages for
delivering material improvements to constituencies, building electoral support
and consolidating their grip over the province.

On October 12, 2009, Governor Daniel Peralta led a public ceremony cele-
brating the twenty-fourth anniversary of the founding of El Chaltén. Town residents and members of the media gathered in the central plaza on the cold spring
day. In the distance, the snow-covered Chaltén Massif periodically emerged
from the thick cloud cover. The park rangers and the border police, wearing their
uniforms, stood at attention and saluted as the national anthem was played. Flags
rippled in the wind. Peralta was a member of the "Frente para la Victoria" political bloc within the Partido Justicialista led at the national level by the Kirchners
(see Figure 8.1). As a Kirchnerista, he played a key role in continuing the legacy
established by Kirchner and Fernández during the 1990s and early 2000s as provincial politicians, which included strong state spending on public-sector
employment, infrastructure programs, and an "all of the above" approach to economic development through resource exploitation. Though becoming part of
the opposition, Governor Kirchner unexpectedly benefited from Menem's neoliberal reforms, which included the privatization of state-owned companies and
the decentralization of power to the provinces by devolving control over subsoil
rights (Salvia and Panaia 1997). This included the royalties deriving from
resource exploitation. Kirchner gained a key source of revenue following the
privatization of the national oil company, Yacimientos Petrolíferos Fiscales
(YPF), which had operations in Santa Cruz. Kirchner used the oil rents paid to
the province to expand state employment at a time when Menem was implementing significant structural adjustments across the nation (Allan 2007).

Following the ceremony, members of the public moved into the primary
school auditorium for a set of speeches that included a formal address by Peralta.
This political ritual was well established; the governor thanked the people for

FIGURE 8.1. Electioneering posters for the 2011 campaign (photo by author)

their devotion to the village. Following the pleasantries, he moved to the heart of the address: the detailing of the public revenues that the state would invest in El Chaltén that year. The administration earmarked funds for specific public projects, such as the building of clinics, schools, or roads. The governor sought to personalize the transfer of funds. Rather than overtly expecting any return offering, he framed the revenue transfer as a gift bestowed on the village. The personalization of the state treasury has long been criticized as a form of political corruption and so-called clientelism (Auyero 2002), since it establishes a tacit quid pro quo that links voting to public investment. If Chaltenenses dared to vote against Peralta and the Kirchners, then the size of future gifts would be reduced—or so the logic ran. But the Santa Cruz system also created a hyperpersonalized democratic politics in which the fortunes of leaders rose and fell depending on their ability to deliver material improvements to their constituents. Without the growth of public investment, residents had less incentive to vote for the incumbents. Every year, the governor was forced to genuflect before the voters.

The political ritual of the governor directly addressing the residents on the anniversary of the pueblo was a time-tested event that had also included Néstor Kirchner. In 2000, nine years before Peralta's address, Kirchner had spoken to Chaltenenses, who—more than eight years into his tenure as governor—were well acquainted with him, his wife, and his political entourage. In the previous year, Kirchner had sided with the village in the 182 Bis land dispute, which resulted in the designation of Fitz Roy as a provincial natural monument. He had also traveled to El Chaltén in June to sign a state contract to build a new medical center.

During his speech, Kirchner positioned the pueblo as on the nation's periphery. He called on President Fernando de la Rúa (1999–2001) to visit Santa Cruz, arguing that the province needed the help of the affluent, powerful "north": "[There] is a Santa Cruz that awaits remembrance because we are also an active part of this Argentina and we want to stop being a periphery of the *patria* [homeland]." Kirchner continued: "Fifteen years after the creation of El Chaltén we know what this word signifies: the past, because it is a voice coming from the Tehuelche culture—that which links us to the roots of this land, considered as a sacred site by the indigenous inhabitants for thousands of years; the present, because it is a reality that day to day grows and consolidates more each time as one of the localities with the most growth in the province; and the future because this is the place where many men and women chose to come and live with half measures, with the zeal of making each day in this pueblo a better place for our children" (*La Opinion Austral* 2000). In the address, Kirchner highlighted the growth of the village in terms of its numbers of permanent residents and tourists. However, he also identified the pueblo as having suffered from "half measures" during its existence, perennially underresourced by the very state he ran. Kirchner was well aware of discontent in the village and its residents' demands for greater investment in public services and infrastructure. Anticipating this line of criticism, he deflected it by positioning El Chaltén and Santa Cruz within the discourse of Patagonian underdevelopment. This discourse constructed a center-periphery hierarchy subordinating Patagonia to the national center of Buenos Aires, the hegemon that appropriated resources and wealth while returning very little to the periphery. This center-periphery dynamic marginalized the voices of the people of Santa Cruz. Kirchner called on the "north" to help his people, allowing them to cease being a "periphery" within the homeland.

Kirchner's speech highlighted the public investments being made to promote the green economy and address underdevelopment. He had gained goodwill in El Chaltén by backing the popular sustainability position during the 182 Bis dispute. His political message targeted a constituency based on an understanding of differentiated messaging across resource domains. Indeed, Kirchner took an "all of the above" approach to economic development that included petroleum, mining, agriculture, and tourism. Since the late 1800s, Santa Cruz had been known for its sheep farming. However, this sector fell on hard times as a result of overproduction in fragile steppe ecosystems, which led to desertification. With the decline of agriculture, Kirchner focused on the extraction and conservation industries, which were sited within a spatial division of production. Transnational firms developed the oil sector primarily on the Atlantic coast. Foreign mining corporations and their national subsidiaries invested in the interior parts of the province, on the steppe once dominated by sheep farming. The green economy covered the Andean zone on the western side of the province. Kirchner oversaw the deepening of global capitalist integration within Santa Cruz's mining, petroleum, and tourism industries. Nevertheless, the macroeconomic conditions under Menem greatly constrained national recovery. Beyond the conditions of Patagonian underdevelopment, an overvalued peso hurt the extractive and conservation industries promoted by the Kirchners at the provincial level.

As provincial politicians, the Kirchners oversaw the increasing specialization of the Southern Patagonian Andes as an "eco-region" committed to green development (Mendoza et al. 2017, 110). This binational zone embraced ecotourism and protected area conservation as its key nature industry (Martínez-Reyes 2016). Entrepreneurs in El Chaltén and El Calafate began to build transportation networks linking their communities with Chilean protected areas and tourism destinations. Moving beyond livestock farming, the eco-region developed through the transboundary movement of tourists, a quiet trend that ran counter to the vituperative debates and nationalist rhetoric of the period. In El Chaltén and other Andean communities, the Kirchners worked to strike the right balance between conservation, tourism infrastructure, and urbanization. The harmonization of these three elements required flexibility and attunement to local social dynamics. The Kirchners' light green politics was pro-environment but couched within a developmental logic that sought to build a stronger state and accumulate capital to support jobs, markets, and larger populations.

The Kirchnerist support for the green economy derives from a provincial political history of economic development based on the exploitation of natural resources and targeted political messaging to build electoral coalitions across resource domains. Not only did they support the growing turn toward eco-regionalism, but the Kirchners also worked to defend Argentine territorial sovereignty, capitalizing on the political opening given them by Menem to advance a renewed vision of Peronism.

THE ARGENTINE RENTIER STATE
AND THE GREEN ESTATE

Once they were in the presidential palace in Buenos Aires, the Kirchners advanced a green developmentalist agenda as part of a national economic strategy to revitalize the country in the aftermath of neoliberal crisis, working to overcome underdevelopment and direct massive investments toward Patagonia (Savino 2016, 408). This agenda communicated the emphasis of Kirchnerismo on natural resource exploitation and an environmentalist politics that did not constrain market development greatly. Indeed, green productivism emerged out of a provincial historical context in which the Kirchners secured the Andean electorate by delivering growing public investment to the nascent green economy. As presidents, Kirchner and Fernández advanced a green agenda that intersected with the broader aim of communicating and achieving stronger state control over the nation's natural resources. They built a rentier state that operated across multiple resource domains and mobilized different politics to justify the growing capture of revenues that fed institutional growth.

In April 2013, President Fernández appointed Carlos Corvalán head of the National Parks Administration of Argentina (Administración de Parques Nacionales, or APN). Corvalán had served for many years as the superintendent of the PNLG, overseeing the dramatic expansion of ecotourism in this protected area. As one of his first acts as APN head, Corvalán instructed the ranger station in El Chaltén to begin preparing to charge entrance fees to tourists. A senior park ranger and the director of the ranger station in El Chaltén, Alejandro "Capa" Caparrós remarked: "Today there are forty parks in the nation state and only ten cover the expenses. This money goes into an APN fund, which is an autarkic entity. Fines, fishing permits, commercial permits also go there, and with all this one has to resolve a ton of issues, in places that no one visits. . . . I want to organize meetings between those who are in charge of [El Chaltén's] institutions so we can talk, and share proposals, because there are many issues that bring us together as a settlement. To see the form in which we could cooperate" (Mendoza 2016, 174). Capa's narrative provided an institutional justification for the move to extract rents in the form of tourist user fees from El Chaltén as an access point into the PNLG. He noted that only one-fourth of Argentine parks generate the revenues needed to support the other three-fourths that have far fewer visitors. However, Capa was keenly aware of the entrenched local opposition to this new policy, particularly among tourism entrepreneurs. Entrepreneurs viewed free access to the park as a comparative market advantage they had over the competing destinations throughout southern Patagonia. Since this was a directive from the very top of the APN, Chaltenenses had little hope of reversing the change.

The political appointment of Corvalán and his immediate communiqué to the ranger station in El Chaltén underscores the ascent of the Argentine rentier state across various resource domains under Presidents Kirchner and Fernández. The first resource domain is the "green estate" (Mendoza 2016), consisting of national parks, monuments, and reserves. A federal agency, the APN operates as a public landlord with dominion over the green estate, capturing ground rent to fund its operations and expand investments. The top income earners—the PNLG, Nahuel Huapi, and Iguazú—provide operating funds that are redistributed across the system to subsidize parks with few visitors, along with annual federal appropriations from Buenos Aires. This green rentier state does not generate enormous sums of money for the federal government. Instead, it aims more narrowly to grow the APN and create the monopoly conditions for the ecotourism industry to prosper. The appointment of Corvalán as APN head elevated a Santa Cruz official with whom the Kirchners had worked on conservation issues for many years and signaled the importance of ecotourism-led development to the mission of the APN. Corvalán had overseen the rapid expansion of tourism that had made the PNLG a crown jewel within the national park system. The

APN kept user fees relatively low for the guiding industry and set up a tiered cost system so that foreign tourists paid more money than Argentine tourists did to enter parks, while local residents were eligible for waivers. Though there were local conflicts regarding the imposition or raising of park entrance fees, these debates never became politicized at the provincial or national levels. Instead, superintendents and ranger stations dealt with them on a case-by-case basis. With over 65,000 tourists annually, El Chaltén provided a key opportunity—despite local objections—for the APN to generate revenue to make the SLV station fiscally autonomous and create a surplus to fund other protected areas.

The Kirchnerist APN moved not only to develop its capacity to capture rent from user fees to fund the expansion of the conservation state, but also to expand its territorial holdings. Kirchnerist support for expanding the green estate emerged against the backdrop of long-standing political efforts—from across the ideological spectrum—to expand the federal system. Despite seeking to privatize state companies, utilities, and assets, the Menem administration never viewed the national park system as a set of public assets that needed to be privatized and sold off to investors. Indeed, the period from 1991 to 2000 saw the greatest increase in the number of new protected areas (eight) as well as territory (822,743 hectares) in the federal park system since the period from 1931 to 1940 (Administración de Parques Nacionales 2007, 21). Most of these new parks were not zoned for intensive tourism activities. National parks were on the far side of the bright line between public and private ownership that privatization did not cross. The Kirchners expanded the federal system even further. From 2003 to 2015, the APN gained nineteen new protected areas (terrestrial and marine) that expanded the federal system by some 645,967 hectares. Again, most of these new parks were not zoned for tourism activities (Administración de Parques Nacionales 2012 and 2018). Presidents Kirchner and Fernández brokered an accord between the APN and the Ministry of Defense to incorporate as national reserves land used by the armed forces (Administración de Parques Nacionales 2012, 292–293). Since the founding of the federal system, governments from both the right and left—whether military dictatorships or civilian democracies—have worked to expand the publicly owned and managed green estate. To draw upon Annette Weiner, who in turn was reflecting on Marcel Mauss's The Gift (1967), this patrimony of nature is the "inalienable wealth" to which each successive Argentine presidential administration has contributed since the 1930s (Weiner 1985). These are the "possessions" that communicate "affective qualities of sacredness that constitute the social self in relation to a past and a future" (212). They are untouchable and entrusted to the state as custodian of this common wealth, symbolically communicating the inviolability of the public trust. The Kirchner and Fernández administrations have expanded the green estate—both its territorial and marine holdings and its capacity to capture rent—to create a stronger conservation state.

The Argentine rentier state also emerged within a second resource domain: the agro-extractive sector. Following the devolution of subsoil rights with the 1994 constitutional reform, provincial governments gained control over the petroleum and mineral rents generated by the extractive industry (Schein 2016). Kirchner and Fernández turned to the agricultural industry—soy production in particular—for a new source of discretionary federal revenue that was exempt from provincial revenue-sharing laws. Argentine governments had long levied *retenciones*—export taxes on agricultural commodities that appropriated the rent understood to be the excess or windfall proceeds earned due to high global commodity prices—on the agricultural sector to provide fiscal revenue and protect the domestic market from inflation driven by global price swings. However, these taxes were almost completely eliminated as part of Menem's liberalization strategy (Richardson 2009, 241). Initially reinstituted by the interim administration of President Eduardo Duhalde (2002–2003), the Kirchners quickly ratcheted up export taxes to generate the discretionary funds needed to promote stronger state control over the economy and rebuild the social safety net in the aftermath of national crisis. They established price controls and subsidies (for transportation, energy, and food) to protect real wages, created antipoverty and cash-transfer programs, and funded public works projects (P. Lewis 2009; Richardson 2009). The agricultural sector thus offered the Kirchners a source of public revenue that they could spend on achieving specific political ends: to promote the social state and materially improve the lives of voters. Put differently, agricultural commodity rents became the cornerstone of the surplus recycling system (Varoufakis 2015) constructed by the Kirchners to implement their brand of post-neoliberal politics. But in 2008 the farming sector started a nationwide campaign to protest the further raising of export taxes, which included a general strike, the blocking of highways, and mass mobilization and ultimately resulted in a defeat for Fernández (P. Lewis 2009, 171–188). Unlike the green estate, the state extraction of agricultural rent became heavily politicized at the national level.

Kirchner and Fernández facilitated the creation of a rentier state across various resource domains and different scales of governmental jurisdiction and authority.[2] The politics of the APN and the green estate are markedly different from those involved in the agricultural sector and the drive to levy export taxes to fund the social state. Whereas the fight to capture agricultural rents allowed the Kirchners to represent their fiscal policy as motivated by resource redistribution and social justice, the capture of green rental income within the national park system signaled a politics of decentralized governance, community participation in resource management, and environmental education for visitors, as well as growth in jobs and businesses. In the case of agriculture, the Kirchners employed an authoritative, antagonistic approach to garner greater revenues that supported the social state. By contrast, green developmentalism rests upon efforts to forge popular environmental fronts for sustainability. Kirchnerist post-neoliberal resource politics thus involves a pluralized rentier state that applies different modes of governance and justification to growing revenue extraction and institution building.

THE GREEN ECONOMY VERSUS EXTRACTIVE INDUSTRY

Green developmentalism intersects with a political agenda to promote stronger state control over the economy through rent capture within natural resource domains. The Kirchners have relied upon global capital investment—particularly within capital-intensive extractive industries—to foster resource exploitation. With mobile capital searching out the highest rates of return, extractive industries have increasingly encroached upon the green economy and protected areas. In Andean Patagonia, this has generated increasing tension between the green and extractive industries.

A high-placed APN official discussed the problem of the lack of land management beyond the green economy. Extractive industries such as mining have sought to expand to mountain environments and lands surrounding protected areas. The official observed:

From the [perspective of] protected areas, effectively there is a large conflict that has two causes. One is the tremendous growth of mining activities—the boom that exists and that was not foreseen by those of us who work in conservation. We did not anticipate this, not so that we could necessarily impede it, but rather so we could create a land management plan. Now mining appears and wants to develop all over the place, in all areas. But in Argentina, there is no land management master plan—not just for mining, for nothing, for not one economic activity. [The second cause is that] there is no plan that says that we are going to develop mining here and forestry there. No. So, all economic forces potentially affect all territories. . . . And so the problem with mining, to go back to your question, is that there is not a territorial management plan. The great economic power of this activity makes it very difficult for governments to put on the brakes. . . . Due to this boom we are worried about the contamination that might be caused near national parks, for example Bosques Petrificado [National Monument]. In this case there is an inequality between mining and national parks—not just between conservation and mining, but also between conservation and forestry and other activities: that they [mining, forestry, and other extractive sectors] are not planned activities.

This official underscored the threat to protected areas posed especially by transnational mining corporations. Based on land management, ecological science, and territorial planning, the green economy is at odds with the unplanned movement of extractive capital across Patagonia in pursuit of higher profits. This has created a highly unregulated terrain for the development of natural resources.

Presidents Kirchner and Fernández applied their Santa Cruz developmental approach to the national economy. This involved strong support for global market integration and an emphasis on exploiting natural resource endowments, which allowed them to expand public-sector spending and shore up their political alliances. As provincial politicians, they relied on oil rents. As national leaders, they turned to agricultural rents. Like other members of the New Left in Latin America, the Kirchners espoused a form of progressive extractivism (Ebenau and Liberatore 2013). Across the region, governments have turned to petroleum, mining, and other forms of extraction to generate the growth and tax revenues needed to expand social welfare programs, support real wages, and engage in modest or more expansive forms of redistribution. One downside of progressive extractivism is the socio-environmental toll it takes on exploited areas. In Argentina, extractivism and the expansion of soy production have resulted in land grabs, evictions, and acts of violence against communities, while also precipitating social movements of opposition (Svampa and Antonelli 2009; Gordillo 2014; Brent 2015; Savino 2016; Schein 2016).

In Andean Patagonia, the incursions of mining corporations and hydropower projects have generated social movements to defend eco-regionalism: the formal and informal zoning of this environment for green economic activities like eco-tourism and conservation (Mendoza et al. 2017). Social movements have worked to resist extraregional actors ranging from national governments to transnational corporations. In 2002, Meridian Gold, Inc., proposed an open-pit mining project in a tourism-dominated zone of Esquel that abuts Los Alerces National Park in Argentina. A social movement arose in opposition to Meridian that led not only to a local plebiscite rejecting the mining project, but also to a province-wide moratorium that cost the company hundreds of millions of dollars (Herz, La Vina, and Sohn 2007, 28–30). Other transnationals have sought to open up parts of the Southern Patagonian Andes for mining projects, but they have faced local coalitions of resistance in places like Perito Moreno, Los Antiguos, and Futaleufú.

National governments and energy companies have promoted the "green energy" potential of hydropower, attempting to harmonize megadam projects with the wider framework of eco-regionalism (Mendoza et al. 2017, 107). From 2006 to 2014, HidroAysén was the key site of protest around which the Patagonia Sin Represas (Patagonian without Dams) campaign consolidated into a trans-Andean movement (Silva 2016). HidroAysén is a state-backed corporate venture by the Italian energy conglomerate Enel and the Chilean utility Colbún to build five hydroelectric dams on the Baker and Pascua Rivers in Chile's Aysén region. Due to the amount of publicity surrounding the protest campaign, President

Michelle Bachelet withdrew state support for HidroAysén, temporarily shutting down this highly controversial development project. On the other side of the border, the Fernández administration pushed forward the Represas Patagonia project to build two hydroelectric dams—the Jorge Cepernic and Néstor Kirchner Dams—on the Santa Cruz River, which flows from Lake Argentino to the Atlantic Ocean (Mendoza et al. 2017). The dams became a rallying point for a coalition of environmental NGOs to oppose this Argentine-Chinese venture. Represas Patagonia was the largest public works project initiated under the banner of Kirchnerismo, signaling the commitment of the Kirchners to overcoming regional and provincial underdevelopment. Capitalizing on the sovereign glacier and water resources defended by the Kirchners during the 1990s, these dams would provide an enormous source of energy to power development and resource exploitation across the region. Environmental NGOs filed a lawsuit against the federal government for failing to comply with environmental law, which required an environmental impact study to be carried out before the project began. The environmental coalition cited scientists who argued that the dams had the potential to raise the water level of Lake Argentino, potentially affecting the lacustrine glaciers of the PNLG (Gaffoglio 2014).

Green developmentalism has succeeded in building a stronger green economy within the Patagonian eco-region. This success has provided the conditions of possibility for popular resistance to the incursions of foreign extractive capital into the region, as well as ostensibly green energy projects—like hydroelectric dams—supported by governments. Taking an "all of the above" approach, Kirchnerist resource politics has led to growing tension between the extractive and green industries. Defending the eco-region, communities and NGOs have fought against threats to popular visions of sustainable development.

THE POLITICS OF THE GREEN ECONOMY

In March 2015, President Fernández addressed a crowd of supporters gathered outside the PNLG superintendent's office in her family home of El Calafate. Flanked by her sister-in-law, Alicia Kirchner, who was running for provincial governor, Fernández proudly announced the opening of a new tourism information center for the PNLG. As discussed in the opening pages of the introduction, Fernández took this opportunity to provide a brief history of economic growth in El Calafate as a metaphor for national development under Kirchnerismo. Continuing with her speech, she mentioned the almost 272 million pesos (equivalent to $30,900,000 at the time) that were being invested in El Calafate for the tourism center and a new boardwalk named in honor of her late husband. Referring to the source of this public investment, Fernández praised the "soybean fund": the "fund that we are giving and sending to each of the provinces and municipalities, precisely so projects can be undertaken with participation in the rights to soy exportation" (Fernández de Kirchner 2015). Presenting agricultural rents as the source of money for national public works, Fernández linked the green economy to the surplus recycling system at work within the Argentine rentier state. Moreover, there was an explicitly individualized politics at work in this granting of public money. Fernández sought not only to personalize this transfer of funds to improve the ecotourism industry, but also to memorialize her husband by building the boardwalk—thereby reinforcing the political symbolism and identification of Santa Cruz as the base for Kirchnerismo.

Since the 1990s, Kirchnerismo has thus developed across the domains of provincial and federal politics. The green productivist agenda is part of the battles waged by the Kirchnerist center left against the Menemist center right over the direction of the Peronist party. This green agenda communicates key values of Kirchnerismo: the securing of territorial sovereignty over land near the Chilean border; the promotion of natural resource exploitation as a strategy for employment, accumulation, and material improvements to the lives of voters; and the creation of a diversified rentier state and surplus recycling system to promote the social state and public investment. However, this approach has fostered growing tension between the green and extractive industries in Andean Patagonia. The very success of building popular environmental fronts of support for sustainable development has provided the bases of social opposition to transnational mining interests and state-corporate hydropower ventures.

CONCLUSION

This book has examined the intersection of Argentine post-neoliberal politics and the green economy. The green productivist agenda initiated by Presidents Néstor Kirchner and Cristina Fernández de Kirchner sought to accelerate ecotourism-led development to promote a form of sustainable capitalism that supports entrepreneurship and business, generates growing employment, recruits seasonal and permanent residents, and expands the revenue base of the National Parks Administration (Administración de Parques Nacionales, or APN). This project worked to build a mixed economy in which capital accumulation fostered both market expansion and the strengthening of the conservation state. Under the Kirchners, the green capitalist economy witnessed a near doubling of tourist numbers, the rapid growth of commerce and service work, the strengthening of the APN's regulatory power, and increasing public and private investment in park landscapes. Enacting this green agenda, the Kirchners communicated their commitment to territorial sovereignty, their support for natural resource exploitation and environmental protection, and their endorsement of the creation of a differentiated rentier state across resource domains. Ecotourism-led growth centrally involved the selling of sublime alpine landscape (see Figure C.1). Though there are other commercially important landscapes, Andean Patagonia has been the focal point for national ecotourism based on adventure leisure pursuits such as trekking, mountaineering, kayaking, and boating. To manage the growth of ecotourism, the APN used community-based conservation to generate consent for scientific sustainability protocols developed by land managers and enforced by park rangers. As a political intervention, the green productivist agenda sought to build popular environmental fronts of support for the conservation state and Kirchnerist post-neoliberal rule.

Despite accelerating ecotourism-led growth, green productivism led to a series of contradictions that drew attention to the limits of the social state, inclusive development, and resource redistribution associated with Kirchnerismo as a political ideology. The ecotourism industry was based on rentier capitalism and the creation of what I termed the "semiotic estate": the exercising of

FIGURE C.1. The Patagonian sublime: Chaltén Massif (© Dörte Pietron)

monopoly control over the symbolic and territorial dimensions of parkland. The conservation state and entrepreneurial capital forged public-private alliances to control the park, create place brands, and upgrade the alpine landscape to satisfy affluent consumers' tastes. The green economy established a robust middle class of formalized, property-owning citizens. Ecotourism successfully brought growing numbers of tourists to the trekking capital of Argentina, among other destinations. However, ecotourism involved a highly classed form of consumption available only to the upper-middle and upper classes. Moreover, the entrepreneurial class angled to dominate the service working class, maintaining a largely informal labor market that stripped workers of the social rights associated with labor-based citizenship. The APN embraced community-based conservation as a strategy of democratic rule but implemented policies that did little to halt growing inequality and stratification within communities. Green development thus fostered a set of outcomes that ran counter to Kirchnerist political ideology: the elitist consumption of iconic spaces of national nature, the solidification of tiered citizenship dividing the formalized middle class from the informalized service class, and the establishment of state-capital rule at the expense of subaltern actors.

Moreover, the green capitalist economy was defined by a concrete ecology of risk. The spheres of production, consumption, and the state depended on distinct risk subjectivities. In El Chaltén, tourism consumption focused on the vertical and horizontal terrains of alpine adventure pursued by mountaineers and trekkers, respectively. Service workers and tourism entrepreneurs struggled to control or gain access to socioeconomic opportunities. Land managers and park rangers sought to generate a public conservation subject position that incorporated tourists, residents, and state actors into the discourse of scientific sustainability. This capitalist ecology of risk stabilized positional understandings and practical engagements with multidimensional types and scales of risk. As Karl Marx (1990) recognized, capitalist economies are inherently unstable because they are based on market competition and creative destruction, which work to upend and undermine existing social relations and conditions. As the field of political ecology has shown, capital moves in and out of localities in pursuit of the highest rates of accumulation, generating risk exposure and contributing to environmental devastation. The global discourse of sustainable development emerged as a critical response to the tendency for capital to undermine the ecological conditions upon which accumulation is based. Sustainability sought to restore faith in the capacity for capitalism to correct itself and incorporate environmental externalities into the market system. In Patagonia, the discourse of scientific sustainability has articulated this gospel of salvation. Land managers and park rangers have labored to establish and adjust the social and legal conditions of the green economy to ensure that ecotourism is sustainable, mobilizing shifting visions of ecological risk and security.

However, the green productivist agenda fostered inequality and marginalization alongside wealth creation, thereby partly eroding the social bases of legitimacy for the post-neoliberal turn. Patagonian communities promoted sustainable ecotourism but also fashioned a political culture of Kirchnerismo based on concrete understandings of the state, governance, and citizenship. This political culture—the double state, ambiguous governance, and tiered citizenship—served as the framework for Chaltenenses and others to read the spectral presence of Kirchnerist power into the licit and illicit dimensions of the green economy. Residents struggled to interpret inflation statistics, public projects like bridges and highways, and the wealth of empresarios, uncertain how to decode their meaning. Residents viewed center-left Kirchnerismo as a legitimate political agenda. However, they also identified the personalized state of los Kirchners with the corrupt use of political power that threatened the viability of the community. This was the ethnographic insight that I found most perplexing and challenging: how to depict the opacity and instability of meaning for subjects within everyday life. To represent this insight ethnographically, I developed the model of the ecology of risk to place uncertain potentiality for being at the ontological foundation of social life.

Responding to the crisis of Argentine neoliberalism, the Kirchner and Fernández administrations sought to rebuild the social state, strengthen national sovereignty, and create a more progressive form of capitalism. To do so, they pursued a neo-developmentalist approach based on resource exploitation and domestic consumption. Hamstrung by revenue-sharing agreements with the provinces, the Kirchners raised export taxes on agricultural commodities to provide sources of discretionary income that could be used in politically expedient ways. Kirchner and Fernández justified the appropriation of agricultural rents as a way to channel a capitalist surplus into social programs, antipoverty measures, subsidies to protect wages, and public works projects. However, especially during her second term as president, Fernández faced a suite of problems such as high inflation, debt repayment litigation, devaluation, capital flight, and eroding terms of trade. Kirchner and Fernández built political alliances with center-left and leftist governments throughout Latin America to advance trade and commerce, secure allies to defend Argentine claims to sovereignty over the Islas Malvinas (also known as the Falkland Islands), and forge a front to oppose—in a selective, politically resonant fashion—U.S. empire building and the global neoliberal order. In Argentina, this antagonistic front celebrated an anti-neoliberal creed and pursued practices such as domestic subsidies, tariffs, currency controls, and nationalization that were derided as irrational, crude, and destructive by Euro-American politicians, media, and public intellectuals. The Kirchner and Fernández administrations promoted the green economy as part of a strategic emphasis on natural resource exploitation. The green economy became one pillar of a broader program to deliver material improvements to constituencies and to communicate the values of social equity, territorial sovereignty, the defense of the patrimony of nature, and global economic integration.

The Patagonian Sublime makes a number of critical contributions to scholarship through its theorization of post-neoliberal green development and politics. First, it provides a model for the study of the capitalist economy through attention to the trinity form of capital, labor, and land, as well as the mediating role of the state in shaping consumer access to resources. Developing the concept of the semiotic estate, I have sought to illuminate how the green economy is shaped by rentier capitalism and ground rent capture. This model may be useful to anthropologists, political ecologists, and others studying capitalist dynamics around the world, directing long overdue attention to rent. Second, the book delineates the green productivist agenda used by the Kirchner and Fernández administrations as part of a broader strategy of resource exploitation. Contributing to scholarship on Latin American resource politics, I demonstrate the need to bring conservation and extraction together into the same framework to assess the multifaceted rentier state that develops across various resource domains. I highlight the Kirchnerist political strategy of building popular environmental fronts for sustainable development, as well as the genesis of political cultures of the state, governance, and citizenship. Third, the book develops an ecology of risk approach to understanding the intersection of the risk society and global capital. This ethnographic model highlights the plurality of risk subject positions that simultaneously exist within a capitalist space, as well as political efforts undertaken to integrate these positions into a hegemonic vision for collective security. Scholarly attention to the interactional convergence or conjuncture of risk positionalities is long overdue, as is a multiperspectival, multiscalar understanding of a capitalist ecology in the making. Fourth, the book challenges political ecologists to examine the role of post-neoliberal politics—among governments, political parties, civic groups, and indigenous movements—in articulating counterhegemonic fronts in opposition to global neoliberalism. Such an examination would require scholars to move beyond the totalizing strains of thinking within scholarship on neoliberal conservation, turning instead to spaces of dissent, resistance, and alternative development. I have made a case for positioning the rentier state much more centrally in analyses of topics like ecotourism, conservation politics, and sustainable development. In doing so, I have drawn attention to how Argentine post-neoliberal conservation is built upon particular strategies of political rule, capitalist growth, and national representation that converge within the making of the semiotic estate.

Following twelve years of Kirchnerismo, Argentines elected as president Mauricio Macri, a center-right politician and wealthy businessman. Daniel Scioli, the Peronist party candidate, lost the October 2015 election by three percentage points. The Macri administration began to dismantle the Kirchnerist macroeconomic framework that relied upon intervention into foreign exchange markets, a devalued peso, and currency controls, while also seeking to eliminate consumer subsidies. However, Macri has struggled to contain high inflation and manage the economic recession that dominated his first year in office. After taking power, he reshuffled the federal bureaucracy and moved the APN out of the Ministry of Tourism and into the newly reorganized Ministry of the Environment and Sustainable Development. Macri sacked the Kirchnerist-appointed APN president, Carlos Corvalán, and replaced him with Eugenio Breard, a former executive at Philip Morris. Macri tapped Emiliano Ezcurra for APN vice president. Ezcurra was the director of Banco de Bosques, an environmental NGO. These appointments signaled a new approach to the green economy that looked outside the conservation state to include corporate and NGO perspectives. Moreover, the bureaucratic reorganization represented a criticism of Kirchnerist green productivism. Macri sought to communicate that the APN was returning to its primary mission of environmental protection. The new APN leadership soon came out against the Represas Patagonia hydroelectric dam project in Santa Cruz, the public works project with the largest investment under the Kirchners (see chapter 8). Under Corvalán, the APN had refrained from commenting on the dams, despite their potential environmental impact on Lake Argentino and Parque Nacional Los Glaciares. Though signaling support for the antidam coalition, the Macri administration ultimately approved the Represas Patagonia project and allayed the concerns of the Chinese government and Chinese corporate investors. Under its new leaders, the APN has continued to promote ecotourism-led growth and has sought to expand the federal protected area system in Patagonia.

More broadly across Latin America, the first wave of post-neoliberal governments appears to have peaked, with the deposing of President Dilma Rousseff in
Brazil and with Venezuela teetering on the brink of civil war. Perhaps Macri's
victory will usher in a second generation of neoliberal leaders across the continent, who will be more attuned to the importance of the social state and the
need to tackle inequality, poverty, and environmental destruction. For now,
though, the Kirchnerist New Left has become part of the opposition, representing a vibrant source of social mobilization, heterodox economic thinking, and
political imagination in Argentina. During the 2015 election, Alicia Kirchner—
the sister of Néstor Kirchner—became governor of Santa Cruz, while Máximo
Kirchner—the son of Néstor and Cristina—was elected as a national deputy. In
October 2017, Cristina Fernández de Kirchner was once again elected as a national
senator, this time as the leader of the newly formed Unidad Ciudadana (Citizen's
Unity party). She is expected to become the chief opponent to Macri's center-
right coalition. It remains to be seen how the politics of Kirchnerismo will be
modified to articulate a new popular front for post-neoliberal development and
continue the project of building twenty-first-century Peronism.

ACKNOWLEDGMENTS

This book has developed through various phases over the past decade. The idea for it emerged during a year spent with my wife in Santiago de Chile, teaching English to Pinochet-sympathetic businesspeople. Originally, we had thought about living in Buenos Aires, but this was in the immediate aftermath of the Argentine economic crisis of 2001–2002. Our prospects of eking out a living seemed greater on the other side of the Andes, so we settled into the Parque Forestal neighborhood and traveled during holidays. Some of those trips were to Patagonia. Taking a bus to the far south was a uniquely inspiring experience, since one cannot travel directly from Santiago to Punta Arenas, the capital of the Magallanes region. Instead, one must cross the Andes into Argentina and travel east to the Atlantic coast before going south—a journey that is over 3,000 kilometers long. In the process, one gets a sense not only for the expansiveness of this vast region, but also for the territorial division of capitalist production that separates the Andean green economy from the arid steppe and coastal zones.

In 2006, I began field research on the topic of the politics of the Patagonian green economy, with a focus on the Argentine village of El Chaltén and Parque Nacional Los Glaciares. I owe a tremendous debt to the people of El Chaltén for their kindness and patience. In particular, I would like to acknowledge Alejandra Chanampa, Aristides Aieta, Leonardo Wozniak, Andrea Torres, Juan José Landucci, Marco Cravea, Gerardo Sans, Andrea Randazzo, Mela Iribarren, and Cecilia Sanchez Izaguirre. I would especially like to thank Rolando Garibotti for his long-standing guidance on all matters related to conservation and mountaineering, as well as for his efforts as an informal research assistant. I have benefited greatly from the research support provided by: the Administración de Parques Nacionales de Argentina; the Corporación Nacional Forestal de Chile; the Instituto Argentino de Nivología, Glaciología y Ciencias Ambientales; Estancia Los Huemules; and Conservación Patagónica. I consulted historical documents at the Biblioteca Central y Centro de Documentación Perito Francisco P. Moreno in Buenos Aires, the Biblioteca de Parque Nacional Nahuel Huapi in Bariloche, the Archivo Histórico Provincial de Santa Cruz in Río Gallegos, and the Biblioteca de Parque Nacional Los Glaciares in El Calafate—all in Argentina.

The University of Chicago provided the intellectual environment in which this project took shape. John Comaroff, William Mazzarella, and Stephan Palmié offered invaluable support and critical commentary on my dissertation. Joe Masco has been an incredible mentor, professionally and intellectually. This manuscript has benefited immensely from his close reading and suggestions over the years. I would also like to thank faculty members and students in the

Department of Anthropology, the Workshop on the Anthropology of Latin America and the Caribbean, the Workshop on the Global Environment, and the Center for Latin American Studies for their feedback on earlier drafts. The Division of Social Sciences provided financial support during my graduate studies, including the Provost/Markovitz Fellowship and the Trustees Fellowship. Initial fieldwork was undertaken with the support of a Tinker Field Research Grant from the Center for Latin American Studies and a Leiffer Field Research Fellowship from the Department of Anthropology. The Social Science Research Council supported the bulk of the fieldwork in Argentina through a generous International Dissertation Research Fellowship grant.

The manuscript became much more interdisciplinary after I arrived at the University of Mississippi as a faculty member in 2013. In the Department of Sociology and Anthropology, I would especially like to thank James Thomas, Robbie Ethridge, Jay Johnson, Kate Centellas, Tony Boudreaux, Kirsten Dellinger, Jeff Jackson, Willa Johnson, Kirk Johnson, Catarina Passidomo, Amy McDowell, Carolyn Freiwald, Maureen Meyers, Miguel Centellas, and Simone Delerme. I would also like to thank Conor and Carey Dowling, Jesse Cromwell and Laura Martin, Will Townes, Pato and Shannon Cohn, Afton Thomas, and Darren Grem. The College of Liberal Arts has provided generous support for research and travel. I have enriched my own understanding of political ecology, sociocultural anthropology, risk studies, and Latin American studies through conversations with countless students over the years, as well as with thesis advisees from the Sally McDonnell Barksdale Honors College and the Croft Institute for International Studies.

The book has been greatly improved by collaborations and conversations with scholars working in Argentina and Chile, particularly a group of Patagonia-focused researchers that includes Rob Fletcher, Laura Ogden, George Holmes, and Colombina Schaeffer. I am grateful to Kim Guinta and Rutgers University Press for their enthusiasm and support for the project, as well as to reviewers for offering sharp feedback on the proposal and manuscript. Stephen G. Harris from the Center for Archaeological Research at the University of Mississippi created the two maps that appear in the book, using geospatial data from the Biblioteca del Congreso Nacional de Chile and DIVA-GIS. Rolando Garibotti provided the cover photo and a figure for chapter 1. Photos by Dörte Pietron appear in the introduction and conclusion. The rest of the photos are my own. I am grateful to the American Anthropological Association and the editors of two journals for permission to reprint and update previously published articles. Portions of the introduction, chapter 3, and chapter 4 appeared in "Post-Neoliberal Labor in Patagonia: Informality and Citizenship in the Green Economy," *Dialectical Anthropology* 41 (1): 55–76. Sections of chapter 5 and chapter 6 appeared in "Educational Policing: Park Rangers and the Politics of the Green (E)State in Patagonia," *Journal of Latin American and Caribbean Anthropology* 21 (1): 173–192.

Lastly, this project has emerged out of a highly supportive network of kin and close friends. I am thankful to my wonderful parents, Abel and Sherry Mendoza, and my siblings, Abel C. Mendoza and Adriana DalSoglio, for their enduring love and support. I would like to thank Atif Haque, Lisa Haque, and Azam Ahmed for their friendship. I am grateful to Judith Aronson and Christopher Ricks for the kindness and generosity they have shown me over the years. Finally, Alice Ricks—my wife and editor—has read through each draft and proposal over the past decade, giving feedback on everything from argumentation and storytelling to the use of images. I cannot begin to express my appreciation for all that she has done. This book is dedicated to Alice and my sharp, funny, and joyful daughters, Sylvie and Nadia Mendoza.

NOTES

INTRODUCTION

1. James Ferguson (2015) has explored the "new politics of distribution" at work in southern African countries, which challenges the scholarly narrative of hegemonic neoliberalism. In Euro-America, the far right has increasingly promoted an antiglobalization ideology that blames immigrants and racial others, the technocratic elite, and open borders for deindustrialization, the decline of sovereignty, and the dilution of national culture.

2. Many Latin American governments sought to accelerate industrialization by imposing protective tariffs on foreign commodities and subsidizing national industries that produced goods and services for the domestic market. The goal of import substitution industrialization was to reduce dependency on foreign countries by gradually expanding domestic production and consumption.

3. I have used pseudonyms throughout the book to protect the identity of my research subjects, unless they explicitly requested otherwise. However, I have used the real names of public officials in state agencies and people whose names appear in journal, newspaper, or magazine articles I have cited.

4. The Hielos Continentales includes both the Southern and Northern Patagonian Ice Fields.

5. In the peak season from October 2007 to March 2008, El Calafate and the southern zone of the PNLG received 433,882 visitors. During the Argentine recession of 2008–2009, there was a significant dip to 369,212 visitors, with incremental gains over the next five years.

6. The concept of a green economy could be applied to the foraging, pastoralist, horticultural, or agricultural economies long studied by anthropologists. It could refer to state or nonstate societies as well as to socialist, anarchist, feudal, or capitalist productive arrangements, among others. However, the green economy and sustainable development are often narrowly understood in terms of the capitalist economy. They are part of what Martin O'Connor (1993) calls the ecological phase of capitalism, which is based upon the attempt to internalize environmental destruction and ecological systems within an encompassing system of self-managing accumulation.

7. See also Walley 2004, West and Carrier 2004, Carrier and Macleod 2005, Vivanco 2007, and Stronza and Gordillo 2008.

8. Current research within the anthropology of capitalism is voluminous. Scholars have focused on a number of key topics, such as neoliberalism (Jean Comaroff and Comaroff 2000), industry and the corporation (Rajan 2007; Ong 2010; Shever 2012; Kirsch 2014), finance and banking (LiPuma and Lee 2004; Zaloom 2006; Ho 2009; Miyazaki 2013; Appadurai 2016), ethnic economies and consumption (Colloredo-Mansfeld 1999; Appadurai 2000; John Comaroff and Comaroff 2009; West 2012), money and debt (Maurer 2005; Cattelino 2008; Graeber 2011), marketing and advertising (Miller 1997; Mazzarella 2005), and resource exploitation (Tsing 2005; Escobar 2008; Li 2014).

9. According to Marx (1991), landowners accrue ground rents by leasing out their lands to capitalist farmers, miners, foresters, and other resource exploiters, appropriating a portion of the surplus value generated by these activities. Marx's model of rent depends upon the labor theory of value in which surplus value (extracted from surplus labor) is unevenly distributed within and across industries.

10. Coronil (1997) primarily focuses on the political history of oil rents in Venezuela.

11. Rent capture is a contentious issue for both the right and the left. The right critiques the pursuit of rent because it suggests a lack of entrepreneurial zeal and dependence on a mono- poly position that undermines market competition. The left criticizes the pursuit of rent because of its association with aristocratic landownership and class stratification. The rentier state is typically associated with authoritarianism, corruption, and the resource curse (Coronil 1997; Watts 2001; Dunning 2008; Mitchell 2013). I argue that scholars need to provide more fine-grained analyses of the multilateral rentier state that develops across various resource regimes, including the green economy and protected areas.

12. The concept of the semiotic estate could be fruitfully extended to the tourism industry at large, artisan craft production, wine making, liquor distilleries, specialty coffee, or the local food movement—anything that involves the monopolization of coupled territorial and symbolic spaces that allow landowners to regulate and dictate the terms of consumer access.

13. The literature on neoliberal conservation is extensive, but there are a number of theoretical overviews (Brockington, Duffy, and Igoe 2010; Igoe, Neves, and Brockington 2010; Büscher, Dressler, and Fletcher 2014) and ethnographies specific to protected areas or green develop- ment spaces (Büscher 2013; Martínez-Reyes 2016). George Holmes and Connor Cavanagh have defined neoliberal conservation as a trend characterized by "practices and discourses of finan- cialisation, marketization, privatization, commodification, and decentralisation within conser- vation governance" (2016, 199). Robert Fletcher, Wolfram Dressler, and Bram Büscher concep- tualize "Nature™ Inc." as the "new frontiers of neoliberal conservation," highlighting concrete practices, discourses, and modes of circulation of natural capital (2014, 5). Initially revolving around ecotourism and CBC, neoliberal conservation—as Nature™ Inc.—has increasingly developed more complex forms of environmental protection such as payments for ecosystem services, bioprospecting, carbon markets, species banking, and so-called REDD+ programs to reduce emissions from deforestation and forest degradation.

14. Perhaps the best-known theorization of risk society comes from Ulrich Beck (2012). Beck's notion of risk society refers to a form of reflexive modernization generated by planetary socioecological hazards that undermine confidence in expert risk management systems. Working in the ethnographic tradition of risk scholarship, I focus instead on the translocal risk society of the Patagonian green economy. My approach is similar to that of Bruce Braun, who conceptualizes the risk society as a product of the different fields of risk exposure of actors to "capitalist development" tied up with the "social production of space, place, and nature" (2003, 178).

15. This book provides an examination of the Patagonian green economy as a risk society integrated into global capital networks. One potential approach that could be developed is based on risk governmentality (Dean 2010). Drawing upon Michel Foucault's (1991 and 2009) concept of governmentality, scholars have examined the shifting parameters of risk governance across the liberal, social welfare, and neoliberal periods (Ewald 1991; O'Malley 1996; Baker and Simon 2002; Aradau and van Munster 2008; O'Malley 2008). The question then becomes how post-neoliberal governments—which seek to create stronger welfare states and socialize risk in certain arenas of public life—have altered risk governance logics. One problem with the risk governmentality approach is that it tends to provide a flattening, monochromatic picture of how risk subjectivity operates, eliminating the plural visions of risk that exist in social life—that is, how subjects experience and act from a position of multilateral risk exposure. Rather than reducing risk experience to either a purported neo- liberal entrepreneurial ethos or a post-neoliberal mixed approach (that is, one with multi- ple governmentalities) of market individualization intertwined with social welfarism, I

focus ethnographically instead on the ecology of risk that is operative in the Patagonian green economy to understand the different modes of risk subjectivity that are produced and sustained.

CHAPTER 1   ALPINE-STYLE MOUNTAINEERING

1. I follow Martin Heidegger (1962) in conceptualizing death as involving not just the biological demise of organisms but also an authenticating relationship to resolute "being."

2. Resolve is a key principle of the climbing habitus (Dutkiewicz 2015; see also Bunn 2016). Pierre Bourdieu defines the habitus as embodied systems of "durable, transposable *dispositions* . . . enabling agents to cope with unforeseen and ever-changing situations" (2004, 72; emphasis in original).

3. I follow Denis Cosgrove's definition of landscape ideology, which refers to the "way in which certain classes of people have signified themselves and their world through their imagined relationship with nature, and through which they have underlined and communicated their own social role and that of others with respect to external nature" (1998, 15).

4. As late as the 1970s, Jorge Luis Borges—the celebrated Argentine author—drew upon the long-standing notion that Patagonia was a land of nothingness, likening it to an Argentine "Sahara" (quoted in Theroux 1980, 402).

5. For a discussion of the Tehuelche Aonikenk, see Pero (2002). For a first-hand account of life in the El Chaltén zone in the early twentieth century, see Madsen (2006).

6. Mountain landscapes became acceptable destinations for the cosmopolitan leisure class in the eighteenth and nineteenth centuries (Schama 1996).

7. There is a growing literature on the politics of wilderness and its impacts on indigenous and rural communities. Peter Coates (1998) discusses the history of the multifaceted concept of nature. William Cronon (1996) provides a seminal critique of mythic wilderness, while Roderick Neumann (1998), Dan Brockington (2002), and Mark Dowie (2011) discuss the legacy of expropriation and resettlement in the building of protected wilderness areas around the world.

8. The popular understanding of free climbing—that it means climbing without ropes—is mistaken. Climbing entirely without ropes is called free soloing. A free climber can use a rope, bolts, or other tools to protect the climber in the event of falling, but not to aid his or her upward progress.

9. In 2014, Red Bull Media House released the film, *Cerro Torre: A Snowball's Chance in Hell*, which showcased the first free ascent of the Compressor Route by David Lama and his climbing partner, Peter Ortner.

10. Climbing scholars have drawn attention to the politics of risk implicit in debates over climbing styles (N. Lewis 2000; Kiewa 2002; Bogardus 2012).

11. Jan Dutkiewicz discusses the "haptic vocabulary" used by climbers to describe categories and sizes of different rock holds, as well as the "static" and "dynamic" moves employed for progress (2015, 30).

12. Contrary to the assertion that extreme sports are built on an illusion of control (Lyng 1990), climbers recognize that random factors can kill even the most alert, accomplished alpinist.

13. This is what William Mazzarella calls the ongoing attempt to close the "structural 'gap' at the heart of the commodity form" between the "embodied resonance" of products and their abstract "discursive elaboration" by marketers (2005, 20–21).

CHAPTER 2   ADVENTURE TREKKING

1. Adventure trekking is a particular form of what John Urry has called the "romantic" tourist gaze that idealizes "solitude, privacy and a personal, semi-spiritual relationship with the object of the gaze" (2008, 43). The use of the Foucauldian "gaze" to theorize trekking tourism can be problematic, however, if it occludes attention to the other senses of the body. The gaze model runs the risk of imposing a far too ocular-centric approach, tacitly introducing a hierarchy of the senses into the analysis. Urry recognizes the limitations of the gaze model (152–156). My representation of trekking seeks to foreground kinesthesis (the sense of movement) and the mobile tourist body.

2. This is indicative of what Claudia Bell and John Lyall refer to as the "accelerated sublime" (2002).

3. John and Jean Comaroff note that this "Argentina-as-brand" campaign is fashioned around the making of "corporate nationhood" in which nationality becomes an object of ownership for citizens and a vehicle by which "Argentina recognizes itself and fixes its place in the world" through tourism (2009, 123). Though for the Comaroffs this points toward the expansion of the global ethnic economy, the Argentina-as-brand campaign also serves as a rentier strategy by which post-neoliberal governments have sought to capitalize on the consumer value of patrimonial nature and culture.

4. Kinesthesis refers to the "sense of movement" that is part of the "somatic senses" of the body—which includes the five classic senses as well as "the underexplored background feelings of embodiment," such as "proprioception (felt muscular position) and the vestibular system (sense of balance)" (Paterson 2009, 768). As an integral feeling of mobility, kinesthesis helps establish the orientation of the body within the environment.

5. Trekking draws upon the nature-society dualism. Trekking invokes the long history of the wilderness concept as a site for the recuperation of a natural subjectivity (Tsing 2005, 95–101).

6. One exception is the small Kaweshkar (Alacalufe) community living in Puerto Edén, a remote village in Bernardo O'Higgins National Park.

CHAPTER 3   *COMERCIANTE* ENTREPRENEURSHIP

1. Entrepreneurs note that that the high proportion of public-sector jobs is associated with Governor Kirchner. This proportion continued once Kirchner and Fernández moved to Buenos Aires to occupy the presidential palace. There was a public-works boom in Santa Cruz implemented under the Kirchners that channeled federal money to the province. Beyond this, entrepreneurs point to the Kirchnerist patronage machine that is thought to control the provincial government.

2. The capitalist market cannot be viewed as a space in which actors pursue their self-interest according to the natural laws of competition encapsulated in the image of *homo economicus* (Sahlins 1972). Instead, shifting cultural perspectives are constitutive of market capitalism, fostering different understandings of where the market does or does not exist, what has value, how money can and cannot facilitate exchange relations, and how competition should occur (Wolf 1982; Zelizer 1997; Verdery 2003; Zaloom 2006; Cattelino 2008; Ho 2009; West 2012; D'Avella 2014). These perspectives allow some market actors to be framed as more or less virtuous than others, and the market to be seen as a space in which the social and moral bonds of solidarity may be present or absent. Rather than creating market distortion, these acts of solidarity are everyday business practices used by middle-class owners to make a globally integrated tourism market viable under inflationary conditions.

3. Though Alicia Kirchner, Néstor Kirchner's sister, was elected governor of Santa Cruz in 2015, the Kirchner family did not hold the provincial governorship from 2003 to 2015. From 2007 to 2015, Governor Daniel Peralta ruled Santa Cruz as a member of the Kirchnerist political wing (Frente para la Victoria) within the Partido Justicialista, though the relationship had grown strained by the end of the Fernández presidency.

CHAPTER 4   *GOLONDRINA* LABORING

1. Poverty and extreme poverty, defined as surviving on $4 per day and $2.50 per day, respectively, fell from 2002 crisis highs of 45.5 percent and 29.2 percent of the national population to 14.3 percent and 6.6 percent in 2010 (Weisbrot et al 2011, 8).
2. Lucía Trujillo and Martín Retamozo argue that informality declined from 47 percent in 2003 to 33 percent in 2014 (2017, 49). Mariano Féliz places informality in 2010 as high as 44.7 percent in the private sector, with 13 percent of public-sector workers having what are called "trash contracts" (2012, 112). These are arrangements in which employers hire employees for a "probationary period" without benefits, which can translate into a permanent state of informal employment (Whitson 2007a, 128).
3. A political discussion of the Madsen issue ensued during the 2007–2008 season. A series of proposals emerged in the face of service workers' public disagreement with the idea of closing the camp. Initially supporting closure, the Cámara de Comercio shifted toward a more accommodating stance that kept the camp open. The possibility arose of the Club Andino, the local mountaineering club, or some other civil society group taking over the administration of Madsen. From the perspective of the National Parks Administration of Argentina (Administración de Parques Nacionales, or APN), however, this would have violated its jurisdiction over park territory.
4. In Argentina, the health care system is tripartite. There is private health care for the affluent, a high-quality public health care system for legal workers run by unions, and an underfunded and basic public system (Cavagnero, Carrin, and Torres 2010).
5. The Argentine state is legally allowed to employ "contract" and "fellowship" workers for "no more than 6 months without formalizing them," but in practice it is common for casualized laboring conditions to persist for years (Whitson 2007b, 2924, note 4).

CHAPTER 5   COMMUNITY-BASED CONSERVATION

1. On neoliberal conservation, also see Igoe and Brockington (2007), Fletcher (2010), Arsel and Büscher (2012), Brondo (2013), Büscher, Dressler, and Fletcher (2014).
2. In a similar vein, Nora Haenn and coauthors have examined the notion of disorganized neoliberal conservation in which the state, communal property, and even socialism play important roles in Mexican protected areas (2014). Moreover, José Martínez-Reyes (2016) examines Mayan post-conservation and post-development (see also Escobar 1995 and 2010), which can be understood as a mode of post-neoliberal conservation deriving from indigenous action.
3. See Aagesen (2000) for a concise historical overview of the APN and changing approaches to protected area conservation.
4. Anthropologists have drawn attention to the hollow promise of CBC and participatory development, examining the divergence between hype and practice (Walley 2004; West 2006; Garner 2013). Others have examined popular resistance to environmental governance and state surveillance (Haenn 2005; Hoffman 2014).

5. Land managers had included this new regulation in the 1997 PMLG, citing the successful example of the rescue system at Cerro Aconcagua Provincial Park (Administración de Parques Nacionales 1997, 84–85).

CHAPTER 6   CONSERVATION POLICING

1. To become a full ranger, a person must complete the competitive, multiyear university program at the Escuela Nacional de Guardaparques (National Ranger School) of the National Parks Administration of Argentina.

2. In 2013, Fernández appointed Corvalán president of the APN. Corvalán had overseen the vast expansion of tourism in the PNLG. During the 2012–2013 season alone, the APN collected 26 million pesos ($4,753,000 at the time) in revenue from the over 500,000 visitors who entered the southern zone of PNLG (Mendoza 2016, 174–75).

3. Civilian rule returned to Argentina in 1983, leading to a tumultuous discussion about how to hold military and paramilitary forces accountable for the tens of thousands of people who were disappeared, tortured, and executed during the Dirty War (Feitlowitz 1999). Discourses of corruption and impunity arose during the 1980s and 1990s related to the perpetrators of mass violence and human rights violations. Kirchner won plaudits from human rights organizations for the vigor with which his administration reversed the course of his predecessors and sought to prosecute those responsible for the crimes committed under the dictatorship (Faulk 2013).

4. The concept of the green estate refers not only to public protected areas, but also to private ones controlled by cooperatives, corporations, and individual investors (Mendoza 2016). There is a growing literature on private protected areas in Patagonia (Meza 2009; Holmes 2014; Tecklin and Sepulveda 2014; Serenari et al. 2016), as well as public protected areas, tourism, and resident communities (Aagesen 2000; Martín and Chehébar 2001; Otero et al. 2006; Miniconi and Guyot 2010; Mendoza 2016 and 2017; Mendoza et al. 2017).

5. The National Oceanic and Atmospheric Administration's Air Resources Laboratory is the weather service used by rangers, climbers, and guides.

6. This day celebrates the founding gift that is at the historical basis of the national park system. In 1903, Francisco "Perito" Moreno—a Patagonian explorer, anthropologist, and geographer—ceded land to the Argentine government to create the first national park, near the city of Bariloche.

CHAPTER 7   DEFENDING POPULAR SUSTAINABILITY IN *LA COMUNA*

1. Not just the nation, but also the local community must be constructed as an imagined community. The imagination of the community is an ongoing process wedded to the production and reproduction of the sociopolitical order (West 2006). Though historically constituted, the sociopolitical order is also anticipatory and future oriented. A major element in the creation of a sociopolitical imaginary among a group of actors is the taking account of its own collective futurity by defining key characteristics of its evolving identity. Festivals help to stabilize and objectify specific markers of identity.

2. In addition to a section of Monte Fitz Roy, 182 Bis included Aguja Mermoz, Cerro Pollone, Aguja Pollone, Cerro Domo Blanco, Torre Piergiorgio, and parts of the Marconi, Pollone, and Fitz Roy Norte Glaciers.

CHAPTER 8   KIRCHNERISMO AND THE POLITICS OF THE GREEN
              ECONOMY

1. The OAS arbitration panel accepted Argentina's claim to some 530 square kilometers of disputed territory, including Lake del Desierto.

2. This suggests that scholars should move beyond viewing the rentier state as a monolithic entity automatically associated with authoritarianism, corruption, and antidemocratic governance (Coronil 1997; Dunning 2008). There are different modalities of the rentier state that emerge across resource domains.

REFERENCES

Aagesen, David. 2000. "Rights to Land and Resources in Argentina's Alerces National Park." *Bulletin of Latin American Research* 19 (4): 547–569.

Abrams, Philip. 1988. "Notes on the Difficulty of Studying the State (1977)." *Journal of Historical Sociology* 1 (1): 58–89.

Abramson, Allen, and Robert Fletcher. 2007. "Recreating the Vertical: Rock-Climbing as Epic and Deep Eco-Play." *Anthropology Today* 23 (6): 3–7.

Administración de Parques Nacionales. 1997. *Plan preliminar de manejo, Parque Nacional Los Glaciares.* Buenos Aires: Administración de Parques Nacionales.

———. 2004. *Auditoría ambiental área de uso público de El Chaltén—Parque y Reserva Nacional Los Glaciares.* Buenos Aires: Administración de Parques Nacionales.

———. 2007. *Las áreas protegidas de la Argentina: Herramienta superior para la conservación de nuestro patrimonio natural y cultural.* Buenos Aires: Administración de Parques Nacionales.

———. 2012. *Guía visual parques nacionales de la Argentina.* Madrid, Spain: Administración de Parques Nacionales—Ministerio de Medio Ambiente.

———. 2014. *Compendio Estadístico del Turismo en Parque Nacional Los Glaciares.* El Calafate, Argentina: Intendencia de Parque Nacional Los Glaciares.

———. 2018. "Historia institucional." Administración de Parques Nacionales. Accessed February 14, 2018. https://www.parquesnacionales.gob.ar/institucional/historia-institucional/.

Agrawal, Arun. 2005. *Environmentality: Technologies of Government and the Making of Subjects.* Durham, NC: Duke University Press.

———. 2010. "Environment, Community, Government." In *In the Name of Humanity: The Government of Threat and Care,* edited by Ilana Feldman and Miriam Ticktin, 190–217. Durham, NC: Duke University Press.

Aguiló, Tomy. 2009. "Una Buena Temporada." *Vertical Argentina* 3 (April): 46–49.

Allan, Laurence. 2007. "Nestor Kirchner, Santa Cruz and the Hielos Continentales Controversy, 1991–1999." *Journal of Latin American Studies* 39 (4): 747–770

Alonso, Miguel Angel. 2004. *Lago Argentino & Glaciar Perito Moreno Handbook.* Buenos Aires: Zagier & Urruty Publications.

Alvarez, Juan José. 2007. *Crisis de gobernabilidad y control en Argentina: Propuestas para una reforma institucional.* Buenos Aires: Ciudad Argentina.

Anderson, Benedict. 2000. *Imagined Communities: Reflections on the Origin and Spread of Nationalism.* London: Verso.

Appadurai, Arjun. 2000. *Modernity at Large: Cultural Dimensions of Globalization.* Minneapolis: University of Minnesota Press.

———. 2016. *Banking on Words: The Failure of Language in the Age of Derivative Finance.* Chicago: University of Chicago Press.

Aradau, Claudia, and Rens van Munster. 2008. "Taming the Future: The *Dispositif* of Risk in the War on Terror." In *Risk and the War on Terror,* edited by Louise Amoore and Marieke de Goede, 23–40. London: Routledge.

Arsel, Murat, and Bram Büscher. 2012. "Nature™ Inc.: Changes and Continuities in Neoliberal Conservation and Market-Based Environmental Policy." *Development and Change* 43(1): 53–78.

Arsel, Murat, Barbara Hogenboom, and Lorenzo Pellegrini. 2016. "The Extractive Imperative in Latin America." *Extractive Industries and Society* 3 (4): 880–887.

Auyero, Javier. 2002. *Poor People's Politics: Peronist Survival Networks and the Legacy of Evita.* Durham, NC: Duke University Press.

Auyero, Javier, and Débora Alejandra Swistun. 2009. *Flammable: Environmental Suffering in an Argentine Shantytown.* Oxford: Oxford University Press.

Babb, Sarah L. 2001. *Managing Mexico: Economists from Nationalism to Neoliberalism.* Princeton, NJ: Princeton University Press.

Bacigalupo, Ana Mariella. 2016. *Thunder Shaman: Making History with Mapuche Spirits in Chile and Patagonia.* Austin: University of Texas Press

Baker, Tom, and Jonathan Simon, eds. 2002. *Embracing Risk: The Changing Culture of Insurance and Responsibility.* Chicago: University of Chicago Press.

Ban, Cornel. 2013. "Brazil's Liberal Neo-Developmentalism: New Paradigm or Edited Orthodoxy?" *Review of International Political Economy* 20 (2): 298–331.

Bandieri, Susana. 2005. *Historia de la Patagonia.* Buenos Aires: Editorial Sudamericana.

Bayer, Osvaldo. 2008. *La Patagonia rebelde.* Buenos Aires: Booket.

Beck, Ulrich. 2012. *Risk Society: Towards a New Modernity.* London: Sage Publications.

Beedie, Paul. 2003. "Adventure Tourism." In *Sport and Adventure Tourism*, edited by Simon Hudson, 203–239. New York: Haworth Hospitality.

Bell, Claudia, and John Lyall. 2002. *The Accelerated Sublime: Landscape, Tourism, and Identity.* Westport, CT: Praeger.

Benwell, Matthew C., and Klaus Dodds. 2011. "Argentine Territorial Nationalism Revisited: The Malvinas/Falklands Dispute and Geographies of Everyday Nationalism." *Political Geography* 30 (8): 441–449.

Bogardus, Lisa M. 2012. "The Bolt Wars: A Social Worlds Perspective on Rock Climbing and Intragroup Conflict." *Journal of Contemporary Ethnography* 41 (3): 283–308.

Bourdieu, Pierre. 2002. *Distinction: A Social Critique of the Judgement of Taste*, translated by Richard Nice. Cambridge, MA: Harvard University Press.

———. 2004. *Outline of a Theory of Practice*, translated by Richard Nice. Cambridge: Cambridge University Press.

Brand, Ulrich, and Nicola Sekler. 2009. "Postneoliberalism: Catch-All Word or Valuable Analytical and Political Concept?–Aims of a Beginning Debate." *Development Dialogue* 51 (1): 5–14.

Braun, Bruce. 2003. "'On the Raggedy Edge of Risk': Articulations of Race and Nature after Biology." In *Race, Nature, and the Politics of Difference*, edited by Donald S. Moore, Jake Kosek, and Anand Pandian, 175–203. Durham, NC: Duke University Press.

Brent, Zoe W. 2015. "Territorial Restructuring and Resistance in Argentina." *Journal of Peasant Studies* 42 (3–4): 671–694.

Bresser-Pereira, Luiz Carlos. 2016. "New Developmentalism as a Weberian Ideal Type." In *Macroeconomics and Development: Roberto Frenkel and the Economics of Latin America*, edited by Mario Damill, Martín Rapetti, and Guillermo Rozenwurcel, 373–383. New York: Columbia University Press.

Briones, Claudia, and José Luis Lantana. 2002. "Living on the Edge." In *Archaeological and Anthropological Perspectives on the Native Peoples of Pampa, Patagonia, and Tierra Del Fuego to the Nineteenth Century*, edited by Claudia Briones and José Luis Lantana, 1–12. Westport, CT: Bergin and Garvey.

Brockington, Dan. 2002. *Fortress Conservation: The Preservation of the Mkomazi Game Reserve, Tanzania.* Oxford: International African Institute.

Brockington, Dan, Rosaleen Duffy, and Jim Igoe. 2010. *Nature Unbound: Conservation, Capitalism and the Future of Protected Areas*. London: Earthscan.

Brondo, Keri Vacanti. 2013. *Land Grab: Green Neoliberalism, Gender, and Garifuna Resistance in Honduras*. Tucson: University of Arizona Press.

Bunn, Matthew. 2016. "Habitus and Disposition in High-Risk Mountain-Climbing." *Body & Society* 22 (1): 92–114.

Burke, Edmund. 1990. *A Philosophical Enquiry into the Origin of Our Ideas of the Sublime and Beautiful*, edited by Adam Phillips. Oxford: Oxford University Press.

Büscher, Bram. 2013. *Transforming the Frontier: Peace Parks and the Politics of Neoliberal Conservation in Southern Africa*. Durham, NC: Duke University Press.

Büscher, Bram, Wolfram Heinz Dressler, and Robert Fletcher, eds. 2014. *Nature™ Inc.: Environmental Conservation in the Neoliberal Age*. Tucson: University of Arizona Press.

Bustillo, Exequiel. 1999. *El despertar de Bariloche: Una estrategia Patagónica*. Buenos Aires: Editorial Sudamericana.

Calvo, Ernesto, and M. Victoria Murillo. 2012. "Argentina: The Persistence of Peronism." *Journal of Democracy* 23 (2): 148–161.

Carrier, James G., and Donald V. L. Macleod. 2005. "Bursting the Bubble: The Socio-Cultural Context of Ecotourism." *Journal of the Royal Anthropological Institute* 11 (2): 315–334.

Castañeda, Jorge G. 2006. "Latin America's Left Turn." *Foreign Affairs* 85 (3): 28–43.

Cattelino, Jessica. 2008. *High Stakes: Florida Seminole Gaming and Sovereignty*. Durham, NC: Duke University Press.

Cavagnero, Eleonora, Guy Carrin, and Rubén Torres. 2010. *A National Social Health Insurance Plan for Argentina: Simulating Its Financial Feasibility*. Geneva: World Health Organization.

Chouinard, Yvon. 2006. *Let My People Go Surfing: The Education of a Reluctant Businessman*. New York: Penguin Books.

Chouinard, Yvon, Dick Dorworth, Chris Jones, Lito Tejada-Flores, and Doug Tompkins. 2013. *Climbing Fitz Roy 1968: Reflections on the Lost Photos of the Third Ascent*. Ventura, CA: Patagonia Books.

Coates, Peter A. 1998. *Nature: Western Attitudes since Ancient Times*. Berkeley: University of California Press.

Colloredo-Mansfeld, Rudolf Josef. 1999. *The Native Leisure Class: Consumption and Cultural Creativity in the Andes*. Chicago: University of Chicago Press.

Comaroff, Jean, and John L. Comaroff. 2000. "Millennial Capitalism: First Thoughts on a Second Coming." In *Millennial Capitalism and the Culture of Neoliberalism*, edited by Jean Comaroff and John L. Comaroff, 291–343. Durham, NC: Duke University Press.

———. 2012. *Theory from the South, or, How Euro-America Is Evolving toward Africa*. Boulder, CO: Paradigm Publishers.

Comaroff, John L., and Jean Comaroff. 1992. *Ethnography and the Historical Imagination*. Boulder, CO: Westview Press.

———. 2009. *Ethnicity, Inc.* Chicago: University of Chicago Press.

Cordes, Kelly. 2014. *The Tower: A Chronicle of Climbing and Controversy on Cerro Torre*. Ventura, CA: Patagonia.

Coronil, Fernando. 1997. *The Magical State: Nature, Money, and Modernity in Venezuela*. Chicago: University of Chicago Press.

———. 2011. "The Future in Question: History and Utopia in Latin America (1989–2010)." In *Business as Usual: The Roots of the Global Financial Meltdown*, edited by Craig Calhoun and Georgi Derluguian, 231–264. New York: New York University Press.

Cosgrove, Denis E. 1998. *Social Formation and Symbolic Landscape*. Madison: University of Wisconsin Press.

Cronon, William. 1996. "The Trouble with Wilderness: Or, Getting Back to the Wrong Nature." *Environmental History* 1 (1): 7–28.

Crouch, Gregory. 2002. *Enduring Patagonia*. New York: Random House.

Darwin, Charles. 1989. *Voyage of the Beagle*, edited by Janet Browne and Michael Neve. London: Penguin Books.

D'Avella, Nicholas. 2014. "Ecologies of Investment: Crisis Histories and Brick Futures in Argentina." *Cultural Anthropology* 29 (1): 173–199.

Dean, Mitchell. 2010. *Governmentality: Power and Rule in Modern Society*. London: Sage.

Dezalay, Yves, and Bryant G. Garth. 2002. *The Internationalization of Palace Wars: Lawyers, Economists, and the Contest to Transform Latin American States*. Chicago: University of Chicago Press.

Dodds, Klaus. 2012. "Stormy Waters: Britain, the Falkland Islands and UK-Argentine Relations." *International Affairs* 88 (4): 683–700.

Dowie, Mark. 2011. *Conservation Refugees: The Hundred-Year Conflict between Global Conservation and Native Peoples*. Cambridge, MA: MIT Press.

Duffy, Rosaleen. 2002. *A Trip Too Far: Ecotourism, Politics, and Exploitation*. London: Earthscan.

Dumont, Guillaume. 2015. "Co-Creation and New Media: The Entrepreneurial Work of Climbing Photographers in Digital Times." *Anthropology of Work Review* 36 (1): 26–36.

Dunning, Thad. 2008. *Crude Democracy: Natural Resource Wealth and Political Regimes*. Cambridge: Cambridge University Press.

Dutkiewicz, Jan. 2015. "Pretzel Logic: An Embodied Ethnography of a Rock Climb." *Space and Culture* 18 (1): 25–38.

Duviols, Jean-Paul. 1997. "The Patagonian 'Giants.'" In *Patagonia: Natural History, Prehistory and Ethnography at the Uttermost End of the Earth*, edited by Colin McEwan, Luis A. Borrero, and Alfredo Prieto, 127–139. Princeton, NJ: Princeton University Press.

Ebenau, Matthias, and Victoria Liberatore. 2013. "Neodevelopmentalist State Capitalism in Brazil and Argentina: Chances, Limits and Contradictions." *Der Moderne Staat—Zeitschrift Fur Public Policy, Recht Und Management* 6 (1): 105–125.

Echeverri Cañas, Lina Maria, and Christian Estay-Niculcar. 2013. "El rol del turismo en la consolidación de la marca país de Argentina." *Visión Del Futuro* 17 (2): 186–199.

Ellner, Steve, ed. 2014. *Latin America's Radical Left: Challenges and Complexities of Political Power in the Twenty-First Century*. Lanham, MD: Rowman and Littlefield.

Escobar, Arturo. 1995. *Encountering Development: The Making and Unmaking of the Third World*. Princeton, NJ: Princeton University Press.

———. 2008. *Territories of Difference: Place, Movements, Life, Redes*. Durham, NC: Duke University Press.

———. 2010. "Latin America at a Crossroads: Alternative Modernizations, Post-Liberalism, or Post-Development?" *Cultural Studies* 24 (1): 1–65.

Etchemendy, Sebastián, and Ruth Berins Collier. 2007. "Down but Not Out: Union Resurgence and Segmented Neocorporatism in Argentina (2003–2007)." *Politics & Society* 35 (3): 363–401.

Ewald, François. 1991. "Insurance and Risk." In *The Foucault Effect: Studies in Governmentality with Two Lectures by and an Interview with Michel Foucault*, edited by Graham Burchell, Colin Gordon, and Peter Miller, 197–210. Chicago: University of Chicago Press.

Faulk, Karen Ann. 2013. *In the Wake of Neoliberalism: Citizenship and Human Rights in Argentina*. Stanford, CA: Stanford University Press.

Feitlowitz, Marguerite. 1999. *A Lexicon of Terror: Argentina and the Legacies of Torture*. New York: Oxford University Press.

Féliz, Mariano. 2012. "Neo-Developmentalism: Beyond Neoliberalism? Capitalist Crisis and Argentina's Development since the 1990s." *Historical Materialism* 20 (2): 105–123.

Ferguson, James. 2015. *Give a Man a Fish: Reflections on the New Politics of Distribution*. Durham, NC: Duke University Press.

Fernández de Kirchner, Cristina. 2015. "El logro más importante es haber empoderado a una sociedad de derechos." March 20. Accessed February 16, 2018. http://www.cfkargentina.com/la-presidenta-cristina-kirchner-inauguro-obras-en-el-calafate-santa-cruz-dni-24-creacion-del-iumer-en-cordoba/.

Fletcher, Robert. 2008. "Living on the Edge: The Appeal of Risk Sports for the Professional Middle Class." *Sociology of Sport Journal* 25 (3): 310–330.

———. 2010. "Neoliberal Environmentality: Towards a Poststructuralist Political Ecology of the Conservation Debate." *Conservation and Society* 8 (3): 171–181.

———. 2014. *Romancing the Wild: Cultural Dimensions of Ecotourism*. Durham, NC: Duke University Press.

Fletcher, Robert, Wolfram Dressler, and Bram Büscher. 2014. "Nature™ Inc.: The New Frontiers of Environmental Conservation." In *Nature™ Inc.: Environmental Conservation in the Neoliberal Age*, edited by Bram Büscher, Wolfram Dressler, and Robert Fletcher, 3–21. Tucson: University of Arizona Press.

Flores-Macias, Gustavo. 2012. *After Neoliberalism? The Left and Economic Reforms in Latin America*. Oxford: Oxford University Press.

Foucault, Michel. 1979. *Discipline and Punish: The Birth of the Prison*, translated by Alan Sheridan. New York: Vintage Books.

———. 1991. "Governmentality." In *The Foucault Effect: Studies in Governmentality with Two Lectures by and an Interview with Michel Foucault*, edited by Graham Burchell, Colin Gordon, and Peter Miller, 87–104. Chicago: University of Chicago Press.

———. 2009. *Security, Territory, Population: Lectures at the Collège de France, 1977–1978*, translated by Graham Burchell. New York: Picador.

Gaffoglio, Loreley. 2014. "Energía que duele: Impacto ambiental de las represas sobre el Santa Cruz." *La Nacion*. November 17. Accessed July 8, 2016. http://www.lanacion.com.ar/1744545-energia-que-duele-impacto-ambiental-de-las-represas-sobre-el-santa-cruz.

Garibotti, Rolando. 2004. "Mountain Unveiled: A Revealing Analysis of Cerro Torre's Tallest Tale." *American Alpine Journal* 46 (78): 138–155.

Garner, Andrew. 2013. "Uncivil Society: Local Stakeholders and Environmental Protection in Jamaica." In *Virtualism, Governance and Practice: Vision and Execution in Environmental Conservation*, edited by James G. Carrier and Paige West, 134–154. New York: Berghahn Books.

Godbout, Jacques T., and Alain Caillé. 2000. *The World of the Gift*. Montreal: McGill-Queen's University Press.

Goffman, Erving. 1990. *The Presentation of Self in Everyday Life*. New York: Anchor Books.

Goodale, Mark, and Nancy Grey Postero, eds. 2013. *Neoliberalism, Interrupted: Social Change and Contested Governance in Contemporary Latin America*. Stanford, CA: Stanford University Press.

Gordillo, Gastón. 2004. *Landscapes of Devils: Tensions of Place and Memory in the Argentinean Chaco*. Durham, NC: Duke University Press.

———. 2014. *Rubble: The Afterlife of Destruction*. Durham, NC: Duke University Press.

Gott, Richard. 2007. "Latin America as a White Settler Society." *Bulletin of Latin American Research* 26 (2): 269–289.

Graeber, David. 2011. *Debt: The First 5,000 Years*. Brooklyn, NY: Melville House.

Gramsci, Antonio. 2000. *The Gramsci Reader: Selected Writings, 1916–1935*, edited by David Forgacs. New York: New York University Press.

Grugel, Jean, and Pía Riggirozzi. 2009. "The End of the Embrace? Neoliberalism and Alternatives to Neoliberalism in Latin America." In *Governance after Neoliberalism in Latin America*, edited by Jean Grugel and Pía Riggirozzi, 1–23. New York: Palgrave Macmillan.

———. 2012. "Post-Neoliberalism in Latin America: Rebuilding and Reclaiming the State after Crisis." *Development and Change* 43 (1): 1–21.

Haenfler, Ross. 2013. *Goths, Gamers, and Grrrls: Deviance and Youth Subcultures*. New York: Oxford University Press.

Haenn, Nora. 2005. *Fields of Power, Forests of Discontent: Culture, Conservation, and the State in Mexico*. Tucson: University of Arizona Press.

Haenn, Nora, Elizabeth Olson, José Martínez-Reyes, and Leticia Durand. 2014. "Introduction: Between Capitalism, the State, and the Grassroots: Mexico's Contribution to a Global Conservation Debate." *Conservation and Society* 12 (2): 111–119.

Harvey, David. 2001. *Spaces of Capital: Towards a Critical Geography*. New York: Routledge.

———. 2007. *A Brief History of Neoliberalism*. Oxford: Oxford University Press.

Heidegger, Martin. 1962. *Being and Time*, translated by John Macquarrie and Edward Robinson. New York: Harper Collins.

Herz, Steven, Antonio La Vina, and Jonathan Sohn. 2007. *Development without Conflict: The Business Case for Community Consent*. Washington, DC: World Resources Institute.

Hielos: Día clave en Diputados. 1996. *La Nacion*. December 17. Accessed February 14, 2018. https://www.lanacion.com.ar/174554-hielos-dia-clave-en-diputados.

Ho, Karen Zouwen. 2009. *Liquidated: An Ethnography of Wall Street*. Durham, NC: Duke University Press.

Hoffman, David M. 2014. "Conch, Cooperatives, and Conflict: Conservation and Resistance in the Banco Chinchorro Biosphere Reserve." *Conservation and Society* 12 (2): 120–132.

Holmes, George. 2014. "What Is a Land Grab? Exploring Green Grabs, Conservation, and Private Protected Areas in Southern Chile." *Journal of Peasant Studies* 41 (4): 547–567.

Holmes, George, and Connor J. Cavanagh. 2016. "A Review of the Social Impacts of Neoliberal Conservation: Formations, Inequalities, Contestations." *Geoforum* 75 (October): 199–209.

Honey, Martha. 2008. *Ecotourism and Sustainable Development: Who Owns Paradise?* Washington: Island Press.

Hristov, Jasmin. 2014. *Paramilitarism and Neoliberalism: Violent Systems of Capital Accumulation in Colombia and Beyond*. London: Pluto Press.

Igoe, Jim. 2004. *Conservation and Globalization: A Study of National Parks and Indigenous Communities from East Africa to South Dakota*. Belmont, CA: Wadsworth Publishing Company.

Igoe, Jim, and Dan Brockington. 2007. "Neoliberal Conservation: A Brief Introduction." *Conservation and Society* 5 (4): 432–449

Igoe, Jim, Katja Neves, and Dan Brockington. 2010. "A Spectacular Eco-Tour around the Historic Bloc: Theorising the Convergence of Biodiversity Conservation and Capitalist Expansion." *Antipode* 42 (3): 486–512.

Irrazábal, Fernando, and Luis Soto Jr. 2009. "Dossier: Chaltén/Patagonia." *Vertical Argentina* 6 (December): 30–40.

James, Daniel. 2001. *Resistance and Integration: Peronism and the Argentine Working Class, 1946–1976*. Cambridge: Cambridge University Press.

Johnston, Barbara R., and Ted Edwards. 1994. "The Commodification of Mountaineering." *Annals of Tourism Research* 21 (3): 459–478.

Kalous, Chris. 2012. "Episode 6: Hayden Kennedy: Alpine Taliban or Patagonian Custodi-an™? (Part 1)." *The Enormocast: A Slice of the Climbing Life*. March 1. Accessed February 16, 2018. https://enormocast.com/episode-6-hayden-kennedy-alpine-taliban-or-patagonian -custodian-part-1/.

Kant, Immanuel. 1951. *Critique of Judgement*, translated by J.H. Bernard. New York: Haffner Press.

Keane, Webb. 1997. *Signs of Recognition: Powers and Hazards of Representation in an Indonesian Society*. Berkeley: University of California Press.

Kearney, Alan. 1993. *Mountaineering in Patagonia*. Seattle: Cloudcap.

Keynes, John Maynard. 1920. *The Economic Consequences of the Peace*. London: Macmillan

———. 1997. *The General Theory of Employment, Interest, and Money*. Amherst, NY: Prometheus Books.

Kiewa, Jackie. 2002. "Traditional Climbing: Metaphor of Resistance or Metanarrative of Oppression?" *Leisure Studies* 21 (2): 145–161.

Kirsch, Stuart. 2014. *Mining Capitalism: The Relationship between Corporations and Their Critics*. Oakland: University of California Press.

Klubock, Thomas Miller. 2014. *La Frontera: Forests and Ecological Conflict in Chile's Frontier Territory*. Durham, NC: Duke University Press.

Laclau, Ernesto. 2007. *On Populist Reason*. London: Verso.

Laclau, Ernesto, and Chantal Mouffe. 2014. *Hegemony and Socialist Strategy: Towards a Radical Democratic Politics*. London: Verso.

La Opinión Austral. 1999. "Preocupación por venta de tierras." December 14, 1999.

———. 2000. "El mensaje de los pioneros en el aniversario de El Chaltén." October 13, 2000.

Lavigne, Joshua, and Sharon Wood. 2012. "Carlyle Norman Accident Report." *Alpinist*. January 30. Accessed February 16, 2018. http://www.alpinist.com/doc/web12w/newswire -carlyle-norman.

Laviolette, Patrick. 2016. *Extreme Landscapes of Leisure: Not a Hap-Hazardous Sport*. London: Routledge.

Lazar, Sian. 2012. "A Desire to Formalize Work? Comparing Trade Union Strategies in Bolivia and Argentina." *Anthropology of Work Review* 33 (1): 15–24.

Le Breton, David. 2000. "Playing Symbolically with Death in Extreme Sports." *Body & Society* 6 (1): 1–11.

Lewis, Neil. 2000. "The Climbing Body, Nature and the Experience of Modernity." *Body & Society* 6 (3–4): 58–80.

Lewis, Paul H. 2009. *The Agony of Argentine Capitalism: From Menem to the Kirchners*. Santa Barbara, CA: Praeger.

Li, Tania. 2014. *Land's End: Capitalist Relations on an Indigenous Frontier*. Durham, NC: Duke University Press.

Limón, José Eduardo. 1994. *Dancing with the Devil: Society and Cultural Poetics in Mexican-American South Texas*. Madison: University of Wisconsin Press.

LiPuma, Edward, and Benjamin Lee. 2004. *Financial Derivatives and the Globalization of Risk*. Durham, NC: Duke University Press.

Logan, Joy. 2011. *Aconcagua: The Invention of Mountaineering on America's Highest Peak*. Tucson: University of Arizona Press.

Lyng, Stephen. 1990. "Edgework: A Social Psychological Analysis of Voluntary Risk Taking." *American Journal of Sociology* 95 (4): 851–886.

MacDonald, Laura, and Arne Ruckert. 2009. "Post-Neoliberalism in the Americas: An Introduction." In *Post-Neoliberalism in the Americas*, edited by Laura MacDonald and Arne Ruckert, 1–20. Basingstoke, UK: Palgrave Macmillan.

Madsen, Andreas. 2006. *La Patagonia vieja*. Ushuaia, Argentina: Zagier & Urruty.

Mallon, Florencia E. 2005. *Courage Tastes of Blood: The Mapuche Community of Nicolás Ailío and the Chilean State, 1906–2001*. Durham, NC: Duke University Press.

Manica, Mario. 2012. "Enduring Freedom." *Planet Mountain*. February 9. Accessed February 16, 2018. http://www.planetmountain.com/it/notizie/alpinismo/schiodatura-del-torre -le-riflessioni-di-mario-manica-e-manuel-lugli.html.

Martín, Carlos, and Claudio Chehébar. 2001. "The National Parks of Argentinian Patagonia— Management Policies for Conservation, Public Use, Rural Settlements, and Indigenous Communities." *Journal of the Royal Society of New Zealand* 31 (4): 845–864.

Martínez-Reyes, José. 2016. *Moral Ecology of a Forest: The Nature Industry and Maya Post-Conservation*. Tucson: University of Arizona Press.

Marx, Karl. 1990. *Capital: A Critique of Political Economy*. Vol. 1, translated by Ben Fowkes. London: Penguin Books

———. 1991. *Capital: A Critique of Political Economy*. Vol. 3, translated by David Fernbach. London: Penguin Books.

Masco, Joseph. 2006. *The Nuclear Borderlands: The Manhattan Project in Post–Cold War New Mexico*. Princeton, NJ: Princeton University Press.

———. 2014. *The Theater of Operations: National Security Affect from the Cold War to the War on Terror*. Durham, NC: Duke University Press.

Maurer, Bill. 2005. *Mutual Life, Limited: Islamic Banking, Alternative Currencies, Lateral Reason*. Princeton, NJ: Princeton University Press.

Mauss, Marcel. 1967. *The Gift: Forms and Functions of Exchange in Archaic Societies*, translated by Ian Cunnison. New York: Norton.

Mazzarella, William. 2005. *Shoveling Smoke: Advertising and Globalization in Contemporary India*. Durham, NC: Duke University Press.

Melgarejo, Juan Ignacio. 1999. *Hielos Continentales*. Buenos Aires: printed by the author.

Mendoza, Marcos. 2016. "Educational Policing: Park Rangers and the Politics of the Green (E)State in Patagonia." *Journal of Latin American and Caribbean Anthropology* 21 (1): 173–192.

———. 2017. "Post-Neoliberal Labor in Patagonia: Informality and Citizenship in the Green Economy." *Dialectical Anthropology* 41 (1): 55–76.

Mendoza, Marcos, Robert Fletcher, George Holmes, Laura A. Ogden, and Colombina Schaeffer. 2017. "The Patagonian Imaginary: Natural Resources and Global Capitalism at the Far End of the World." *Journal of Latin American Geography* 16 (2): 93–116.

Merleau-Ponty, Maurice. 1981. *Phenomenology of Perception*, translated by Colin Smith. London: Routledge and Kegan Paul.

Meza, Laura E. 2009. "Mapuche Struggles for Land and the Role of Private Protected Areas in Chile." *Journal of Latin American Geography* 8 (1): 149–163.

Miller, Daniel. 1997. *Capitalism: An Ethnographic Approach*. Oxford: Berg.

Miniconi, Renaud, and Sylvain Guyot. 2010. "Conflicts and Cooperation in the Mountainous Mapuche Territory (Argentina): The Case of the Nahuel Huapi National Park." *Revue de Géographie Alpine* 98 (1): 138–153.

Ministerio de Turismo de Argentina. 2014. *Anuario estadístico de turismo*. Ministerio de Turismo de Argentina. http://www.yvera.gob.ar/estadistica/info/anuarios-estadisticos -turisticos.

Mitchell, Timothy. 1991. "The Limits of the State: Beyond Statist Approaches and Their Critics." *American Political Science Review* 83 (1): 77–96.

———. 2013. *Carbon Democracy: Political Power in the Age of Oil*. London: Verso.

Miyazaki, Hirokazu. 2013. *Arbitraging Japan: Dreams of Capitalism at the End of Finance*. Berkeley: University of California Press.

Moreno, Francisco P. 2002. *Perito Moreno's Travel Journal: A Personal Reminiscence*. Buenos Aires: El Elefante Blanco.

———. 2006. *Viaje a la Patagonia austral*. Buenos Aires: El Elefante Blanco.

Muir, Sarah. 2016. "On Historical Exhaustion: Argentine Critique in an Era of 'Total Corruption.'" *Comparative Studies in Society and History* 58 (1): 129–158.

Munn, Nancy D. 1992. *The Fame of Gawa: A Symbolic Study of Value Transformation in a Massim (Papua New Guinea) Society*. Durham, NC: Duke University Press.

Nash, Roderick Frazier. 2001. *Wilderness and the American Mind*. New Haven, CT: Yale University Press.

Navarro Floria, Pedro. 1999. *Historia de la Patagonia*. Buenos Aires: Ciudad Argentina.

Neumann, Roderick P. 1998. *Imposing Wilderness: Struggles over Livelihood and Nature Preservation in Africa*. Berkeley: University of California Press.

Nietzsche, Friedrich Wilhelm. 1966. *Beyond Good and Evil: Prelude to a Philosophy of the Future*, translated by Walter Kaufmann. New York: Vintage Books.

Nouzeilles, Gabriela. 1999. "Patagonia as Borderland: Nature, Culture, and the Idea of the State." *Journal of Latin American Cultural Studies* 8 (1): 35–48.

O'Connor, Martin. 1993. "On the Misadventures of Capitalist Nature." *Capitalism Nature Socialism* 4 (3): 7–40.

Ogden, Laura. 2011. *Swamplife: People, Gators, and Mangroves Entangled in the Everglades*. Minneapolis: University of Minnesota Press.

Oltremari, Juan V., and Royal G. Jackson. 2006. "Conflicts, Perceptions, and Expectations of Indigenous Communities Associated with Natural Areas in Chile." *Natural Areas Journal* 26 (2): 215–220.

O'Malley, Pat. 1996. "Risk and Responsibility." In *Foucault and Political Reason: Liberalism, Neo-Liberalism and Rationalities of Government*, edited by Andrew Barry, Thomas Osborne, and Nikolas S. Rose, 189-207. Chicago: University of Chicago Press.

———. 2008. "Governmentality and Risk." In *Social Theories of Risk and Uncertainty: An Introduction*, edited by Jens Zinn, 52–75. Malden, MA: Blackwell.

Ong, Aihwa. 2010. *Spirits of Resistance and Capitalist Discipline*. Albany: State University of New York Press.

Organisation for Economic Co-operation and Development. 2014. "Argentina." In *OECD Tourism Trends and Policies 2014*, 334–339. OECD Publishing. http://www.oecd-ilibrary .org/content/book/tour-2014-en.

Ortner, Sherry B. 1999. *Life and Death on Mt. Everest: Sherpas and Himalayan Mountaineering*. Princeton, NJ: Princeton University Press.

Otero, Adriana, Lía Nakayama, Susana Marioni, Elisa Gallego, Alicia Lonac, Andrés Dimitriu, Rodrigo González, and Claudia Hosid. 2006. "Amenity Migration in the Patagonian Mountain Community of San Martín de Los Andes, Neuquén, Argentina." In *The Amenity Migrants: Seeking and Sustaining Mountains and Their Cultures*, edited by Laurence A. G. Moss, 200–211. Wallingford, UK: CABI Publishing.

Paley, Julia. 2001. *Marketing Democracy: Power and Social Movements in Post-Dictatorship Chile*. Berkeley: University of California Press.

Pastoriza, Elisa. 2011. *La conquista de las vacaciones: Breve historia del turismo en la Argentina*. Buenos Aires: Edhasa.

Paterson, Mark. 2009. "Haptic Geographies: Ethnography, Haptic Knowledges and Sensuous Dispositions." *Progress in Human Geography* 33 (6): 766–788.

Pero, Alejandro. 2002. "The Tehuelche of Patagonia as Chronicled by Travelers and Explorers in the Nineteenth Century." In *Archaeological and Anthropological Perspectives on the Native Peoples of Pampa, Patagonia, and Tierra Del Fuego to the Nineteenth Century*, edited by Claudia Briones and José Luis Lantana, 103–119. Westport, CT: Bergin and Garvey.

Petryna, Adriana. 2002. *Life Exposed: Biological Citizens after Chernobyl*. Princeton, NJ: Princeton University Press.

Radcliffe, Sarah A. 2012. "Development for a Postneoliberal Era? Sumak Kawsay, Living Well and the Limits to Decolonisation in Ecuador." *Geoforum* 43 (2): 240–249.

Rajan, Kaushik Sunder. 2007. *Biocapital: The Constitution of Postgenomic Life*. Durham, NC: Duke University Press.

Richards, Patricia. 2010. "Of Indians and Terrorists: How the State and Local Elites Construct the Mapuche in Neoliberal Multicultural Chile." *Journal of Latin American Studies* 41 (1): 59–90.

Richardson, Neal P. 2009. "Export-Oriented Populism: Commodities and Coalitions in Argentina." *Studies in Comparative International Development* 44 (3): 228–255.

Robinson, William I. 2010. *Latin America and Global Capitalism: A Critical Globalization Perspective*. Baltimore, MD: Johns Hopkins University Press.

Rojas, Juan José Ramón. 1975. "Operación Desierto." Gendarmería Nacional Agrupación Patagonia Austral. Archivo Histórico Provincial de Santa Cruz, Río Gallegos, Argentina.

Sahlins, Marshall. 1972. *Stone Age Economics*. New York: Aldine de Gruyter.

Salvia, Agustín, and Marta Panaia, eds. 1997. *La Patagonia privatizada: Crisis, cambios estructurales en el sistema regional Patagónico y sus impactos en los mercados de trabajo*. Buenos Aires: Centro de Estudios Avanzados, Oficina de Publicaciones del Ciclo Básico Común, Universidad de Buenos Aires.

Santiso, Javier. 2007. *Latin America's Political Economy of the Possible*. Cambridge, MA: MIT Press.

Savino, Lucas. 2016. "Landscapes of Contrast: The Neo-Extractivist State and Indigenous Peoples in 'Post-Neoliberal' Argentina." *Extractive Industries and Society* 3 (2): 404–415.

Schama, Simon. 1996. *Landscape and Memory*. New York: Vintage Books.

Schein, Daniel Roy Torunczyk. 2016. "The Socio-Political Dynamics of Transnational Mining in Argentina: The Cases of Puerto San Julián and Esquel in Patagonia." *Extractive Industries and Society* 3 (4): 1067–1074.

Scheper-Hughes, Nancy. 1992. *Death without Weeping: The Violence of Everyday Life in Brazil*. Berkeley: University of California Press.

Schiller, Friedrich. 1982. *On the Aesthetic Education of Man: In a Series of Letters*, translated by Elizabeth M. Wilkinson and L.A. Willoughby. Oxford: Clarendon Press of Oxford University Press.

Serenari, Christopher, M. Nils Peterson, Tim Wallace, and Paulina Stowhas. 2016. "Private Protected Areas, Ecotourism Development and Impacts on Local People's Well-Being: A Review from Case Studies in Southern Chile." *Journal of Sustainable Tourism* 25 (12): 1792–1810.

Shever, Elana. 2012. *Resources for Reform: Oil and Neoliberalism in Argentina*. Stanford, CA: Stanford University Press.

Silva, Eduardo, 2016. "Patagonia, without Dams! Lessons of a David vs. Goliath Campaign." *Extractive Industries and Society* 3 (4): 947–957.

Smith, Adam. 1976. *An Inquiry into the Nature and Causes of the Wealth of Nations*, edited by Edwin Cannan. Chicago: University of Chicago Press.

Sopeña, Germán. 2008. *Memorias de Patagonia: Crónicas, escenarios, personajes*. Buenos Aires: Booket.

Stiglitz, Joseph E. 2003. *Globalization and Its Discontents*. New York: W. W. Norton.

Stronza, Amanda, and Javier Gordillo. 2008. "Community Views of Ecotourism." *Annals of Tourism Research* 35 (2): 448–468.

Sutton, Barbara. 2008. "Contesting Racism: Democratic Citizenship, Human Rights, and Antiracist Politics in Argentina." *Latin American Perspectives* 35 (6): 106–121.

Svampa, Maristella, and Mirta A. Antonelli, eds. 2009. *Minería transnacional, narrativas del desarrollo y resistencias sociales*. Buenos Aires: Editorial Biblos.

Tecklin, David R., and Claudia Sepulveda. 2014. "The Diverse Properties of Private Land Conservation in Chile: Growth and Barriers to Private Protected Areas in a Market-Friendly Context." *Conservation and Society* 12 (2): 203–217.

Theroux, Paul. 1980. *The Old Patagonian Express: By Train through the Americas*. London: Penguin Books.

Trujillo, Lucía, and Martín Retamozo. 2017. "Economía política de la desigualdad en Argentina (2003–2015). Instituciones laborales y protección social." *Temas y Debates* 33 (June): 35–61.

Tsing, Anna L. 2005. *Friction: An Ethnography of Global Connection*. Princeton, NJ: Princeton University Press.

United Nations Environmental Programme. 2011. *Towards a Green Economy: Pathways to Sustainable Development and Poverty Eradication*. Accessed February 16, 2018. https://sustainabledevelopment.un.org/index.php?page=view&type=400&nr=126&menu=35.

Urry, John. 2008. *The Tourist Gaze*. London: Sage Publications.

Varoufakis, Yanis. 2015. *The Global Minotaur: America, Europe and the Future of the Global Economy*. London: Zed Books.

Verdery, Katherine. 2003. *The Vanishing Hectare: Property and Value in Postsocialist Transylvania*. Ithaca, NY: Cornell University Press.

Villalba, Unai. 2013. "*Buen Vivir* vs Development: A Paradigm Shift in the Andes?" *Third World Quarterly* 34 (8): 1427–1442.

Vivanco, Luis A. 2007. *Green Encounters: Shaping and Contesting Environmentalism in Rural Costa Rica*. New York: Berghahn Books.

Vivanco, Luis, and Robert J. Gordon, eds. 2009. *Tarzan Was an Eco-Tourist: And Other Tales in the Anthropology of Adventure*. New York: Berghahn Books.

Wacquant, Loïc. 2006. *Body and Soul: Notebooks of an Apprentice Boxer*. Oxford: Oxford University Press.

Walley, Christine. 2004. *Rough Waters: Nature and Development in an East African Marine Park*. Princeton, NJ: Princeton University Press.

Watt, Peter, and Roberto Zepeda. 2012. *Drug War Mexico: Politics, Neoliberalism and Violence in the New Narcoeconomy*. London: Zed Books.

Watts, Michael. 2001. "Petro-Violence: Community, Extraction, and Political Ecology of a Mythic Commodity." In *Violent Environments*, edited by Nancy Lee Peluso and Michael Watts, 189–212. Ithaca, NY: Cornell University Press.

Webber, Jeffery R., and Barry Carr, eds. 2013. *The New Latin American Left: Cracks in the Empire*. Lanham, MD: Rowman and Littlefield.

Weber, Max. 2004. *The Protestant Ethic and the Spirit of Capitalism*, translated by Talcott Parsons. London: Routledge

Weiner, Annette B. 1985. "Inalienable Wealth." *American Ethnologist* 12 (2): 210–227.

Weisbrot, Mark. 2015. *Failed: What the "Experts" Got Wrong about the Global Economy*. New York: Oxford University Press.

Weisbrot, Mark, Rebecca Ray, Juan A. Montecino, and Sara Kozameh. 2011. *The Argentine Success Story and Its Implications*. Washington: Center for Economic and Policy Research.

West, Paige. 2006. *Conservation Is Our Government Now: The Politics of Ecology in Papua New Guinea.* Durham, NC: Duke University Press.

———. 2012. *From Modern Production to Imagined Primitive: The Social World of Coffee from Papua New Guinea.* Durham, NC: Duke University Press.

West, Paige, and James G. Carrier. 2004. "Ecotourism and Authenticity: Getting Away from It All?" *Current Anthropology* 45 (4): 483–498.

Wheaton, Belinda. 2004. *Understanding Lifestyle Sports: Consumption, Identity, and Difference.* London: Routledge.

Whitson, Risa. 2007a. "Beyond the Crisis: Economic Globalization and Informal Work in Urban Argentina." *Journal of Latin American Geography* 6 (2): 121–136.

———. 2007b. "Hidden Struggles: Spaces of Power and Resistance in Informal Work in Urban Argentina." *Environment and Planning A* 39 (12): 2916–2934.

Willis, Michael J., Andrew K. Melkonian, Matthew E. Pritchard, and Andrés Rivera. 2012. "Ice Loss from the Southern Patagonian Ice Field, South America, between 2000 and 2012." *Geophysical Research Letters* 39 (17).

Wolf, Eric R. 1982. *Europe and the People without History.* Berkeley: University of California Press.

World Bank. 2018a. Argentina: GDP Growth (Annual %). Accessed February 16, 2018. https://data.worldbank.org/indicator/NY.GDP.MKTP.KD.ZG?end=2015&locations =AR&start=2003.

———. 2018b. Argentina: GNI Per Capita, Atlas Method (Current US$). Accessed February 16, 2018. https://data.worldbank.org/indicator/NY.GNP.PCAP.CD?locations=AR.

Wylde, Christopher. 2012. *Latin America after Neoliberalism: Developmental Regimes in Post-Crisis States.* Basingstoke, UK: Palgrave Macmillan.

Zaloom, Caitlin. 2006. *Out of the Pits: Traders and Technology from Chicago to London.* Chicago: University of Chicago Press.

Zelizer, Viviana A. 1997. *The Social Meaning of Money.* Princeton, NJ: Princeton University Press.

INDEX

Page numbers in italic type refer to illustrations.

absentee landlords, 70, 83–84, 85
Ackermann, Jorge, 33, 35, 38, 41
Administración de Parques Nacionales
   (APN), 7–8, 9, 28, 81, 82, 110, 112, 114, 120,
   183, 187; and *Auditoría Ambiental*
   (environmental audit), 119; and Camp
   Madsen, 197n3; on climate change, 165; and
   community-based conservation (CBC), 13,
   111–113, 117, 184; and conservation policing,
   129–130, 136, 138, 139, 141, 144, 145; Corvalán
   as head of, 176; and ecotourism, 11, 47; and
   education for rangers, 198n1; and extractive
   industries, 179; and *la comuna*, 153, 166;
   levels of bureaucracy at, 109; and Parque
   Nacional Los Glaciares (PNLG) revenue,
   198n2; and rentier state, 176–177, 178; and
   road from El Calafate to Perito Moreno
   Glacier, 159; and scientific sustainability,
   126, 127; and sustainable trails project
   (STP), 120, 122, 123–124; and tourism, 45;
   and Viedma highway project, 160. *See also*
   conservation policing by SLV rangers
Africa, 193n1
Agrawal, Arun, 112
agriculture. *See* farms/farming
agro-extraction, 5, 178
Aguiló, Tomy, 33, 35, 38, 41
Aguja de la S, 140
Aguja Mermoz, 36, 198n2
Aguja Poincenot, 87
Aguja Pollone, 198n2
Aguja Saint-Exupéry, 37–38
Alaska, 41
Alberdi, Juan Bautista, 27
alpine-style climbing, 31–32, 35–36
alpine sublime, 15, 16, 19, 20, 183, 196n2; and
   climate change, 164; and conservation, 112;
   defined, 15, 53; and green productivism, 19;
   and Kirchnerismo, 16, 168; in mountaineer-
   ing, 34; as political project, 15; in trekking,
   45–46, 47, 52–53, 54, 58, 62–63

alpinism. *See* mountaineering
American Alpine Club, 39, 120
analytic of the conjuncture, 9, 10, 16
Animal Farm (Orwell), 73
anthropology/anthropologists, xiv, 11, 16, 109,
   186, 193n6, 193n8, 197n4
Aonikenk Tehuelche people, 27, 61, 75, 103,
   104, 156, 174, 195n5
Arce, Carlos, 57
Arenal National Park, 61
Argentina: economy of, 1–2, 7, 10, 47, 48, 69,
   85, 88, 124; El Chaltén as trekking capital
   of, 45; in ethnographic research, xiii;
   Cristina Fernández de Kirchner as
   president of, 1; in history of Patagonian
   region, 27–28, 29; and indigenous
   populations, 103; Néstor Kirchner as
   president of, 1; as part of Patagonian
   region, xi; post-neoliberal politics in, xi;
   and sustainable development, 8
Argentine Institute for Snow, Glacier and
   Environmental Sciences, 163
Artigas, Manolo, 67, 73, 80–81, 97
Årtun, Bjørn, 36, 37, 41
Asociación de Vecinos (Association of
   Neighbors), 154, 155, 156, 158
Auditoría Ambiental (environmental audit),
   116–119, 120, 121, 128, 151
authentic self, 50
Auyero, Veronica, 131, 132, 134
Aylwin, Patricio, 170

Bachelet, Michelle, 180–181
backcountry, 45, 52, 53, 58, 62, 105, 122
Banco de Bosques, 187
Bariloche, xiii, 28, 45, 60, 87, 88, 116, 127
Barros, Marcela, 81, 130, 133, 143–144, 151–152,
   160
Beagle, 27
Beagle Channel arbitration case, 170
Beck, Ulrich, 194n14

Bell, Claudia, 196n2
Bernardo O'Higgins National Park, 6, 170, 196n6
Black Diamond, 30
blanco/negro. *See* formal/informal (blanco/negro) labor
bola, 61
Bolivia, 165
bolts, 30, 31–32, 101, 195n8
Borges, Jorge Luis, 195n4
Bosques Petrificado National Monument, 179
bouldering, 101–102
Bouldering Festival, 149
Bourdieu, Pierre, 195n2
branding, 19, 184; and Administración de Parques Nacionales (APN), 110; and Argentina, 196n3; and comerciantes, 85; and ecotourism, 10, 11, 12; and El Chaltén, 45, 56, 77, 104, 131; and empresarios, 82; and green economy, 12, 63; and Kirchnerismo, 168; and *la comuna*, 150, 152; and mountaineering, 34, 39; of national park estates, 68; tourism policy based on, 48; and trekking, 43, 46
Braun, Bruce, 194n14
Brazil, 28, 61, 99, 188
Breard, Eugenio, 187
bridges, 158–159, 161–163, 166, 167, 185
Bridges, Domingo, 82–83, 84
brigadistas, 123, 128
British Mountaineering Council, 157
Brockington, Dan, 195n7
Buenos Aires, xiii, 196n1; Administración de Parques Nacionales (APN) office in, 109; and entrepreneurship, 69, 73, 75, 81, 82; and politics of green economy, 174; and rentier state, 176; and seasonal workers/golondrinas, 87; as tourist destination, 10, 48; and trekking, 56, 62
Bulgakov, Servando, 93–94, 95
Burke, Edmund, 53
Büscher, Bram, 194n13
business owners. *See* comerciantes; empresarios; entrepreneurs
Bustillo, Exequiel, 15–16, 28

Caldwell, Tommy, 35
Cámara de Comercio (Chamber of Commerce), 68, 70, 77, 79, 80, 85; and *Auditoría Ambiental* (environmental audit), 118; and Camp Madsen, 92–93, 138, 197n3; and conservation policing, 144; and De las Vueltas River bridge, 158; and *la comuna*, 154; and 182 Bis land dispute, 156–157; and sustainable trails project (STP), 120
Cambiaso, Estela, 74–75
Camp Confluencia, 137–138, 140, 143–144
Camp Madsen, 89, 91–93, 96, 100, 104, 137, 144, 197n3
Camp Poincenot, 134–135
Camp Prestadores, 143
Canadian Rockies, 15, 25, 165
Caparrós, Alejandro "Capa," 176
capital, entrepreneurial, 104–105, 150, 152, 168
capitalism, xiv, 185, 196n2; and analytic of the conjuncture, 9; anthropology of, 193n8; and class, 63; ecological phase of, 193n6; and ecotourism, 11, 43; and entrepreneurs, 75; global, xi, 3, 4, 16; and green economy, 8, 44; industrial, 11; and Kirchners, 183; market, 2, 4; Marx on, 11, 16; and Parque Nacional Los Glaciares (PNLG), 45; progressive, 3; and risk, 16; and scientific sustainability, 127. *See also* rentier capitalism
Carrier, James, 60
Casa de Gobierno (Provincial Government Palace), 98
Castillo, Alejandro, 158, 163
Cavanagh, Connor, 194n13
Cerro Aconcagua Provincial Park, 198n5
Cerro Chaltén. *See* Monte Fitz Roy
Cerro Domo Blanco, 198n2
Cerro Pollone, 198n2
Cerro Torre, 132; mountaineering on, 25, 28–29, 30, 32–33, 36, 38; photo of, 29, 37; and sustainable trails project (STP), 124; in trekking, 54
Cerro Torre: A Snowball's Chance in Hell (film), 195n9
Chaltén Massif, 6, 19, 162; and mountaineering, 25, 28, 29, 39, 42, 149; and 182 Bis land dispute, 154, 156, 157; and Patagonia, Inc., 40; photo of, 184; and trekking, 53, 54, 58
Chamber of Commerce. *See* Cámara de Comercio (Chamber of Commerce)
Chamber of Deputies, 170
charlas, 131–134

Chávez, Hugo, xi
Chavez, Patricio "Pato," 87–88
Chehébar, Claudio, 116, 117, 122, 124
Chile, xi, 58, 60, 169, 170, 171, 175, 182; in ethnographic research, xiii; in history of Patagonian region, 27–28, 29; and indigenous populations, 103; seasonal worker/golondrina from, 88; and trekking, 43. See also Torres del Paine National Park
Chiloé park, 61
Chouinard, Yvon, 33, 40, 120, 121, 157
Chubut, xi
citizenship, 19, 70–71, 76, 186; and comerciantes, 86; of empresarios, 84; labor-based, 71, 72, 75, 86, 90, 94, 97, 98, 100, 104, 105; and seasonal workers/golondrinas, 89, 94, 96; tiered system of, 18–19, 20, 90, 99, 100, 104, 184, 185
Citizen's Unity party (Unidad Ciudadana), 188
class, 10, 12, 74, 88, 105, 196n2 (chap. 3); and citizenship, 72; comerciantes as middle, 67; and ecotourism, 44, 48; in El Chaltén, 75–76; and empresarios, 85; entrepreneurial, 69, 96, 98, 184; green economy and middle, 184; and indigenous populations, 104; and labor, 99–100, 104, 105; and mountaineering, 25; oligarchic, 70; and owners of rental units, 83; and progressive capitalism, 63; and race, 99; and rangers, 128; and rent capture, 194n11; and seasonal workers/golondrinas, 88–89, 94, 97, 104; and tourism industry, 68; and trekking, 50, 59, 60, 61; unionized working, 71; upper, 184
clientelism, 173
climate change, 8, 16, 57, 163–166
clothing/equipment, 50–51, 53, 57, 59, 100, 101, 131, 195n8
Club Andino, 120, 197n3
Coates, Peter, 195n7
Colbún, 180
Colorado, Elena, 134, 135–136, 141–142
Comaroff, Jean, 4, 196n3
Comaroff, John, 4, 196n3
comerciantes, 67–70, 73–86; and absentee landlords, 83–84, 85; defined, 67; difficulties for, 67–68, 69; and empresarios, 69–70, 73–74, 77, 80–82; and laboring *a*

pulmón, 75, 79, 84, 85; laboring culture of, 70; market solidarity for, 76–79; risk for, 86. See also formal/informal (blanco/ negro) labor; market individualism
Comisión de Fomento (Development Commission), 77, 154
community-based conservation (CBC), xi, xiv, 16, 110, 111, 126–127, 183, 194n13; and alpine sublime, 15; anthropologists on, 197n4; and *Auditoría Ambiental* (environmental audit), 117, 119; and conservation policing, 129, 136–139, 145; and conservation state, 20; and ecotourism, 11, 13–14; and green productivism, 12, 19; and Kirchnerismo, 168; and *la comuna*, 152; national politics of, 111–113; and rentier logic, 14. See also scientific sustainability
community/collective. See la comuna (collective/community)
compañeros de rubro (market-sector partners), 77–78
Compressor Route, 29, 30–33, 37, 195n9
Consejo Agrario Provincial (CAP), 72, 80, 83, 94, 96, 154, 156
conservation, 5, 120, 174–175, 187; and *Auditoría Ambiental* (environmental audit), 118; at Delegación Técnica Regional de Patagonia (DTP), 110; in El Calafate, 2; and extractive industries, 180; and green economy, 2, 9; in history of Patagonian region, 29; and light green politics, 172; and neoliberal politics, xiv, 13–14, 194n13, 197nn1–2, and 182 Bis land dispute, 157; and scientific sustainability, 126, 127; at Seccional Lago Viedma (SLV) ranger station, 109; and sustainable trails project (STP), 121, 124. See also community-based conservation (CBC); conservation policing by SLV rangers; conservation state
conservation policing by SLV rangers, 128–145; authoritative/punitive practices for, 128, 140–142; campground management in, 137–140; charlas in, 131–134; educational practices for, 128, 129, 131–132, 134, 135–136, 139, 141, 143–145; guiding sector in, 128, 138, 140–141; and political culture of conservation state, 129–131; trail patrolling in, 134–137

conservation state, 9, 20, 104, 105, 119, 183, 184; and analytic of the conjuncture, 9; and *Auditoría Ambiental* (environmental audit), 117; controlling access to parkland, 44; and corruption, 82; and ecotourism, 48; and El Chaltén, 68–69; and green economy, 110; and Kirchner-Fernández administrations, 117; and Kirchnerismo, 168; and *la comuna*, 150, 152; and land management, 110; and mountaineering, 41; and rentier state, 177; and scientific sustainability, 110, 126; and seasonal workers/golondrinas, 89, 104; and semiotic estate, 12, 20; and trekking, 46; *See also* community-based conservation (CBC); conservation; conservation policing by SLV rangers
Contrera, Enrique, 140–141
Coronil, Fernando, 11, 193n10
corporate nationalism, 34
corruption, 18, 20, 76, 79, 129–130, 173, 185, 198n3, 199n2; and conservation policing, 138, 144, 145; increasing concern about, 10; Jimenez on, 161; and Lake Viedma concession, 80–82, 85; networks of, 72; and Viedma highway project, 159–160
Corvalán, Carlos, 93, 122, 130, 143, 176, 187
Cosgrove, Denis, 195n3
Costa Rica, 61
crampons, 57, 59
Cronon, William, 195n7
Crouch, Gregory, 38
Cundin, Griselda, 88, 103
Cundin, Jorge, 88, 103

dams, 180–181, 187
Darwin, Charles, 27
Davis, Rick, 48–51
De Angelis, Ernesto, 122–126, 129, 133, 134, 136, 142
De las Vueltas River, 6, 7, 96, 158–159, 159, 161–163, 166, 167
Delegación Técnica Regional de Patagonia (DTP), 109–110, 117, 130; and *Auditoría Ambiental* (environmental audit), 116, 119; and conservation, 113; and scientific sustainability, 126; and sustainable trails project (STP), 121, 125
deregulation, 1, 4, 71, 170
Detassis, Bruno, 29

Development Commission: *See* Comisión de Fomento (Development Commission)
"dirtbag" image, 52
Dirty War, 13, 198n3
Dos Santos, Alejandra, 73–74, 85
double state, 18–19, 72, 85, 105, 129, 160, 167, 185
Dowie, Mark, 195n7
Dressler, Wolfram, 194n13
Duhalde, Eduardo, 2, 178
Dutkiewicz, Jan, 195n11

ecology of risk, xiv, 16–17, 105, 184, 185, 186. *See also* risk
economy: of Argentina, 1–2, 7, 10, 47, 48, 69, 85, 88, 124; capitalist, 15, 17, 62, 96, 104, 105, 145, 184, 186, 193n6; credit, 82–83; and Kirchnerismo, 70. *See also* global economy; inflation
ecotourism, xi, xiv, 3, 16, 61, 131, 175, 184, 187, 194n13; and Administración de Parques Nacionales (APN), 110; based on rentier capitalism, 69; boom, 7, 69, 78, 89, 94, 116, 128; and branding, 12; bubble, 60; and class, 60, 61; and comerciantes, 68; and conservation, 13–14, 112, 126, 133, 142; described, 10–11; and development, 15; and El Chaltén, 61, 62, 69; and empresarios, 82, 85; and extractive industries, 180; farming replaced by, 45; and green economy, 2, 9; and green productivism, 12, 14–15, 19; in history of Patagonian region, 28; and Kirchnerismo, 168, 171, 182; and Kirchners, 69, 183; and *la comuna*, 150, 152; and mountaineering, 26, 63; narrative from tourists on Patagonian region, 43–44; and national parks, 26; and neoliberal politics, 13; and 182 Bis land dispute, 157; politics of, 47–48; and rentier logic, 20, 85; and rentier state, 176; and risk, 17; and scientific sustainability, 126; and Seccional Lago Viedma, 128; slowing of development of, 10; and trekking, 46–47, 60, 63
Ecuador, 61
Egger, Toni, 40
El Calafate, 81, 159, 175, 181; as community, 74; and Delegación Técnica Regional de Patagonia (DTP), 113; in ethnographic research, xiii; glaciers in, 12, 43; and Kirchners, 1–3, 72; number of visitors to, 47, 193n5; and rent capture, 131; and

seasonal workers/golondrinas, 87; slow
growth history of, 2; and tourism, 60–61;
and trekking, 56, 58
El Chaltén, xi–xiv, 5, 10, 20, 120, 174, 175, 184;
anniversary celebration for, 172–173; and
branding, 45, 46, 59, 104, 131; and
community-based conservation (CBC),
127; and corruption, 129; credit economy in,
82–83; and Delegación Técnica Regional de
Patagonia (DTP), 113; described, 5–6, 6; and
ecotourism, 61, 62, 144; in ethnographic
research, 3, 4; and financial crisis, 7; frontier
history of, 75; and green economy, 8; green
productivism in, 41; in history of Patagonian
region, 27, 28–29; and indigenous
populations, 104; and Kirchnerismo, 71–72,
171; and Kirchners, 2–3, 18, 169; and Lake del
Desierto, 170; and mountaineering, 25–26,
32, 33, 35, 38, 40–41; number of visitors to,
47; and Patagonia, Inc., 40; photo of, 7, 46;
and *Plan Preliminar de Manejo, Parque
Nacional Los Glaciares* (PMLG), 114, 115;
and politics of labor, 90; and post-neoliberal
politics, 8, 72; and rentier state, 176; and
seasonal workers/golondrinas, 87, 88,
93–97; and semiotic estate, 68; and slowing
economic growth, 7–8; and sustainable
trails project (STP), 120, 122–126; and
trekking, 39, 45–50, 56, 58–62. See also
Auditoría Ambiental (environmental audit);
Camp Madsen; comerciantes; conservation
policing by SLV rangers; *la comuna*
(collective/community)
Eléctrico River, 69–70, 170
empresarios, 70, 73–74, 77, 80–82, 84, 155, 185
Enduring Patagonia (Crouch), 38
Enel, 180
entrepreneurs, 19, 96, 104, 175, 183, 196n1; and
alpine sublime, 63; and closing of Madsen,
138; and conservation policing, 144; and
economy, 10; in El Chaltén, 151; and
indigenous heritage, 61; and *la comuna*, 153,
154, 160; and mountaineering, 39; and 182
Bis land dispute, 157; as owners of rental
units, 83–84; and rentier state, 176;
tourism, xii, xiii, 3–4, 9, 11, 184. See also
comerciantes; empresarios
equipment/clothing. See clothing/equipment
escaladores (climbers), 101, 102

Escuela Nacional de Guardaparques, 198n1
Espina, Héctor, 160, 162
Esquel, 180
estancias, 27, 28, 62, 158, 161
Estancia Verde Hostel, 59, 73
estancieros, 45, 151, 152
ethnicity, 12, 74, 75, 140
ethnography, xii–xiv, 3–4, 16, 185, 193n3,
194–195n15, 194nn13–14
Europe: and climate change, 163; and
ecotourism in Patagonian region, 43, 60;
entrepreneurs from, 69; in history of
Patagonian region, 26, 27, 29; and
indigenous populations, 103; and
mountaineering, 25, 31, 38, 41, 42;
Patagonian region tourists from, 44;
workers from, 88
European Alps, 15, 25, 165
extractive industries, 28, 169, 172, 174–175,
178–182
Ezcurra, Emiliano, 187

farms/farming, 6, 15, 48, 61, 62, 175, 178,
181–182, 186; and green economy, 8,
193n6; in history of El Chaltén, 75; in
history of Patagonian region, 27, 28; and
la comuna, 152; and mountaineering, 26;
in *Plan Preliminar de Manejo, Parque
Nacional Los Glaciares* (PMLG), 114–115;
replaced by ecotourism, 45; in Santa
Cruz, 174
Fawkes, Josh, 43–44
Ferguson, James, 193n1
Fernández de Kirchner, Cristina, 10, 170–171;
in address to supporters in 2015, 1;
appointed Corvalán president of APN,
198n2; beginnings of political career of, 2;
and ecotourism, 47, 69; electioneering
posters, 173; and green economy, 69; in
history of Patagonian region, 29; and
inflation, 79, 95; in Santa Cruz, 18; and
seasonal workers/golondrinas, 89, 96–97;
as senator, 188; and slowing economic
growth, 7. See also Kirchner-Fernández
administrations; Kirchnerismo; Kirchners
(Néstor and Cristina)
financial crisis, xi–xii, 7, 43, 78, 91, 129. See also
Great Recession
FitzRoy, Robert, 40

Fitz Roy Norte Glacier, 198n2

Fitz Roy Range, 33, 173; and conservation policing, 140; and 182 Bis land dispute, 154, 155, 157; and Patagonia, Inc., 40; and sustainable trails project (STP), 124; and trekking, 48, 54

Fitz Roy Traverse, 33, 35

Fitz Roy Valley, 50, 134–135

Fletcher, Robert, 15, 194n13

formal/informal (blanco/negro) labor, 71, 72, 75, 77, 83, 84, 97–100, 184, 197n2, 197n5; and conservation policing, 142; and seasonal workers/golondrinas, 87–90, 95, 103, 104

Foucault, Michel, 194n15

free climbing, 31, 32, 195n8

free soloing, 195n8

Frías, Juan, 102

frontcountry, 45, 47, 53, 58, 62, 105, 135

Futaleufú, 180

Garibotti, Rolando, 5, 7–8, 10, 33, 34–35, 120–122, 154–155

gauchos/paisanos, 6, 45, 61–62, 151, 152

gaze. See tourist gaze

gender, 10, 12, 44, 95, 105

gente humilde, 96

Gift, The (Mauss), 177

Gillespie, Adam, 123

glaciers, 104, 114, 198n2; and climate change, 163–164, 165; and El Calafate, 1, 6, 12, 43; and mountaineering, 39; and 182 Bis land dispute, 157; and Parque Nacional Los Glaciares (PNLG), 12; in Patagonian region, 14; in Patagonian region ecotourism, 44; retreating, 8; and trekking, 9, 46, 47, 49, 53, 54, 55, 56–59, 62. See also Grande Glacier; Perito Moreno Glacier; Viedma Glacier

Glaciers National Park. See Parque Nacional Los Glaciares (PNLG)

global economy, 1, 7, 14, 15, 19; and Kirchner-Fernández administrations, 63; and mountaineering, 41, 42; and risk, 16, 17; and trekking, 47

golondrinas. See seasonal workers/golondrinas

Gore, Al, 164

Grande Glacier, 49, 58, 143

Grand Teton National Park, 121, 122–123, 125, 126

Great Recession, xii, 7, 10, 85, 119, 130, 153, 161; and comerciantes, 69; and seasonal workers/golondrinas, 87, 89; and sustainable development, 17. See also financial crisis

green developmentalism, 175, 178–179, 181

green economy, xi, xii, xiv, 2–4, 20, 127, 181–182, 183; and analytic of the conjuncture, 9; applied to other economies, 193n6; and Auditoría Ambiental (environmental audit), 116, 117, 118; and branding, 12, 63; and climate change, 165; and conservation, 9, 110, 131, 145; defined, 8; described as capitalistic, 44; and ecotourism, 9, 48; and El Chaltén, 8–9; and empresarios, 70; in ethnographic research, xii–xiii; and extractive industries, 169, 180; focuses of, 11; and green productivism, 47; as grounded in global tourism, 61; and indigenous populations, 103; and Kirchner-Fernández administrations, 5, 169, 186; and Kirchners, 18, 20–21, 43, 63, 69, 72, 85, 168, 171, 172, 175; and la comuna, 153, 166; and land managers, 113; and market capitalism, 8; and middle class, 184; and mountaineering, 26, 63; new approach to, 187; and 182 Bis land dispute, 157; and Plan Preliminar de Manejo, Parque Nacional Los Glaciares (PMLG), 114; and popular sustainability, 166; risk consciousness within, xi; and scientific sustainability, 126; and seasonal workers/golondrinas, 103, 104; and trekking, 45, 63; and weakening of community/solidarity, 74

green estate, 175–179, 198n4

Greenpeace, 164

green productivism, xi, xiv, 16, 185, 187; and community-based conservation (CBC), 110, 126, 127; and conservation policing, 129, 145; and ecotourism, 12, 14–15, 48; in El Chaltén, 41; and entrepreneurs, 74, 76, 85–86; and green economy, 47; and Kirchner-Fernández administrations, 186; and Kirchnerismo, 10, 12–13, 19, 21, 168, 182; and Kirchners, 5, 71, 175, 183; and labor, 91; and mountaineering, 26, 41; and national parks, 47; and politics of labor, 89, 90; and rent capture, 130; and seasonal workers/golondrinas, 89, 104, 105; and sustainable trails project (STP), 125

ground rents, 11, 110, 186, 193n9
guiding sector, 68, 81; and *Auditoría Ambiental* (environmental audit), 118–119; and climate change, 163; and community-based conservation (CBC), 111; and conservation policing, 128, 138, 140–143; and frontcountry vs. backcountry, 62; and rentier state, 177; and seasonal workers/golondrinas, 87, 95, 96, 101, 102; and trekking, 58–59; and Francisco de la Vega, 155

Haenn, Nora, 197n2
haptic vocabulary, 195n11
health care/insurance, 98, 197n4
Heidegger, Martin, 195n1
HidroAysén, 180, 181
Hielos Continentales, 6, 193n4
Himalayas (Nepal), 15, 25, 41, 44
Holmes, George, 194n13
Honnold, Alex, 35
horses, 27, 61, 118–119, 120, 152
Hostel Cerro Solo, 73
Hostel Lago Viedma, 87, 91, 99
Hostel La Rimaya, 155
Hostel Verde, 80
Hostería Nunatak Viedma, 76, 84

Ibañez, Raquel, 67–69, 73, 77, 78, 85, 95–96
icebergs, 1, 46
ice fields, 1, 6, 114, 163–164, 171
Iguazú Falls, 14
Iguazú National Park, 14, 28, 47, 176
IMF. *See* International Monetary Fund (IMF)
indigenous societies/peoples, 15, 26–27, 61, 62, 96, 103–104, 187, 195n7
Indonesia, 9
inflation, 78–79, 89, 90, 95, 96, 104, 170, 178, 185, 186, 187
informal labor. *See* formal/informal (blanco/negro) labor
Instituto Argentino de Nivología, Glaciología y Ciencias Ambientales (IANIGLA). *See* Argentine Institute for Snow, Glacier and Environmental Sciences
Instituto Nacional de Estadística y Censos (INDEC), 79, 119
Intergovernmental Panel on Climate Change, 163
International Monetary Fund (IMF), 1, 2, 4

Irrazábal, Fernando, 91–92
Islas Malvinas/Falkland Islands, 169, 186
Israelis, 140

James, Daniel, 71
Jimenez, Antonio, 161–162
Jorge Cepernic Dam, 181
Juárez, Rafael, 40

Kant, Immanuel, 53
Kaweshkar (Alacalufe) community, 103, 196n6
Kennedy, Hayden, 31–32, 38
Keynes, John Maynard, 16, 75
kinesthesis, 50, 196n4
Kirchner, Alicia, 181, 188, 197n3
Kirchner, Máximo, 188
Kirchner, Néstor, 170, 173–174, 188, 198n3; beginnings of political career of, 2; and ecotourism, 7, 47, 69, 89, 94; and El Chaltén, 45; in history of Patagonian region, 29; as president of Argentina, 1; in Santa Cruz, 18. *See also* Kirchner-Fernández administrations; Kirchners (Néstor and Cristina)
Kirchner-Fernández administrations, xi, xii, 119, 138, 185; and Administración de Parques Nacionales (APN), 117; and comerciantes, 70, 76; and community-based conservation (CBC), 112, 113, 126, 127; and conservation policing, 138–140; and conservation state, 129–130; and De las Vueltas River bridge, 158–159; encouraging increased tourism, 14–15; and green economy, xi, 5, 169, 186; and green productivism, xiv, 5; and informal labor, 104, 105; and *la comuna*, 167; and neo-developmentalism, 4–5; and politics of labor, 89–90; tourism policy of, 48. *See also* Kirchnerismo
Kirchnerismo, 18–19, 75, 105; and alpine sublime, 16; and citizenship, 20; and comerciantes, 75; and defending territorial sovereignty, 169–172; development of, as political ideology, 17–18; and economic development through resource exploitation, 172–175; and empresarios, 85; and entrepreneurs, 76; and extractive industries, 169, 179–181; and green

Kirchnerismo (cont.)
economy, 2; and green productivism, 10, 12–13, 21; introduction to, 1–2; and mountaineering, 41; political culture of, 70–72; and rentier state/green estate, 169, 175–179; and risk, 17
Kirchners (Néstor and Cristina), 185, 186, 196n1, 197n3; and De las Vueltas River bridge, 161–162; as empresarios, 80; and green economy, 20–21, 85, 175; and green productivism, 183; and la comuna, 151, 166–167; and 182 Bis land dispute, 156–157; and Viedma highway project, 159–161. See also Fernández de Kirchner, Cristina; Kirchner, Néstor; Kirchner-Fernández administrations; Kirchnerismo
Kirk, Cullen, 36, 37, 41
Kruk, Jason, 31–32

labor, 11, 19; and alpine sublime, 63; and comerciantes, 70; contracts, 97, 102, 103, 197n2, 197n5; and Kirchner-Fernández administrations, 4; and la comuna, 150, 153, 154; market in ethnographic research, xiii; markets and entrepreneurs, 79; and mountaineering, 25; a pulmón, 75, 79, 84, 85; and risk, 17; See also formal/informal (blanco/negro) labor; seasonal workers/golondrinas; service workers; unions
la comuna (collective/community), 149–167; and climate change, 163–166; and De las Vueltas River bridge, 158–159, 159, 161–163, 166, 167; festivals, 149–150; and history of El Chaltén, 151; 182 Bis land dispute, 154–158, 166; and popular sustainability, 151–153; preservationist aesthetic, 151–152, 158, 166; and Viedma highway project, 159–163, 166, 167
Laguna Capri, 134
Laguna de los Tres (LDLT), 50, 54, 120–121, 125, 132, 135
Laguna Sucia, 54
Laguna Torre (LT), 49, 50, 132
Lake Argentino, 181, 187
Lake del Desierto, 88, 169–170, 199n1
Lake Viedma, 6, 27, 49, 81, 82, 155, 159, 161
Lama, David, 32, 38, 195n9

land grants, 94, 128
land managers, 7–8, 110, 120, 183; at Administración de Parques Nacionales (APN), 109; and Auditoría Ambiental (environmental audit), 116–119; and conservation, 9, 110, 130, 145, 185; and conservation state, 20; at Delegación Técnica Regional de Patagonia (DTP), 109–110; and economy, 10; and empresarios, 82; in ethnographic research, xii, 3; and green economy, 11; and la comuna, 152, 153; and Parque Nacional Los Glaciares (PNLG) management plan, 113–116, 198n5; and risk, 17; and scientific sustainability, 126; and sustainable trails project (STP), 124
landscape ideology, 195n3
land scarcity, 104
Lange, Katrina, 48–51
Lanin National Park, 28, 61, 111, 117
La Opinión Austral, 155
La Plata, 102
latifundista regime, 27
Latin America, xi, xiv, 3, 4, 44, 193n2
Li, Tania, 9, 10, 16
light green politics, 172, 175
Lis, Mateo, 79–80, 140
Loma del Pliegue Tumbado, 48–51, 49, 53–54
Lopez, Mateo, 137, 143
Los Alerces National Park, 28, 180
Los Antiguos, 180
Los Cóndores trail, 53
Lyall, John, 196n2

MacDonald, Laura, 4
Macleod, Donald, 60
Macri, Mauricio, 187, 188
Maestri, Cesare, 30, 31, 33
Magellan, Ferdinand, 26–27
Mammut, 30, 50
Mapuche communities/people, 61, 103–104, 111, 117
Marchmain, Evan, 43–44
Marconi, Violeta, 75
Marconi Glacier, 198n2
market individualism, 74–79
market solidarity, 78–79
Marquez, Juliana, 139
Martínez-Reyes, José, 197n2
Marx, Karl, 11, 16, 185, 193n9

Matthews-Johnson, Sam, 59

Mauss, Marcel, 177

Mazzarella, William, 195n12

meditation, 50

Mendoza (in Argentina), 45, 87

Mendoza, Ricardo, 87–88

Menem, Carlos, 76, 119, 129, 168, 170, 171, 172, 178, 182; and inflation, 47, 170; introduction to, 1; and labor, 71, 170; and national park system, 177; and Partido Justicialista/Peronist party, 18, 182

Meridian Gold, Inc., 180

Messi, Claudio, 131, 132, 134

mestizaje, 99

microcartels, 70, 77–78, 79, 85

Ministry of Defense, 177

Ministry of Production, 47

Ministry of the Environment and Sustainable Development, 8, 187

Ministry of Tourism, 187

miradores (scenic viewpoints), 52–53, 56

Monte Fitz Roy, 5, 6, 116, 132, 170, 171, 198n2; mountaineering on, 25, 28–29; and 182 Bis land dispute, 156; and Patagonia, Inc., 40; photo of, 7; and sustainable trails project (STP), 120–121

Montemayor, El Morocho, 87

Monteverde Cloud Forest Reserve, 61

moraine, 8, 49

Moreno, Francisco "Perito," 27, 198n6

mountaineering, 25–26, 28–42, 44, 56, 104, 183, 184, 195n12; Access Fund, 155; and alpine sublime, 15; and branding, 39; in Chaltén Massif, 19; and climate change, 165; clothing/equipment, 195n8; and conservation policing, 131, 140, 143; and De las Vueltas River bridge, 158; and economy, 10; and ecotourism, 26; ethics of style in, 30–33; in ethnographic research, xii, xiii–xiv, 3; global, 29, 30, 34, 38, 39, 41; and green economy, 9, 11, 26; and green productivism, 26; haptic vocabulary in, 195n11; in history of Patagonian region, 28–29, 30; ice, 81; and *la comuna*, 149, 153; number of annual visitors for, 45; and 182 Bis land dispute, 154; and public culture of El Chaltén, 40–41; and resolve, 26, 33, 36–38, 41, 195n2; and retreating glaciers, 8;

risk of injury/death in, 17, 25, 26, 28, 30, 31, 33–38, 41–42, 44, 59, 195n1, 195n10; and seasonal workers/golondrinas, 100, 101; sources of participants in, 25; status hierarchy in, 33–35; and sustainable trails project (STP), 120, 122; and trekking, 26, 39, 41, 52, 59, 62, 63

Munn, Nancy, 34

Nahuel Huapi National Park, 28, 61, 117, 176

National Census and Statistics Institution of Argentina. *See* Instituto Nacional de Estadística y Censos (INDEC)

National Day of Argentine Parks, *139*, 139

National Oceanic and Atmospheric Administration's Air Resources Laboratory, 198n5

national parks: and ecotourism, 26, 44; as estates, 68; farming replaced at, 45; and green productivism, 47; number of annual visitors to, 47; in Patagonian region, 15, 28; and rentier logic, 48. *See also names of individual national parks*

National Parks Administration of Argentina. *See* Administración de Parques Nacionales (APN)

National Parks Directorship, 28

National Ranger School. *See* Escuela Nacional de Guardaparques

National Trekking Festival, 149–150

Nature™Inc., 194n13

neo-developmentalism, 4–5, 19, 63, 89, 105, 112, 185

neoliberal politics, 4, 12, 119, 175, 185, 188, 193n1, 193n8, 197n1, 197n2; and conservation, 13–14, 194n13; and ecotourism, 13; and global capitalism, 4; introduction to, xi; and Kirchnerismo, 2, 70; and labor, 89, 99; and Menem, 1; opposition to, 3, 187; and politics of community-based conservation (CBC), 112, 113

Nepal, 15

Néstor Kirchner Dam, 181

Neumann, Roderick, 195n7

Neuquén, xi

New Left governments, xi, 3, 4, 5, 180, 188

New Zealand, 15

Nietzsche, Friedrich, 38

nongovernmental organizations (NGOs), 3,
13, 111, 116; Banco de Bosques, 187; and
climate change, 164; and community-based
conservation (CBC), 112, 127; and dam
projects, 181; and Delegación Técnica
Regional de Patagonia (DTP), 110; and
scientific sustainability, 126; and sustain-
able trails project (STP), 120, 124
Norman, Carlyle, 37–38
North America: and mountaineering, 25;
Patagonian region tourists from, 44
Northern Patagonian Andes, 61, 103
Northern Patagonian Ice Field, 163, 193n4
North Face (company), 30, 40
Norway, 36

O'Connor, Martin, 193n6
182 Bis land dispute, 154–158, 166, 173, 174,
198n2
Operation Desert, 169
Organization of American States (OAS), 170,
199n1
Ortner, Peter, 195n9
Orwell, George, 73

paisanos. See gauchos/paisanos
Paraguay, 28, 88, 96
Pari, Anita, 93–94, 95
park management plans. See Auditoría
Ambiental (environmental audit); Plan
Preliminar de Manejo, Parque Nacional
Los Glaciares (PMLG)
park rangers. See rangers
Parque Nacional Los Glaciares (PNLG), xi,
28, 69, 170; as adjacent to El Chaltén, xii;
and Camp Madsen, 93; and capitalist
production, 45; and climate change, 164;
and conservation policing, 131, 142; and
Corvalán, 198n2; creation of, 28; and dam
projects, 187; and Delegación Técnica
Regional de Patagonia (DTP), 109; and
economy, 7; and ecotourism, 10; and
empresarios, 81; in ethnographic research,
xiii, 3; and glaciers, 12; and Kirchnerismo,
2–3, 169, 171; and Kirchners, 1–3, 18; and la
comuna festivals, 150; map of, 6; and
mountaineering, 25, 41–42; and 182 Bis
land dispute, 154, 157; park rangers of, 20;
and preservationist aesthetic, 152; and rent

capture, 131; and rentier state, 176; and
scientific sustainability, 126; and Seccional
Lago Viedma, 128; and sustainable trails
project (STP), 122, 125; tourism information center for, 181; tourists visiting, 44, 47,
193n5; and trekking, 5, 12, 19, 46, 49–50, 56,
58, 59, 60, 62; and Viedma highway project,
159. See also Auditoría Ambiental
(environmental audit); Plan Preliminar de
Manejo, Parque Nacional Los Glaciares
(PMLG)
Partido Justicialista/Peronist party, 18, 71, 119,
170, 171, 172, 182, 187, 197n3
Paso del Cuadrado, 154–155, 157
Patagonia, Inc., 30, 33, 34, 40, 120
Patagonian Andes, 25, 41, 44
Patagonian region, 15; described, 14; as
desert, 27, 28, 45, 195n4; history of, 15–16,
26–30; introduction to and description of,
xi, xii; and Patagonia, Inc., 40
Patagonian Regional Technical Delegation.
See Delegación Técnica Regional de
Patagonia (DTP)
Patagonia Salvaje, 81–82, 130, 138, 155
Patagonia Sin Represas (Patagonian without
Dams) campaign, 180–181
Paz, Sonia, 60–61
Peralta, Daniel, 172–173, 173, 197n3
Perito Moreno Glacier, 28, 56, 57, 58, 81, 143,
159, 180
Perón, Eva, 17
Perón, Juan, 17, 28, 70, 171
Peronism, 18, 70–71, 96–97, 171, 175
Peronist party. See Partido Justicialista/
Peronist party
Peru, 165
Peruvian Andes, 15
Piazzolla, Jorge, 138
Piedras Blancas Glacier, 164
Piolín de Oro (Golden Cord) award, 149
Plan Preliminar de Manejo, Parque Nacional
Los Glaciares (PMLG), 113–116, 120, 151,
198n5
Poincenot, Jacques, 40
Pollone Glacier, 198n2
post-neoliberal politics, 183, 186, 187, 188,
194n15; and class, 63; and comerciantes, 76;
and conservation state, 20; described, 4;
and El Chaltén, 8, 72; and entrepreneurs,

85; and farming, 178; and formal/informal labor, 99; and green economy, 48; and green productivism, 19, 127, 185; inflation as condition of, 79; introduction to, xi, xiv, 12, 18; and politics of community-based conservation (CBC), 112; and politics of labor, 90; and rentier state, 179; and seasonal workers/golondrinas, 97, 104

poverty, 89, 99, 197n1 (chap. 1)

preservationist aesthetic, 151–152, 158, 166

price-fixing, 70, 77–78, 85

privatization, 1, 4, 71, 151, 154, 156, 157, 170, 172, 177, 194n13

Provincial Agrarian Council of Santa Cruz. See Consejo Agrario Provincial (CAP)

pseudonyms, 193n3

public-private alliances, 12, 19, 68, 119, 126, 133, 144, 184

Pucón, 88

Puerto Edén, 196n6

Puerto Natales, 12, 43

Punta Arenas, 27

race, 10, 12, 44, 69, 74, 75, 96, 97, 99–100, 105

rangers, 68, 120, 183; and Auditoría Ambiental (environmental audit), 116; on Camp Madsen, 92–93; and climate change, 163; and conservation, 9, 20, 110, 185; and economy, 10; education for, 198n1; and empresarios, 81, 82; in ethnographic research, xii, xiii, 3–4; and green economy, 11; and la comuna, 150, 153, 154, 160; as middle class, 69; and mountaineering, 38; and Plan Preliminar de Manejo, Parque Nacional Los Glaciares (PMLG), 114; and politics of ecotourism, 48; and politics of labor, 90; and risk, 17; and scientific sustainability, 126; and sustainable trails project (STP), 122–125, 123; and trekking, 50. See also conservation policing by SLV rangers; Seccional Lago Viedma (SLV)

recorridas, 134, 136, 140

Red Bull, 32

Red Bull Media House, 195n9

REDD+ programs, 194n13

rental housing, 70, 83–84

rentier, 179, 194n11; dynamics, xiv; ground rents, 68, 110, 186, 193n9; logic, 11, 14, 20, 48,

69, 82, 85; operations, 11, 12; position, 59; processes, 11; rent capture, 12, 19, 21; strategy, 196n3. See also rentier capitalism; rentier state

rentier capitalism, 186; and community-based conservation (CBC), 14; and conservation policing, 145; and ecotourism, 11, 69, 183–184; and park service, 20; and tourism, 11

rentier state, 182, 183, 186, 187, 199n2; and Administración de Parques Nacionales (APN), 125, 130–131; and green economy, 194n11; and green estate, 175–179; and Kirchnerismo, 169

Represas Patagonia hydroelectric dam project, 181, 187

Resolution 83, 170

resolve, 36–38, 41, 195n2

Retamozo, Martín, 197n2

retenciones, 178

Río Blanco Glacier, 5, 54, 55

Río Gallegos, xiii, 170

Río Negro, xi

risk: and Auditoría Ambiental (environmental audit), 119; capitalist ecology of, 105; for comerciantes, 69, 70, 77, 78, 86; consciousness, xi, 3, 16, 17; and conservation policing, 129; and conservation state, 110; and ecology, xiv, 16, 17, 111, 114, 126, 164, 184, 185, 186; and El Chaltén, 75; experience of, 9–10; governmentality, 194n15; and Kirchnerismo, 168; and la comuna, 150, 152, 153, 167; in mountaineering, 25, 28, 30, 31, 33–38, 41–42, 44, 59, 195n10; objective/subjective, 37; and Plan Preliminar de Manejo, Parque Nacional Los Glaciares (PMLG), 115; scales of, 17; and scientific sustainability, 126, 127; and seasonal workers/golondrinas, 89, 97, 105; studies, xiv; in trekking, 45, 47, 57, 58, 62. See also risk society; risk subjectivity

risk society, 194n15; Ulrich Beck on, 194n14; and comerciantes, 70; and community-based conservation (CBC), 110; defined, 17; and ecology of risk, 186; and green capitalist economy, 104; introduction to, 16–17, 19; and la comuna, 167; and 182 Bis land dispute, 157; and seasonal workers/golondrinas, 89; and trekking, 45

risk subjectivity, 19, 184, 194–195n15; and
     conservation policing, 144; of entrepre-
     neurs, 85; and green capitalist society, 10,
     17; and mountaineering, 26, 35, 41, 104; of
     service workers, 89; and trekking, 47, 62,
     104
Rivadavia, Eduardo, 155
rock climbing, 101–102, 140
Rodolfo, Don, 118
Rosales, Veronica, 101–102
Rousseff, Dilma, 188
Rúa, Fernando de la, 1, 174
Ruckert, Arne, 4

Saint-Exupéry, Antoine de, 40
Salinas, Maria Elena, 83, 84
Salta, 45
Sánchez, Alfredo, 154, 155–157
Santa Cruz, 6, 74, 80; dam project in, 187; and
     extractive industries, 174–175; farming in,
     174; and Kirchners, 2, 18, 72, 85, 161, 170, 171,
     173, 174, 188, 196n1, 197n3; as province of
     Argentina, xi; Yacimientos Petrolíferos
     Fiscales (YPF) in, 172
Santa Cruz River, 181
Scheper-Hughes, Nancy, 99
scientific sustainability, 20, 110–111, 120,
     126–127, 183, 185; and Auditoría Ambiental
     (environmental audit), 116, 117; and climate
     change, 165; and conservation policing,
     144, 145; described, 109; and Kirchnerismo,
     168; and la comuna, 150–153, 166–167; and
     politics of community-based conservation
     (CBC), 111, 112; at Seccional Lago Viedma
     (SLV) ranger station, 109; and sustainable
     trails project (STP), 120, 124
Scioli, Daniel, 187
seasonal workers/golondrinas, 20, 68, 69, 70,
     72, 76, 86–105; at Camp Confluencia, 137;
     at Camp Madsen, 89, 91–93, 96, 100, 104;
     and comerciantes, 67, 68; and economy, 10;
     formal/informal labor, 97–100, 103,
     104–105, 128; and green economy/tourism,
     9; and indigenous populations, 103–104;
     and la comuna, 160; land grants for, 94; and
     land scarcity, 96, 104; moving up to middle
     class, 88–89; origin of name "golondrinas,"
     87; at Parque Nacional Los Glaciares
     (PNLG), 44; photo of fixed-contract

workers, 103; and play, 100–104; and
     politics of labor, 89–90; and rental units,
     83; and risk, 97, 105; and skilled vs.
     unskilled labor, 94–97, 102, 105; and social
     hierarchy, 95–96
Seccional Lago Viedma (SLV), 109, 114, 121,
     122–123, 125, 126, 169. See also conservation
     policing by SLV rangers
Secretary of Tourism, 47
Selk'nam, 103
Semiotic estate, 15, 19, 20, 119, 186, 187; and
     alpine sublime, 15; and comerciantes, 68;
     and conservation policing, 144; and
     conservation state, 20; defined, 12, 68; and
     empresarios, 82; and la comuna, 150; and
     public-private alliance, 126; and tourism
     industry at large, 194n12
Sen, Grace, 57
service workers, 19, 184; in ethnographic
     research, xii, xiii, 4; and green economy, 9,
     11. See also seasonal workers/golondrinas
siege tactics, 30–31
simul-climbing, 36
Smith, Adam, 16
Soto, Claudia, 76–78, 84, 85, 95
Soto, Luis, Jr., 91–92
Southern Alps (New Zealand), 15
Southern Patagonia, 61
Southern Patagonian Andes, 6, 25, 103, 175, 180
Southern Patagonian Ice Field, 6, 46, 57, 58,
     163, 165, 169, 170, 193n4
soybean fund, 181–182
Spain, 27
sponsorships, 34–35, 40, 41, 50
sport climbing, 101
Standhardt, Ernst, 40
super-elite status, 34, 39, 40, 41, 42, 101
super gringo, 51
sustainability: and Auditoría Ambiental
     (environmental audit), 119; and conserva-
     tion policing, 129, 145; and De las Vueltas
     River bridge, 158; and la comuna, 162;
     participatory development agenda for, 105;
     and Plan Preliminar de Manejo, Parque
     Nacional Los Glaciares (PMLG), 114–115;
     popular, 151–153, 166, 167; and rentier state,
     179; scientific, 20
sustainable development, 19, 20, 185, 187,
     193n6; in Argentina, 8–9; and climate

change, 166; and conservation policing, 128, 143; and *la comuna*, 150, 152, 166; and politics of ecotourism, 48; and risk, 17
sustainable trails project (STP), 116, 120–126, 136
Sutton, Barbara, 99

Tellez, Marisol, 98
Terray, Lionel, 28–29
Tierra del Fuego (province), xi
Tierra del Fuego National Park, 12
Tompkins, Doug, 40
Torre Expediciones, 81, 155
Torre Piergiorgio, 198n2
Torre Range, 48, 49, 54, 154
Torres del Paine National Park, 6, 12, 58, 59, 114, 137
Torre Valley, 50, 154
tourism: and El Chaltén, 60; global, 61; in history of Patagonian region, 28, 29; infrastructure, 80; and Néstor Kirchner, 174; and mountaineering, 26, 39; park-centered, 44; patterns, 60; and place-making narratives, 59; in Santa Cruz, 174–175. *See also* ecotourism; tourism industry
tourism industry, 12–13, 15, 59, 126; and *Auditoría Ambiental* (environmental audit), 117; and class, 68; and community-based conservation (CBC), 127; and conservation state, 9; and De las Vueltas River bridge, 158; and economy, 7; and El Chaltén, 56, 63; and green productivism, 5; and Kirchners, 2; and *la comuna*, 151, 152–153; and mountaineering, 41–42; and national parks, 68; and park rangers, 20; and Patagonia region, 40; and semiotic estate, 12, 194n12; and slowing economic growth, 8; and trekking, 46
tourist gaze, 42, 46, 93, 132, 150, 196n1
trekking, 19, 104, 183, 184, 196n1, 196n5; and alpine sublime, 15, 45–46, 47, 52–53, 54, 58, 62–63; authentic self/meditation in, 50; and branding, 46; clothing/equipment for, 50–51, 53, 57, 59; commercial guiding sector for, 58–59; and community-based conservation (CBC), 111; and conservation policing, 131, 132, 135, 143; and economy, 10; and ecotourism, 46–47; and El Chaltén, 6,

39, 45; in ethnographic research, xii, xiii, 3; on frontcountry trails, 48–51, 49, 55; and green economy, 9, 11; ice, 56–59, 81; and *la comuna* festivals, 149–150; and mountaineering, 26, 39, 41, 52, 59, 62, 63; number of annual visitors for, 45; and 182 Bis land dispute, 154; in Parque Nacional Los Glaciares (PNLG), 5, 19, 46; place-making narratives in, 59–62; Puerto Natales as trekking capital of Chile, 43; and retreating glaciers, 8; and risk, 17, 47, 57, 58, 62; and seasonal workers/golondrinas, 101; in Torres del Paine National Park, 12
Trujillo, Lucia, 197n2

UNESCO World Heritage Site, 132, 157
Unidad Ciudadana (Citizen's Unity party), 188
Unión Cívica Radical (Radical Party), 171
unions, 71, 77, 83, 90, 94, 99, 128
United Nations Environmental Programme, 8
Upsala Glacier, 164
urban sector, 68–69, 95, 102, 105
U.S. Access Fund, 155, 157
U.S. Agency for International Development, 13
U.S. government, 1
Ushuaia, 12, 43, 59
U.S. Park Service, 120, 122

Valverde, Rodrigo, 102–103
Vega, Francisco de la, 80–82, 85, 154–157
Venezuela, xi, 188, 193n10
Vertical Argentina, 35
Viedma Glacier, 58, 81, 143, 155, 159
Viedma highway project, 159–160, 162–163, 166, 167
Villalba, Ricardo, 163–164, 165
Vuelta de Hielo, 118

Washington Consensus, 1, 3
Weber, Max, 75
Weiner, Annette, 177
World Bank, 1, 13

Yacimientos Petrolíferos Fiscales (YPF), 172
Yaghan, 103
Yungas Ecological Corridor, 111

Zamora, Andreiña, 98

ABOUT THE AUTHOR

MARCOS MENDOZA is an assistant professor of anthropology in the Department of Sociology and Anthropology at the University of Mississippi (UM). He received his doctorate from the University of Chicago in 2013 and then joined the faculty at UM. His current research focuses on Latin American politics, the green economy, risk society, narco-violence, and social movements in Argentina, Chile, and Mexico. His previous work has been published in *Dialectical Anthropology*, the *Journal of Latin American and Caribbean Anthropology*, and the *Journal of Latin American Geography*.